CADOGAN

KU-758-243

Amsterdam

Cadogan Books plc
West End House House (3rd Floor), 11 Hills Place,
London W1R 1AG, UK
becky.kendall@morrispub.co.uk

Ditrsibuted in the USA by
The Globe Pequot Press
6 Business Park Road, PO Box 833, Old Saybrook,
Connecticut 06475–0833

Copyright © Rodney Bolt 1997, 2000
Updated by the author and Gerard Van Vuuren, 2000

Book and cover design by Animage
Cover photographs (front and back) by:
        The Travel Library, Stuart Black
Maps © Cadogan Guides, drawn by Map Creation Ltd
Chapter title pages designed by Kicca Tommasi and Mary-Ann Gallagher
        from photographs by Gerard Van Vuuren

Series Editors: Linda McQueen
Editor: Mary-Ann Gallagher
Indexing: Isobel McLean
Production: Book Production Services

A catalogue record for this book is available from the British Library
ISBN 1–86011–954–9

Printed and bound in Great Britain by the Cromwell Press Ltd.

About the Author

Rodney Bolt is seldom happier than when rattling along the canals of Amsterdam on his Miss Marple Dutch bicycle, or burrowing through papers in the Municipal Archive. Having lived in Greece, South Africa, Britain and Germany, he arrived in Amsterdam in 1991, and now nothing can convince him to leave. He has also written Cadogan Guides to Germany, Bavaria and Madeira, as well as other books and numerous articles on the Netherlands. In 1994 he won the German National Tourist Office's 'Travel Writer of the Year' award.

About the Updater

Gerard van Vuuren is a musician and travel writer who has lived in Amsterdam for many years. He studied in The Hague and Amsterdam, and when he is not playing the harpsichord is to be found behind a camera or hard at work on publications about the Netherlands.

Acknowledgements

Many thanks to Linda McQueen for her ideas and guidance, to Mary-Ann Gallagher for editing this edition, to Map Creation for tackling the awesome task of transferring Amsterdam on to readable maps, and to Gerard for the great new photographs. My special gratitude to all those people who helped with this book the first time round, and in so doing put me on the road to a new career, is undiluted by the passing years.

Contents

You're walking late at night along the Amstel. A frill of gables ends abruptly against the hard lines of the vast new opera house which cut across the evening skyline. A long junkie in ragged red jeans and a flat Spanish hat sways and dances to a frail tune that no one else can hear. A young woman stands up to pedal her heavy black bicycle over a hump-backed bridge, her toddler asleep in a custom-built wicker carrier on

Introduction

the back. Just ahead, an ancient man wearing a chauffeur's cap manoeuvres a wheelchair along the uneven pavement. Its incumbent, a *grande dame* swathed in black fur, nods as they pass with a gracious '*Goedenavond*'. In Amsterdam three strands of life continually interweave: reminders of the wealthy Golden Age trading city dominated by a few Calvinist families, the sleazy port, and the radical hippie mecca of the 1960s grown comfortably liberal.

As a visitor you'll find Amsterdam at once familiar and curious. It has an edge and verve that will keep you on your toes. As Henry James wrote after a visit to the Netherlands in the 1870s, it will 'at least give one's regular habits of thought the stimulus of a little confusion'. You'll be daily launched into a farrago of sleek business people, droves of tourists, scruffs, bohemians and persons of decidedly ill repute. Yet everyone seems to get on remarkably well together; and the chance encounters with people here will be one of the lasting pleasures of your visit.

In the 1980s Amsterdam re-established its importance as a world finance centre. The 1990s saw a burgeoning of traffic through the harbour and Schiphol airport. Copywriters began to overuse the 'Gateway to Europe' epithet, as big-name computer companies and other industries reliant on speedy distribution networks arrived in town. Amsterdam's kernel of job-eager foreign residents, and the locals' facility with languages, made it an ideal location for freefone call-centres—next time your computer is on the blink and you call the number in the handbook, chances are (if you're phoning from within Europe) that you're speaking to someone in Amsterdam, however perfectly they speak your mother tongue. Today the Netherlands has one of the strongest economies in the EU, and the prosperity shows. Brazen, glittering business parks have sprouted on the outskirts of town, though thankfully the centre remains sacrosanct. Soon the entire inner city is to be placed on the World Heritage List of protected monuments, alongside such architectural stalwarts as the Great Wall of China.

Now that Amsterdam has notched up higher status in the business world, it seems anxious to become a little more respectable. Politics are becoming more conservative, police are clearing out junkies and dealers from the more squalid areas of the red-light district, and restaurants and galleries are appearing in their wake. But Amsterdam will never lose its alternative tang. It has a long tradition of liberal tolerance and is, after all, a port, with a port's rough edge. For centuries its heretics, whores and disruptive politicians have nudged and needled other Amsterdammers away from any tendency to complacency. Today you will still find a relaxed and tolerant city. Same-sex couples kiss in the street, whiffs of marijuana waft from psychedelic coffeeshops, clinics and crisis centres exist to help addicts with more severe drug habits. People seem aware of the environment, and in their spotless city are more often to be seen cycling and walking than whizzing about in cars.

This guide shows you Amsterdam in its diversity. It doesn't balk at the darker sides, and delights in the treasures. It is biased towards architecture and art and has a healthy obsession with cafés—for the town's greatest attractions are still its simplest pleasures: strolls along the canals, time spent in front of a painting that takes your breath away and long conversations in quiet cafés where centuries of tobacco smoke have turned the walls quite brown.

Travel

By Air

In 1921 the world's first air travel booking office opened at Amsterdam's **Schiphol Airport**. The dashing Captain Jerry Shaw would fly intrepid passengers, two at a time in a fragile De Havilland, across the Channel to Croydon near London (Heathrow and Gatwick were still meadows). These days Schiphol enjoys a reputation as one of the world's sleekest and most user-friendly airports, and has an impressive mall of duty-free shops. It serves direct flights from London, Manchester, New York, Los Angeles, Toronto, Vancouver and Sydney as well as many other airports around the UK and Americas.

Flights from London take about 45 minutes, from New York about 8 hours. In 1984 the British and Dutch governments passed legislation that broke the monopoly held by KLM and BA over the Amsterdam–London route and the number of airlines offering flights rocketed. A browse through the travel ads in the British press (such as *Time Out* or the *London Evening Standard*) will divulge any number of return flights priced below £100, even on scheduled airlines. Prices direct from New York start at about $200 for special deals and go up to around $800 for more conventional fares. American travellers thinking of stopping over in London might find it cheaper to buy a ticket to Amsterdam in the UK.

KLM, the Dutch national airline, operates in partnership with the American company Northwest Airlines. Together they offer a service that takes in most major US cities, including New York, Baltimore, Los Angeles and Miami. KLM also flies to a number of Canadian cities, including Vancouver, Toronto and Montreal.

airline numbers

Schiphol Airport	(General Info)	✆ (0900) 0141
KLM UK	UK	✆ (0345) 666 777
	Amsterdam	✆ (06) 474 7747
American Airlines	USA	✆ (1 800) 433 7300
	Amsterdam	✆ (06) 022 7844
British Airways	UK	✆ (0345) 222 111
	Amsterdam (Hoofddorp)	✆ (023) 554 7555
British Midland	UK	✆ (0345) 554 554
	Amsterdam	✆ (06) 662 2211
Canadian Airlines	Canada	✆ 416 798 2211 (Toronto)
	UK	✆ (020) 7745 5000
	Rotterdam	✆ (010) 208 3650

KLM	UK	✆ (08705) 074 074
	USA	✆ (1 800) 3 747 747
	Amsterdam	✆ (06) 474 7747
Transavia	UK	✆ (01293) 596 650
	Amsterdam	✆ (06) 604 6555
TWA	UK	✆ (020) 8814 0707
	USA	✆ (1 800) 892 4141
	Amsterdam	✆ (06) 627 4646

transport from the airport

Taxis will cost you at least ƒ60, and hardly seem worth it given the ease, frequency and price of public transport. **Trains** leave for Centraal Station every 15 minutes (until 1am, then hourly until 5am). The journey takes about 20 minutes and tickets cost ƒ5.75.

Alternatively, you can swan into town on the plush **KLM Hotel Bus**. The service is available to anyone, even if you sneaked over on a bucket flight and intend sleeping in the Vondelpark. Buses leave at 15min intervals from 6.30am to 9.15pm and tickets cost ƒ17.50. Route A stops include the Pulitzer, Krasnapolsky, Jolly Carlton and Okura (i.e. manly central Amsterdam). Route B focuses more on southern Amsterdam, stopping at such hotels as the Hilton, Beethoven and Apollo.

By Train

The most convenient method of travelling by train to Amsterdam is going through the tunnel with **Eurostar**, ✆ (0990) 186 186. Although there are plans to extend the Eurostar service to Amsterdam, for the moment you will have to take the Eurostar train to Brussels and make a platform change for a local train to Amsterdam. Fares start at £79 for a standard return and £159 for a first class return (if you book a week in advance).

Stena Line, ✆ (0990) 455 455, offer combined rail and ferry tickets from London to Amsterdam, departing from Liverpool Street via Harwich and the Hook of Holland. The total journey time is about 8 hours, and standard fares start at £79 return, although there are often promotional fares on offer which can bring the price down to a mere £49.

Travelling around Holland by rail is cheap. You don't have to book as services are frequent, and you can hop off a train to explore towns *en route* to your destination without paying extra. The information desk at Centraal Station can give you details of the various cheap tickets and passes offered by the network—a good idea if you're planning a lot of day trips.

By Bus

This is the cheapest way to go, but it can also be the nastiest. Overnight journeys, in particular, seem maliciously planned so that you're woken at a border crossing every few hours. National Express/Eurolines (✆ (01582) 404 511) offer two options from London daily. On the morning departure you cross the Channel by Hovercraft. The overnight trip involves the ferry and takes 2 hours longer. The current return price for either choice is £44, under-26/over-60 £39.

By Car

To bring your car into the Netherlands you'll need a valid insurance document (such as the EU 'green card'), current registration and road safety test certificates, an international identification disc and an EU or international driving licence. Speed limits are 50kph (31mph) in built-up areas, 80kph (50mph) on the open road, and 100kph (75mph) on motorways. Drive on the right, and give way to traffic approaching from the right, except where you have clear right of way. In Amsterdam be wary of sightseeing pedestrians, give way to cyclists and remember that the yellow trams give way to no one.

The shortest ferry crossing is Harwich–Hook of Holland (Stena Line, ✆ (01255) 243 333)—though, depending on where you're setting off from, you might find other lines more convenient: P&O North Sea Ferries (Hull–Rotterdam, ✆ (01482) 377 177) or P&O European Ferries (Dover–Zeebrugge/Ostend, Felixstowe–Zeebrugge, ✆ (0990) 980 980).

Entry Formalities

passports and visas

EU nationals and citizens of Australia, Canada, New Zealand and the USA need only a valid passport to visit the Netherlands if their stay is for less than three months. If you intend to stay for longer than three months you should get your passport stamped on entry, and will need a **residence permit** (*see* 'Living and Working' in Amsterdam, p.20).

customs

People travelling within the European Union are no longer allowed to buy **duty free**, but if you are coming from outside the EU and are over 17, you can enter the Netherlands with 200 cigarettes (or 50 cigars or 250g/8.82oz of tobacco), 1 litre of spirits (or 2 litres of fortified wine) and 2 litres of non-sparkling wine, 50g/1.76oz of perfume and ƒ300 worth of gifts. If you've bought goods tax-paid within the EU then there are no restrictions, within reasonable limits. You should leave any meat, fruit, plants, flowers, illegal radio transmitters and offensive weapons at home. If you bring in your dog or cat it must be accompanied by a certificate stating that it's been inoculated against rabies.

The **exporting of flower bulbs** is permitted to the UK, but you need an inoculation certificate for the USA. It's best to have bulbs posted home to avoid border hassles. Most reputable dealers will do this, and the necessary paperwork, for you.

Getting Around

Amsterdam is a sedate, compact and intimate city. Pedestrians and cyclists set the pace, and you'll find most places you want to visit within comfortable walking distance. If your legs are tired, or you're in a hurry, yellow trams will whisk you to almost anywhere you want to go. A car is a liability. Parking is expensive (when it's possible), and driving in the narrow streets, which throng with bicycles and jaywalking tourists, is a nightmare. Public transport on the other hand is efficient, safe and cheap, and to be recommended.

tickets and travel information

Maps, information and tickets are available from the **GVB** (**Amsterdam Municipal Transport Authority**), Stationsplein 15, opposite Centraal Station (*open Mon–Fri 7am–7pm, Sat and Sun 8am–7pm, © (0900) 9292*). In the summer there's often a mobile branch on Leidseplein. Once you've grasped the quirky logic behind it, the ticketing system seems quite sensible. Although you can buy **single tickets** on boarding, it's cheaper and easier to buy a **strip ticket** (*strippenkaart*, ƒ11.75). This is valid on the metro and on all buses and trains throughout Holland. The *strippenkaart* is divided into 15 units. Each time you make a journey allow 1 unit for 'boarding', then one more for each zone you travel through: a journey in one zone needs 2 units, through two zones needs 3 units, and so on. Fold the card over at the appropriate unit and slip it into the slot of the stamping machine (on board buses and trams and at the entrance to metro stations). Your card is then stamped with the zone and time and is valid for an hour, even if you swap lines. Most tourist sights are within the central zone, but there are maps at all stations and stops, should you be in any doubt.

Strippenkaarten are valid for a minimum of twelve months. You can buy them from stations, newsagents and the GVB. Bus and tram drivers can also sell you an hourly ticket (*uurnetkaart*, pronounced 'oornetkart') for ƒ4.50 which allows you to travel anywhere in Amsterdam within an hour of its validation. If you intend to use a lot of public transport, the most economical ticket will be a day ticket (*dagkaart*). This allows unlimited travel in Amsterdam and costs ƒ12 for 1 day, ƒ15 for 2 days, ƒ19 for 3 days, ƒ23 for 4 days, and ƒ27 for 5 days. You can buy dagkaarten from drivers or the GVB. Weekly, monthly or annual season tickets (*abonnement*) are also available from the GVB, starting from ƒ17.75.

Uniformed and plain-clothes inspectors will spot-fine you ƒ60 if you travel without a valid ticket. Playing the confused foreigner will get you nowhere.

Call ☎ (0900) 9292 for information on all forms of public transport (including trains) nationwide.

By Tram

Trams run from 6am Mon–Fri, 6.30 Sat, and 7.30am Sun. Last trams are around midnight. They hurtle about, bells clanging, scattering cyclists and pedestrians and forcing passengers to hang on for dear life. On most trams you can get on or off through any one of the three doors (which open after you press the adjacent metal button). Some lines have conductors, who sit at the back. On these trams you can only alight through the rear door. If it looks as if you're the only person due to get off, you'll need to tell the driver to stop by pushing one of the bell nipples inside (on older trams these are unmarked and can be quite obscure). Tram stops have yellow boards showing the numbers of the trams they serve and listing further destinations along the route. Of special benefit to visitors is the Circle Tram, running from Centraal Station to all the major sights and back.

By Bus

Buses work on the same system as trams, though you board at the front door. You're much less likely to use them, unless you need a night bus. A black square with the bus number printed on it is shown on the board of night bus stops. By some inscrutable logic the night buses decrease in frequency at about the time the bars close (2am). After this time there is only one bus an hour on some routes, and none at all until 4am on others. So your alternatives are a late night out, a very late night out, or walking home. You can, of course, always get a taxi.

By Metro

The metro is used mainly by commuters from the eastern and southeastern suburbs. There are only two lines, both terminating at Centraal Station. Running times and ticketing are the same as for trams.

By Taxi

Theoretically, you can hail an Amsterdam cab in the street, but you're unlikely to have any luck at all. Best bet is to pick one up at a rank, or telephone the 24-hour central control, ☎ 677 7777 or ☎ (0900) 0724. The main ranks are at Centraal Station, Rembrandtplein and Leidseplein. Cafés, restaurants or night-clubs will usually phone a cab for you, and one will arrive within minutes. The city has its share of grumpy middle-aged male cabbies, familiar the world over, but on the whole taxi drivers are friendly and honest. When you set off, the meter should be blank, except for the minimum charge. Even short journeys are expensive, with a flat rate of ƒ5.80 for starters, then ƒ2.85 a kilometre (ƒ4.50 a mile) and increasing after midnight.

By Bicycle

Cycling is the perfect means of transport in Amsterdam. It's convenient and gets you about at just the right speed to enjoy the city to the full. It's also a very Dutch way to travel. There are 700,000 people living in Amsterdam, and 550,000 bicycles. Hundreds end up dumped in the canals, and from time to time a dredger with a massive iron claw floats round to fish them out. The curious crowd that invariably gathers to watch remains impassive as the crane hauls out old tyres and stringy lumps of mud, but bursts into a patter of applause at the appearance of a mangled, barnacle-encrusted bike.

The city has an excellent network of cycle-lanes, and motorists are either considerate or outnumbered and intimidated. (Amsterdam drivers have a saying that it would be better to run over a queue of old ladies at the bus stop than one cyclist.) Bicycles are cheap to hire, though it can often be more economical to pick up a second-hand one. This you can do from markets or cycle shops for around ƒ150.

Hire charges vary according to season, but start at around ƒ10 a day. You'll need to take your passport, and a deposit. This ranges from ƒ50 to ƒ200, but you can usually get around it by leaving an imprint of your credit card.

Try **Rent-A-Bike** (Pieter Jacobsdwarsstraat 11, ℰ 625 5029) or **Macbike** (Mr. Visserplein 2, ℰ 620 0985) and **Take-A-Bike** (Stationsplein 6, near Centraal Station, ℰ 624 8391), which are a little cheaper.

Bicycle theft is endemic in Amsterdam. Never leave your bike unlocked. The best way to secure it is with a solid metal U-shaped lock (thieves go armed with clippers that cut through chains in seconds). Lock the front wheel and the frame to a railing or high post. It's a good idea, when you're hiring a bike, to check on your liabilities under the rental firm's terms of insurance.

By Water

If you have the time for the leisurely journeys, canal trips can give you an eye-opening perspective on the city. The moment you step on a boat you seem to cross a mysterious boundary. People on shore carry on with their lives—nicking bicycles, arguing, making love—apparently oblivious of you sailing past only a few feet away.

The **Canal Bus** takes you on a gentle dawdle along some fine stretches of canal between the Rijksmuseum and Centraal Station, stopping at Leidseplein, Leidsestraat/Keizersgracht and the Anne Frank Huis. Buses leave at 45-minute intervals between 10am and 6pm. A day ticket costs ƒ22. The new **All Amsterdam Transport Pass** is a day pass that includes all public transport as well as unlimited use of the canal bus and costs a mere ƒ29.50.

Water Taxis can be great fun if you're in a party mood—the company will even lay on a guide, food and drink for appropriate extra charges. If you're lucky you can hail an empty water taxi as it putters past (they can stop anywhere along the canalside). You can also order them from the **Water Taxi Centrale** (Stationsplein 8, ℗ 530 1090; *open daily 9am–1am*; major credit cards accepted). Fares are metered—an 8-seater boat works out at around ƒ125 for the first half an hour irrespective of the number of passengers, and ƒ75 for every subsequent half hour.

If you're feeling energetic you can hire a **Canal Bike** (a pedalboat that seats two or four people; costs ƒ25 per hour for two people and ƒ40 for four; deposit ƒ50; no credit cards, ℗ 626 5574). Explore the canals for a while, then drop it off at any one of the hire company's four moorings—at Leidseplein (between the Marriott and American Hotels), at the Rijksmuseum, at the Anne Frank House, and on the Keizersgracht near Leidsestraat. Remember to keep to the right, and keep an ear open for warning hoots emitted by the long canal boats as they approach sharp corners or narrow tunnels. **Canal Motor Boats** (on Kloveniersburgwal, ℗ 422 7007) offer electric boats for hire at ƒ65 for the first hour, and a declining rate for subsequent hours.

By Car

If you do find yourself lumbered with a car in Amsterdam, you can find covered **car parks** (indicated by a white P on blue background) at De Bijenkorf (on Beursplein), Byzantium (Stadhouderskade, opposite Leidseplein), Europarking (Marnixstraat 250), RAI (on the Europa Boulevard) and under the Muziektheater (Waterlooplein). Charges are around ƒ5 an hour. Parking beside the road works out at about ƒ4 an hour. Street parking works by the 'pay-and-display' method. You put your money into a machine (often cunningly concealed behind a tree halfway down the street), estimate your time of return, then leave the ticket it prints out on your dashboard. If you park illegally your car will be towed away before you've had a chance to buy an ice-cream. It will cost you at least ƒ400 to get it back from the pound (Daniël Goedkoopstraat 7, ℗ 553 0333), and they won't take credit cards. If you overstay your time in a parking bay, your car will be clamped. A yellow sticker on the windscreen tells you where to pay the fine (which will be at least ƒ126). Some meters are free after 7pm and on Sundays, but in the city centre you have to pay up to 11pm, the Sabbath inclusive. It's always best to check before abandoning your car to the clampers.

If you are in Amsterdam for any length of time, it is a good idea to buy a parking card. This costs ƒ30 (9am–7pm) ƒ33 (9am–11pm) or ƒ7 (7pm–11pm), and is available from the Dienst Stadstoezicht (Weesperstraat 105a, Beukenplein 50, Ceintuurbaan 159, Kinkerstraat 17, ✆ 553 0333). A **park-and-ride system** (known to the Dutch as a *Transferium*) operates from the Amsterdam Arena, in Amsterdam South-East.

The national **emergency car-repair service** is ANWB Wegenwacht (✆ (0900) 0888; open 24 hours daily). The most convenient 24-hour petrol stations are at Marnixstraat 250 and Sarphatistraat 225.

If you'd like to **hire a car**, you'll find the international companies well represented:

> **Avis**, Nassaukade 380, ✆ 683 6061
>
> **Budget**, Overtoom 333, ✆ 612 6066
>
> **Hertz**, Overtoom 85, ✆ 612 2441

Local companies provide a good service, sometimes at less than half the price. Try one of these:

> **Diks**, Van Ostadestraat 278–280, ✆ 662 3366
>
> **Drive Yourself**, Cruquiuskade 5, ✆ 627 4001
>
> **Kuperus**, Middenweg 175, ✆ 693 8790

An EU or international driving licence is valid. You'll also need your passport and a credit card (to pay a deposit).

Guided Tours

On the jetties around Centraal Station you'll find a cluster of boat companies offering **canal tours**, candlelight cruises and dinner cruises. Prices and standards are almost uniform, but Lovers Rondvaarten (Prins Hendrikkade 25–27, ✆ 530 1090) has the best reputation.

The Amsterdam Tourist Board (*see* Tourist Information, p.30) not only takes bookings for canal cruises, but constantly comes up with new ideas for touring the city—its staff can suggest all sorts of walking and cycling routes in and about Amsterdam. **Yellowbike** (NZ Kolk 29, ✆ 620 6940) also offers guided cycle tours around the city and surrounding waterlands. **Audiotourist** (Oude Spiegelstraat 9, ✆ 421 5580) will rent you a personal stereo plus guided tour on cassette for ƒ15 (plus deposit). There are three different walks that last two to three hours each.

More rewarding than the commercially organized tours are the informal walk-abouts with old Amsterdam residents offered by **Mee in Mokum** (*open Mon–Fri 1–4pm,* © 625 1390). The guides aren't professional, but give a homely, resident's touch that you're unlikely to find elsewhere. The tours are usually done in Dutch, but since the groups are small (about eight people), it's often possible to arrange an English alternative. **Archivisie** (© 625 8908) offers specialist architectural tours.

Practical A–Z

Addresses

Houses on the main canals are numbered from west to east, even numbers on the outer circumference. The Dutch write the house number *after* the street name, and follow it by Roman numerals indicating the storey: Bloemstraat 56 II would be an apartment two floors above street level at No.56 Bloemstraat. An apartment at street level is shown by the letters 'hs' (*huis*, house).

Amsterdammers seem to have run out of imagination when naming their streets. If they think they've hit on a good name they'll use it again and again—so you get not only Eerste/1e (1st) Helmersstraat but also Tweede/2e (2nd) Helmersstraat and Derde/3e (3rd) Helmersstraat. Transverse streets get the epithet '*dwars*', and also appear in multiples, so Tweede Egelantiersdwarsstraat will be the second street off Egelantiersstraat. The Oudezijd (old side of the city, east of Damrak) and the Nieuwezijd (new side, west of Damrak) are abbreviated in addresses to OZ and NZ—Oudezijds Voorburgwal, for example, is usually written OZ Voorburgwal. Postcodes are written *before* the word 'Amsterdam'. (Postcode directories are available in post offices.)

Climate and Packing

The songs, and all the clichés, about tulips and the **spring** are right. It's a heady time to be in Amsterdam. The city looks sharp and fresh in the clear light that glints off the canals, café owners tentatively put out a few tables and chairs to catch the new sun, there are flowers *everywhere* and everyone seems to be in a good mood. In **summer** the atmosphere becomes almost feverish. Tourists crowd the streets and bars, the air gets heavy and humid and mosquitoes breed abundantly on the canals. Gable-spotters (see pp.61–3) enjoy **autumn and early winter**, as long lines of canalhouses reappear from behind the summer foliage. Brick, cobblestone and leaves mingle in a subtle spectrum of browns. January and February can be punishing. As you teeter along the slippery pavements, icy blasts of wind howl down the narrow streets and lash around corners. But as the door bangs behind you in a warm café or *proeflokaal*, you'll discover the true meaning of the Dutch word *gezelligheid* ('cosiness' and 'conviviality' are about as close as English can get), *see* p.75. The one thing common to all seasons is rain—sudden showers more frequently than the monotonous drenching sort. It's a good idea to pack an umbrella at any time of the year. The temperature can drop suddenly, even in summer, so a few warm clothes are a wise precaution.

Amsterdammers are not ostentatious dressers. The **dress code** seems to be that if it feels good, it looks good. Nightclubbing youth is less self-conscious about fashion than in other cities; you'll find bank clerks wearing jeans to work, and T-shirts as well as black bow-ties at the opera.

English-language **books** are readily available, though expensive, so it's better to buy your holiday reading before you go.

Children

Amsterdam is a diminutive city, perfectly tailored to a small person's needs. Parents don't have to go to extraordinary expense or exercise great feats of imagination to give children a good time. Cycle lanes make bicycling quite safe, a pedalo on the canal can while away hours, even a ride on a clanging tram can be an event. If trams prove to be a hit, try one of the antique trolleys that go to the **Amsterdamse Bos**, a woody parkland where the children can ride horses, eat pancakes, swim and run about to their hearts' content (*see* pp.233).

Walk III is a good one for children—it takes in carnivorous plants, the Anne Frank Huis and a quirky and eventful Theatre Museum. You can start off the walk in the **Zoo**, Plantage Kerklaan 40, © 523 3400 (*open 9–5 daily; entrance adults f25, under-12s f17.50*). It's green and quite attractive, as zoos go, with some interesting outcrops of 19th-century architecture. The complex includes a Planetarium and an aquarium. There's also a museum and a children's farm, where you can stroke various animals (*open same times as zoo; entrance to both included in the zoo ticket*). There's another **city farm** (De Uylenburg, Staalmeesterlaan 420; *open Mon–Fri 9–5, Sat and Sun 10–5; adm free;* © *618 5235*) in the Rembrandtpark, with free horse rides and a playground.

Some museums have special facilities for children. The **New Metropolis Center of Science and Technology,** Prins Hendrikkade, at the entrance to the IJ tunnel, is a paradise for young computer enthusiasts. All the high-tech displays have explanations in English and most invite fiddling fingers. At the other end of the scale is the **Kindermuseum** (Children's Museum) at the Tropenmuseum (Tropical Museum), Linnaeusstraat 2, © 568 8300 (*open Wed for tours at 1.45 and 3.30, Sat and Sun at noon, 1.45, 3.30; special events some Saturdays; adm children f7.50 adults f12.50; children's programme lasts 1½ hours, adults join children after 1 hour. Children between 6 and 12 years old only; reservation recommended*). The staff, who have all had experience of a third world country, create a village-like environment where children can learn first-hand about aspects of another culture—such as drumming, rice-making or dancing.

Of the **theme parks** out of town, by far the most exciting is **De Efteling**, Europalaan 1, Kaatsheuvel, Noord Brabant, 110km from Amsterdam, © (0416) 288 111 (*open daily Easter–Oct 10–6, July and August 10–9; adm f37.50— Dutch Railways offer a special excursion ticket*). This is a surreal fantasy-land with an enormous Enchanted Forest, flying carpets, mysterious boat journeys, a Sleeping Beauty whose breasts heave, and all the usual (and some very unusual) rides. The Amsterdam Tourist Board has information about other parks. Over Christmas there's a popular circus at the Carré Theatre (*see* **Entertainment and Nightlife**, p.210). Other children's theatre is usually in Dutch, but you might be lucky enough to catch the odd mime or puppet show. Check the listings magazines under the following venues: Kindertheater Elleboog, De Krakeling, Poppentheater Diridas, Mirakel Poppentheater.

If you've had enough of the little darlings, you can get hold of vetted and reliable **babysitters** from Oppascentrale Kriterion (✆ 624 5848; *open 24 hours*). Prices start at about ƒ7 an hour and you're expected to provide drinks, food for long sessions and the cost of transport home after midnight. Over weekends there is a minimum charge of ƒ20.

Consulates and Embassies

Australia, Carnegielaan 12, The Hague, ✆ (070) 310 8200
Canada, Sophialaan 7, The Hague, ✆ (070) 361 4111
Great Britain, Koningslaan 44, ✆ 676 4343
New Zealand, Mauristkade 25, The Hague, ✆ (070) 346 9324
USA, Museumplein 19, ✆ 575 5309

For the telephone numbers of other consulates consult the Amsterdam Tourist Board (*see* 'Tourist Information', p.30), or one of the listings magazines.

Crime and Drugs

As far as big cities go, Amsterdam is comfortably safe. You need have little fear of serious street crime at any time of day or night (though women walking alone would be well advised to avoid red-light districts after midnight). At one time the area around Zeedijk in the city centre prickled with drug dealers and junkies and was quite creepy to walk through. A massive police clean-up has made the area safer, but despite council efforts to encourage shops and galleries to move there, it can still seem seedy and tense.

Contrary to received opinion, **soft drugs** are not legal in Holland, though an official blind eye is turned to the possession of under 28g (1oz) of cannabis. The tolerance goes as far as allowing some coffeeshops to sell cannabis over the counter (*see* **Food and Drink**, p.196); here people smoke marijuana on the premises. But this is not true of all coffeeshops and cafés. Anyone found in possession of hard drugs, such as heroin or cocaine, can expect swift prosecution.

Bicycle theft, **theft from cars** and **pickpocketing** are something of a problem. You'll often see quite abusive signs on car windows informing all who might be tempted that there is nothing at all inside to steal. Amsterdammers sometimes spend more on a lock than on their bicycle ('And I'd just bought a new lock!' is a common wail after a bike has been stolen). A favourite trick of pickpockets is to sidle up close and offer to sell you something illicit. In your annoyed efforts to get rid of them (or keenness to see what they've got) you don't notice that your wallet is being gently removed. Sensible vigilance is the only way to avoid these petty crimes: don't leave valuables in your car, always lock your bike securely (see p.7) and don't carry a wallet in your back pocket or leave it on top of a shop counter when paying. Keep traveller's cheques and stubs separate and don't carry large amounts of money in one pocket.

Amsterdam's police generally keep a low profile and are a relaxed and sympathetic lot. If you do need them, the **emergency number is ⊘ 112**. Main **police stations** are at Elandsgracht 117 and Warmoesstraat 44. Report any theft immediately, and get a written statement for your insurance claim. The Amsterdam Tourist Assistance Service (ATAS, NZ Voorburgwal 114/8, ⊘ 625 3246) offers **victim support**, should you have been shaken up by your experience, or feel at a loss as to what to do. If, on the other hand, you find yourself **in trouble** with the police, phone your consulate as soon as you can (but remember that Dutch police are under no legal obligation to allow you a phone call, and can detain you without charge for up to 24 hours). (See also under 'Emergencies', p.16.)

Disabled Travellers

Amsterdam's cobbled streets and tiny houses with narrow doorways and steep stairs pose problems for those with limited mobility. Older **trams** have high steps, and are not accessible at all, though newer models are more wheelchair-friendly. There is, however, a special **taxi service** for wheelchair users (⊘ 613 4134) and the **metro** is accessible. The **Netherlands Railways** publishes timetables in Braille and a detailed booklet on Rail Travel for the Disabled, available at Centraal Station, or through their London office (⊘ (01962) 773646).

The Dutch government takes an enlightened and constructive view of the problems faced by disabled people. They have, for example, introduced banknotes with raised shapes in the corner that indicate their value to the visually impaired. You'll find nearly all museums, cinemas and churches have wheelchair access and many have facilities for the visually impaired and hard of hearing. The **Amsterdam Tourist Board** (near Centraal Station (see p.30) or the London branch of the **Netherlands Board of Tourism** (18 Buckingham Gate, SW1, ⊘ (020) 7828 7900) has lists of accommodation, restaurants, museums and tourist attractions with facilities for the disabled. For information on specialized holidays contact the British organization **RADAR**, 25 Mortimer St, London W1M 8AB, ⊘ (020) 7250 3222 (helpline open between 10am and 4pm).

Discount Cards

The **Amsterdam Culture & Leisure Pass** entitles you to all sorts of discounts on museums and restaurants. It costs ƒ39.50—though it can pay for itself within a few days. It's available from the Amsterdam Tourist Board (*see* 'Tourist Information', p.30). Museums in the Netherlands are seldom free, but for ƒ55 (ƒ25 for under-24s and ƒ45 for over-55s) you can buy an **Annual Museum Card** (Museumjaarkaart) which gets you into most museums in Holland for nothing, or at a substantial discount. Buy one at the museum ticket office. If you're under 26 the **CJP** (Cultureel Jongeren Passport) entitles you to discount at museums, theatres and cultural events. It's available from the AUB Uitburo (Leidseplein 26, © 621 1211, *open Mon–Sat 10–6*), Amsterdam Tourist Board offices and many theatres for ƒ20. You'll need a photograph for all these discount cards, and proof of age for the CJP.

Electricity

The **voltage** in the Netherlands is 220 AC, which is compatible with the UK, but you'll need a transformer for American electrical equipment. Wall sockets take rather flimsy two-pronged plugs.

Emergencies

Police, ambulance, fire brigade, © **112**. The operators speak English. If you are a victim of **rape or sexual abuse** contact De Eerste Lijn (The First Line) on © 613 0245 (24 hours). You'll find main **police stations** at Elandsgracht 117 and Warmoesstraat 44. For insurance purposes, report lost or stolen property to the police as soon as possible. There are **lost property offices** at Centraal Station, GVB Head Office, Prins Hendrikkade 108–114 (*open Mon–Fri 9–4; for items lost on public transport*), and at Waterlooplein 11 (*open Mon–Fri 11–3.30; for items lost in parks and on the streets*). Allow a day or two for your property to filter through the system before trying to reclaim it. For **medical emergencies**, *see* 'Health' p.19. Lost or stolen credit cards can be reported on the following numbers: American Express, stolen cheques © (0800) 022 0100, stolen cards © 504 8000/504 8666 after 6pm; Diners Club © 557 3407; Mastercard/Access © (0800) 022 5821; Visa © 660 0611.

Festivals and Events

Perhaps because of Amsterdam's Puritan heritage, you'll find little civic or royal pomp. Instead, the city lets its hair down at a number of fairs, arts festivals and street parties—the best celebration of all being Koninginnedag on 30 April. Here are some dates to aim for:

February	**Carnival**: Though it's more a southern, Roman Catholic tradition, Amsterdammers (always in the market for a party) have also taken to the traditional dressing up and last-minute boozing before Lent.
25	**Commemoration of the February Strike**—a solemn gathering at the Dokwerker statue on J. D. Meijerplein (*see* p.120).
March	The **Stille Omgang** (Silent Procession) takes place at night on the Sunday closest to the 15 March. Roman Catholics from all over the world walk in silence along the Heiligeweg and up to Sint Nicolaaskerk to celebrate Amsterdam's 'Miracle' (*see* p.33).
	Also in March the Meervaart Theatre hosts a **Blues Festival** and there's a **boat show** featuring the latest pleasure craft at the RAI Congress Centre (on Europaplein).
April	**National Museum Weekend** is usually the third weekend in April. All museums allow free entry and get very crowded. Unless you're exceptionally hard-up, this is a date to avoid.
30	**Koninginnedag** (Queen's Day—a national holiday to celebrate the Queen's birthday). Amsterdam declares a 'free market'. Anyone can sell anything anywhere and all bar and restaurant takings are tax-free. The whole city turns into a cross between the Notting Hill Carnival and a fleamarket. Holland converges on the town to eat, drink, dance and be exceptionally merry, but with the usual charming Dutch relaxed tolerance. Up to three million people throng the streets (Amsterdam's population is only 700,000), yet you hardly see a policeman, there are no barricades, no rules and no problems—seldom upwards of ten arrests over the whole day, and those are usually for pickpocketing. The best time to join in is after midnight on the 29th, when everyone is setting up stalls and people are as fresh and excited as children on Christmas Eve.
	An internationally respected **World Press Photo Exhibition** displays the pick of newspaper and magazine photography from the preceding year. (In the Nieuwe Kerk, mid-April–mid-May.)
	Watch out also for **GRAP Day** at De Melkweg (*see* p.214, **Entertainment and Nightlife**), when Amsterdam's best new bands blast away well into the night.
May 4/5	**Herdenkingsdag** (Remembrance Day) and **Bevrijdingsdag** (Liberation Day) are not the pompous, jingoistic affairs such

occasions often become. Queen Beatrix lays a wreath at the National Monument at 8pm on Remembrance Day and the whole city observes a moving two-minute silence. The next day erupts in street parties, live music and another free market. Vondelpark and Leidseplein are the best places to be.(Nowadays, Bevrijdingsdag is officially celebrated only every five years.)

June The **Holland Festival** runs for the whole month of June. This is Amsterdam's answer to the Edinburgh Festival, with an impressive constellation of international performers booked into opera, dance and theatre venues around the city. The festival forms part of the **Amsterdam Arts Adventure**, which keeps everyone from opera-lovers to movie-buffs entertained well into the summer.

2nd Sunday 5000 people go for a jog around the canals in the Grachtenloop (*see* 'Sport', p.25).

Around the beginning of the month (or at the end of May) the RAI Congress Centre plays host to **Kunst RAI**, an international contemporary art fair. Later in the month, the **World Roots Festival**—nine days of music, dance and theatre from non-Western cultures—takes place at De Melkweg.

July If the Holland Festival sounds too staid for your tastes, try the **July Summer Festival**—a bonanza of the avant-garde that goes on all over town (sometimes in the strangest places).

August For most of the month of August the Martin Luther King Park, beside the Amstel on the southern outskirts of town, is the scene of **De Parade**, a 'theatre funfair'. Various theatre groups and performers arrange bright show booths, some of them dating back to the first half of the century, in a vast circle, and offer everything from cabaret to performance art. The Masters (and Mistresses) of Ceremonies present the players on stages outside the booths, then everyone troops in for the show. There's lots to eat and drink too.

The **Uitmarkt** (Entertainment Market) takes place in the last week of August. Groups from all over the Netherlands offer tantalizing snippets of what the coming cultural season has to offer. It's free, and takes place in theatres, in the open air—in fact anywhere a company can find a suitable space.

More open-air music is played during the three-day-long **Grachtenfestival** (Canal Festival)—this time from boats opposite the Pulitzer Hotel (Prinsengracht 315–31; also in the last week of August).

September	**Bloemen Corso** (Flower Parade) is a parade of floats from Aalsmeer ('the flower capital') to Amsterdam on the first Saturday of the month. Check with the Amsterdam Tourist Board (*see* 'Tourist Information', p.30) for details of the route and arrival times. Vijzelstraat and the Dam are the best places to watch from.

The **Jordaan Festival** is the liveliest of a series of neighbourhood street parties. All over the Jordaan, the residents come out into the streets to booze, barbecue and try their luck in the often unabashedly dire local talent contests.

One weekend in September is given over to **Monumentendag** (Monument Day), when notable buildings that are not usually open to the public allow in streams of curious visitors.

November   In mid-November **St Nicholas (Sinterklaas/Santa Claus) arrives** by steamboat at Centraal Station (supposedly from his home in Spain). He parades through the city on a white horse with his slave Black Pete (an oddly persistent tradition in modern, racially aware Amsterdam) and is given the keys of the city by the *burgemeester* on the Dam. Relax with a coffee on Rembrandtsplein and watch the early part of the procession in relative comfort.

December 5   **Pakjesavond** (Parcel Evening) is the traditional Dutch time to give presents—rather than Christmas Day. It's usual to make up a short rhyme which caricatures the recipient. It's very much a family occasion, and unless you have Dutch friends you'll find the city awfully quiet.

Oudejaarsavond (New Year's Eve), on the other hand, is the perfect excuse for more wild partying. People take to the streets with bottles of champagne, some bars stay open all night and there are fireworks everywhere.

Health and Insurance

Ambulance, ℡ 112

The most useful place to ring if you are ill or need a dentist is the **Central Medical Service** on ℡ (0900) 503 2042. This 24-hour service will refer you to a duty practitioner. The most central **hospital** with an outpatients department is Onze Lieve Vrouwe Gasthuis, Eerste Oosterparkstraat 179, ℡ 599 9111.

Chemists (*drogisterij*) sell non-prescription drugs and toiletries. If you need a prescription made up you should go to an *apotheek*. The Central Medical Service can also advise you on this. If you've crushed your contact lenses or dropped your specs in a canal, try **York Optiek**, Heiligeweg 8, ✆ 623 3295 (*open Mon–Fri 9.30–6, Sat 9.30–5; appointment advisable, major credit cards accepted*). If your dentures take a crunch try **Accident**, Amstelveenseweg 51, ✆ 664 4380 (*open 24 hours*). There's a free and confidential **VD clinic** at Groenburgwal 44, ✆ 555 5822 (*open Mon–Fri 8–10.30 and 1–3, but arrive before 10.30am for first consultation; appointment not necessary*). The Polikliniek Oosterpark, Oosterpark 59, ✆ 693 2151 (*open Mon–Fri 9–5*) offers **contraception, abortion and morning after pills**, but its services are not free.

It is always advisable to take out **travel insurance** before any trip abroad—and to do so as soon as you buy your tickets. Specially tailored travel insurance packages cover medical expenses, lost luggage and theft, and also offer compensation for cancellation and delayed departure. The cost of travel insurance is steadily rising, but is still insignificant when compared to the potential costs of a serious emergency, or even the value of your tickets should you have to cancel your trip. Consult your insurance broker or travel agent. In the event of needing to make a claim, be sure to check the small print of your policy to see what documentation (police report, medical forms, invoices, etc.) is required by the insurance company. That said, EU nations are entitled to receive free or reduced-charge medical treatment in the Netherlands: British visitors will need a **form E111** (fill in application form SA30, available from DSS branches or post offices). Theoretically you should organize this two weeks before you leave, though you can usually do it in one visit. The E111 does not insure personal belongings.

Living and Working in Amsterdam

If you're considering living and working in Amsterdam, you'll need all the energy, imagination and cunning you can muster to find an apartment and a job. Traditional options for English speakers—such as language teaching—barely exist in Amsterdam because the locals speak English so well. It's a small city, and reasonably priced accommodation is very hard to come by—though, of course, once you cross the magic boundary into the world of company lets and luxury rents, problems vanish.

long-term residence and finding a job

Neither EU nor American citizens need a visa for stays of under three months. If you want to stay longer than that you will need some proof of financial independence—usually that means a job in the Netherlands. The situation for EU citizens is not straightforward. The first thing to do is to get your passport stamped when you enter the country. This won't be done automatically, and sometimes you have to be quite insistent. A stamped passport is the only proof of duration of residence that most authorities will accept. Then within five days you should report to the *Bevolkingsregister* section of the City Hall (on Waterlooplein) to register your address and get a residence permit. To do this you must have a permanent address. Hotels and sub-let apartments do not count—and, as everyone in the Netherlands has to register their address, the computer will find you out if you are fibbing. If you are staying 'permanently' with friends, you must have a signed letter from them (and this renders them liable to extra taxes). Armed with a residence permit, you now need a work permit. You cannot legally take on a job unless you have one. You won't get a work permit until you have a residence permit, and you are highly unlikely to find a permanent place to stay if you don't have a job. This is just the first of many Catch 22s waiting to ensnare you.

If you are lucky enough to have a signed contract or firm offer of a job before you enter the country, your employer should be able to organize a work permit for you. If not, then hold tight. You will (eventually) get a work permit from the *Vreemdelingenpolitie* (literally Strangers' Police, Johan Huizinglaan 757, ✆ 559 6300). Be prepared to queue from around 6am in order to get a ticket (when the office opens at 8am) that will place you in an electronic queue. Don't leave the building. Bring all the documentation you can think of, including passport, passport photos (all *exactly* the same), proof that you are medically insured and your residence permit. Even if you have no offer of a job, the *Vreemdelingenpolitie* are obliged to give you an 'EU Letter' that allows you to register with an employment agency. This letter is valid for three months, after which you have to visit the *Vreemdelingenpolitie* again in order to get a work permit for one year. You might be lucky enough to swing an appointment for this second visit, rather than having to queue. A year later, if you have all the valid documents and haven't been anywhere near the Social Security office, you are eligible for a five-year permit.

American citizens are the only non-EU citizens permitted to apply for a residence permit once they're already in the country, rather than before they leave home. The procedure once you arrive is the same one outlined above.

The place to start **looking for a job** is an *uitzendburo* (employment agency) or in newspapers such as *De Volkskrant* (which has a very good jobs section on Saturday). But be warned, unless your Dutch is excellent you're up against very stiff competition from multilingual locals. Two useful agencies are Manpower (Heiligeweg 9, ✆ 622 7081; general office/secretarial) and Tempo Team (Rokin 118, ✆ 523 6110; academic/catering/medical/secretarial/technical).

Shared accommodation is not as common in Amsterdam as in other large cities. The *De Volkskrant* (which day?) or *De Telegraaf* (Wednesdays) newspapers have 'Rented Accommodation Offered' columns (*Woonruinte te huur aangeboden*) and the weekly freebie *De Echo* is also a good bet. The noticeboards in libraries, supermarkets and tobacconists' windows are a good source of medium-term accommodation. Word of mouth is really the best way. Just be prepared to be a bore at parties until you finally find someone who has a friend whose neighbour is moving out.

As a last resort try one of the accommodation agencies (*see* p.206). Be prepared to fork out a whacking fee, plus a month's rent as deposit *and* a month's rent in advance. Consider yourself lucky if you're offered something for under ƒ1500 a month. Sometimes you're also expected to pay *overnamekosten* (literally: taking-over costs) for whatever tatty carpets and fittings the previous tenant has left behind. *Overnamekosten* can run into the thousands of guilders. Haggle a little, but too much quibbling could lose you the apartment.

Maps

Wandering about Amsterdam's labyrinth of canals, you get the feeling that you could set off in any direction and eventually end up where you need to be. (Very often this is true.) It will take some time before you can zig-zag through the back streets with a local's accomplishment, but some moments studying a good map will help. Practically every free tourist leaflet has some sort of street-plan of Amsterdam. By far the clearest of all the commercially produced maps is the colour 3D-effect one published by Carto Studio, available at souvenir shops and book stores. If you need more detail, Falk publish a variety of maps ranging from simple fold-outs to the origami-inspired 'patent-folded' version.

Media

Don't be surprised if you find yourself chatting over a coffee with an Amsterdammer about the previous night's **BBC** TV soap-opera. Amsterdam gets BBC1 and 2, Radio 4 (198kHz Longwave) and the World Service (6045 kHz AM). Even on Dutch television British and American shows tend to be subtitled rather than dubbed. Most homes and hotels are connected to cable. You can get about 20 stations (including CNN) and can decide what to watch by flicking through to Infokanaal—two alternating screens with simultaneous broadcasts of what's on offer on all channels. Non-Dutch speakers might like to tune in to Netherlands Radio 3 (96.8 mHz) for **pop** or Radio 4 (98.9 mHz) for **classical music**. There are also a number of smaller and pirate music stations— Amsterdam FM (106.8 FM) plays the hippest dance music.

International newspapers are available all over Amsterdam, usually on the day of publication. If you want to pigeonhole the Amsterdammer opposite you on the tram by the newspaper he's reading, here's a short list. *De Telegraaf* is right-wing, sensationalist press (though it has good accommodation ads on Wednesdays). It was the only paper allowed to publish during the Nazi occupation. The *NRC Handelsblad* is the favourite of intellectuals. *Het Parool* started life as a Resistance news-sheet during the war. *Trouw* also went underground, and *De Volkskrant* was banned. These three now form the nucleus of the left-wing press. *Het Financieel Dagblad* gives business news, and has an English summary.

Money

The unit of Dutch currency is the **guilder**, which is abbreviated as f, f, fl (for the old Dutch term florin) or NLG (in business and banking contexts). On price tags, 'guilders' is often written as /-. A guilder is divided into 100 **cents** (shortened to 'c'). There are around f3 to the pound sterling, and about f1.66 to the US dollar. The notes are said to be the prettiest in Europe, and come in f10, f25, f50, f100, f250, f500 and f1000 denominations (though you seldom see notes above f100, and may have trouble finding shops that accept larger denominations). There are six types of coin: a **stuiver** (5c, copper); the **dubbeltje** (10c), **kwartje** (25c), f1 and **rijksdaalder** (f2.50)—all silver-coloured; and the f5 (gold-coloured). All prices are rounded up to multiples of five.

Credit cards are not as widely accepted as you might expect. It's always a good policy to double check. A number of shops will charge you extra if you pay by credit card. (For lost credit cards, *see* 'Emergencies', p.16) **Eurocheques** and **traveller's cheques** are a better idea. If you have appropriate identification, many establishments will accept them direct. Nowadays hole-in-the-wall **cash dispensers** are the most convenient way of getting money. Check that your bank card is programmed for overseas withdrawals, and that your bank doesn't charge for the service. You can usually withdraw up to f300 a day.

The **Postbank** (at post offices) and **GWK** (Grens Wissel Kantoor—official *bureaux de change*) are the best places to change your money. Banks are open 9am to 4 or 5pm, Monday to Friday. (Some stay open until 7pm on Thursdays.)

Bureaux de change often offer the same rates as banks, but take more commission. There are *bureaux* open until midnight on Leidsestraat. The GWK exchanges at Centraal Station and Schiphol (both open 24 hours daily) are a better bet than the deals offered by hotel receptions, and even many banks.

If you exchange traveller's cheques at a company branch, you don't have to pay commission at all. You'll find offices of **American Express** at Amsteldijk 166,

Damrak 66 (with 24-hour cash dispenser for cardholders and automatic traveller's cheque refund service) and Van Baerlestraat 39; and **Thomas Cook** at Dam 23–25, Damrak 1–5 (*open Mon–Sat 8am–8pm and Sun 9–8*), and at Leidseplein 31a.

Post Offices

The Dutch postal service logo is a white *ptt post* on a red background. Post offices are generally open Mondays to Fridays from 8.30am to 5pm. Larger branches may also open on Saturdays from 9 to 12 noon. Here you can buy stamps, and send letters, express letters and telegrams (get in the right queue— sometimes counters are labelled for certain functions only). The **main post office** is at Singel 250 (*open Mon–Fri 9–6, Sat 10–1.30; late opening Thurs until 8;* © *556 3311*) and, as well as the usual facilities, has phones, photocopiers, a gift shop and a philately counter. **Parcels** can be sent only through this office, or the sorting office (Oosterdokskade 3, near Centraal Station; *open Mon–Fri 8.30–9, Sat 9–12 noon;* © *622 8272*). Stamps (*postzegels*) can also be bought from tobacconists. At the time of writing it costs ƒ1 to send a postcard to the UK, ƒ1 to send an airmail letter to the UK or a postcard to the USA and ƒ1.30 to send an airmail letter to the USA (prices for letters under 20g). The slot for overseas mail on **post boxes** is marked *Overige*. A **poste restante** service is available. Letters should be addressed to: Poste Restante, Hoofdpostkantoor PTT, Singel 250, 1016 AB Amsterdam. You'll need a passport to claim your mail.

Public Holidays

New Year's Day, Good Friday, Easter Sunday and Monday, Queen's Day (30 April), Ascension Day, Whit Sunday and Monday, Christmas Day and Boxing Day. On these days most things close, and Amsterdam can be very quiet indeed.

Religious Affairs

Roman Catholic services in English are held at an old clandestine church: St John and St Ursula (Begijnhof 30; © 622 1918; Sun 12.15 pm). There's a **Latin High Mass** at De Papegaai (St Peter and Paul, Nieuwezijds Voorburgwal 293; also entrance on Kalverstraat, Sun 11.15am).

Protestant services in English are held in the serene English Reform/Scottish Presbyterian Church (Begijnhof 48; © 624 9665; Sun 10.30am) and at the Anglican Church (Groenburgwal 42; © 624 8877; Sun 10.30am and 7.30pm).

Times of **Jewish services** vary. You can contact the Liberal Community at Jacob Soetendorpstraat 8 (© 642 3562) and the Orthodox Community at PO Box 7967, Van der Boechorstraat 26, 1008 AD (© 646 0046).

Amsterdam is not a very hearty, sporting city. Most people seem to get the exercise they need from all the walking and cycling they do. However, if you're wandering in Amsterdam South, you might be astonished to see brightly dressed figures, swathed in ropes, scaling the walls of the old firemen's barracks. This is the **Netherlands Mountaineering Club** acting out of desperation. They are not alone. Every year, from May to October, squads of eager '**horizontal mountain-climbers**' don shorts and sneakers and slop knee deep through sucking quagmires of black mud off the Frisian coast. This they do for two to four hours at a time, before returning home.

Another odd national pastime is **pole sitting**. Every year, around the beginning of August, men sit on poles in the North Sea (at Noorderwijkerhout just north of The Hague) until they fall off. The last one to do so is the winner.

Korfball is an indigenous hybrid of netball and volleyball played between teams comprising equal numbers of men and women. It's a rule-bound battle of the sexes where players have to toss a ball around at great speed and try to shoot it into a hoop 11 feet (3.5m) off the ground. The nation does, however, also participate in less esoteric sports.

spectator sports

The most popular national sport is **football**. The Dutch team have not had many resounding international successes, but the local Amsterdam team, **Ajax**, has a vociferous and enthusiastic following. Ajax won European Cups three times in the 1970s, and managed again in 1995. If you want to see the team for yourself, head for their flashy new home, the Amsterdam ArenA, © 311 1333, next to the Bijlmer metro station in Amsterdam South East. **Hockey** (field hockey), on the other hand, is a sport in which both the men's and the women's national teams have been world champions. Many national home matches and some good club games are played at the Hockey en Cricket VVV, Aanloop 2, © 640 2464, south of Amstelpark. If your taste inclines towards the faster and more furious, a good **ice hockey** team (S IJ S Amsterdam 89) plays at the Jaap Edenhal rink, Radioweg 64, © 694 9894, from Oct to Feb. The local **basketball** team, Canadians Amsterdam, is one of the best in the country. They play at the Apollohal, Stadionweg, © 671 3910. Fans of **American football** might be lucky enough to catch an Amsterdam Admirals, © 465 0550, home game at the Amsterdam ArenA or at the old Olympic Stadium.

do-it-yourself

Among the numerous well-equipped gyms and **fitness centres** around town are: A Bigger Splash, Looiersgracht 26–30, © 624 8404 (*open daily 7am–midnight; weights, machines, sauna, steam, massage and aerobics; f35 per* day/ƒ87.50 per week/ƒ140 per month all inclusive) and Garden Gym, Jodenbreestraat 158, ℂ 626 8772 (open Mon, Wed, Fri 9–11, Tues and Thurs 12–11, Sat 11–6.30 and Sun 10–7 mainly, though not exclusively, for women; weights, dance, sauna, solarium, massage, self-defence; day pass ƒ16, with sauna/shower ƒ23.50, sauna only ƒ18.50). Sauna Deco, Herengracht 115, ℂ 623 8215 (open Mon–Sat 11–11, Sun 12–6 adm ƒ17.50 before 2pm, or ƒ25 per day) is an exhilarating experience. You sweat away those extra inches in a stylish Art Deco interior rescued from a famous 1920s Parisian department store.

Swimming pools in Amsterdam are clean, well-maintained and supervised. They often have small bars or coffeeshops at the water's edge so you can top up the calories after an energetic swim. Opening times are complicated, with periods set aside for club and naked swimming, so it's a good idea to phone first. The Marnixbad, Marnixplein 9, ℂ 625 4843 (adm ƒ4.75) has waterslides and a whirlpool. The Mirandabad, De Mirandalaan 9, ℂ 642 8080 (adm ƒ7) has tropical temperatures, a pebble beach and a wave machine. There's an outdoor pool for good weather and a slide and whirlpool.

Walking and **cycling** are the two great national pastimes, and the attractive canals and well-laid out cycle paths make both a joy. If you want to be more serious about things, or would like an uninhibited jog, head for the Vondelpark (see **Walk VI**) or the Amsterdamse Bos (see **Day Trips**, p.233). The Amsterdam Tourist Board can offer suggestions for cycling or walking tours (see p.7 for bicycle hire). They will also be able to give you information on the *Grachtenloop* ('canal run'), Amsterdam's equivalent of the London Marathon. One Sunday early in June thousands of people come together to spend the best part of the day jogging set distances up and down the main canals.

In the winter walking gives way to **skating**. If you're lucky you may be in Amsterdam in a year when the canals freeze over, and everyone whizzes around the city on skates. (Be careful, though, the ice can be thin and sometimes doesn't freeze under bridges.) If you don't have your own skates, head for Jaap Edenhal, Radioweg 64, ℂ 694 9894, a large indoor rink where you can hire skates for ƒ10 (you'll need your passport or a ƒ100 deposit). If the weather is really cold you'll hear talk of nothing else but the *elfstedentocht* ('eleven-city marathon') which takes place on the canals and waterways between 11 towns in Friesland. It is only rarely that the freeze is good enough—if you hear it's happening, then it's certainly worth a trip north.

If bats, rackets and balls are your forte, you'll find **squash** and indoor **tennis** courts at the Frans Otten Stadion, Stadionstraat 10, ℂ 662 8767 (open Mon–Fri 9–12, Sat 9–8, Sun 9–10; tennis ƒ45 per hour/ƒ52.50 after 5pm, squash ƒ37.50 per hour; racket hire ƒ5). There are 42 tennis courts, most of them outdoor, at the Amstelpark, Koenenkade 8, ℗ 301 0700 (*open daily 8am–11pm; indoor and outdoor courts ƒ35 per hour*). Squash City, Ketelmakerstraat 6, ℗ 626 7883 (*open Mon–Fri 8.45–midnight, Sat and Sun 8.45–9; ƒ18.50 for 45 minutes after 5pm Mon–Fri and on Sun, ƒ15 before 5pm and on Sat; racket hire ƒ5*) also has a weights room and sauna for players to use. For table tennis enthusiasts, there's the Table Tennis Centre Amsterdam, Keizersgracht 209, ℗ 624 5780 (*open Sun 1pm–7.30pm, Mon 2pm–6pm, Tues–Sat 2pm–1am; ƒ14 per table per hour*).

As gentler form of relaxation, you might try a little **billiards, snooker** or *biljart* (the pocketless Dutch variation). You'll find all three played at the Biljartcentrum Bavaria, Van Ostadestraat 97, ℗ 676 4059 (*open daily 11am–1am; snooker ƒ10 per hour until 2pm, then ƒ15*). The Snookercentrum de Keizer, Keizersgracht 256, ℗ 623 1586 (*open Mon–Thurs and Sun noon–1am, Sat noon–2am; ƒ8.50 per hour before 7pm, then ƒ12 for pool and ƒ15 for snooker*) is in a 17th-century canal house. The tables are in private rooms and you can phone down to the bar for drinks.

Telephones and E-mail

Amsterdam's telephone boxes are green, with a white *ptt telecom* logo. **Payphones** take 25c, ƒ1, ƒ2.50 and coins. Increasingly, **cardphones** are taking the place of payphones. Many accept credit cards, and all operate with phonecards, which you can buy at post offices, railway stations and newsagents. Instructions in phone boxes are clear, but don't be confused by the local ringing tone—a long continuous sound rather like the British 'engaged' signal. A busy line in Holland is indicated by rapid tones. Another surprise is the dalek voice you get when phoning popular numbers such as airports or taxis. You're told: '*Er zijn nog drie (three)/twee (two)/een (one) wachtenden voor u*'—an indication of how many people are patiently waiting ahead of you in an electronic queue. **Kinko's**, Overtoom 62, ℗ 589 0910, ℗ 589 0920 (*open 24 hours*) offers fax, telephone and computer facilities as well as video-conferencing and copy and printing services. Phoning direct from hotel rooms is usually very expensive.

All numbers given in this book which are not preceded by a bracketed code are Amsterdam numbers (*see* below for direct dialling codes). Numbers preceded by 06 are either free, or charged at a special rate, usually between 50c and ƒ1 a minute (a recorded voice will tell you how much you are forking out).

> **Directory Enquiries**: ℗ (0900) 8008
> **International Operator** (also for collect calls): ℗ (0800) 0410
> **International Directory Enquiries**: ℗ (0900) 8418

International direct dialling codes:

> From Amsterdam to USA: ℗ (00 1) + area code without 0
>
> From USA to Amsterdam: ℗ (011 31) 20
>
> From Amsterdam to UK: ℗ (00 44) + area code without 0
>
> From UK to Amsterdam: ℗ (00 31) 20

International calls are cheaper between 8pm and 8am, but calls to other European countries don't count as international.

Uniquely, Amsterdam has **Internet booths** on street corners. These look just like telephone booths, but are marked with an @. A normal telephone card gives you access to the Net and e-mail facilities. The most conveniently situated ones are at Centraal Station, on the Spui, and near Max Euweplein. There are **Internet cafés** dotted all over town, the most impressive being in De Waag on Nieuwmarkt (*see* p.132).

Time

Amsterdam is 2 hours ahead of Greenwich Mean Time in the spring and summer, and 1 hour ahead in winter and autumn.

Tipping, Etiquette and Service

Restaurant and bar bills in Holland are inclusive of tax and service, so a tip isn't really necessary. It's customary, though, to round the amount up to the nearest guilder (or *f*5 for a big bill). If the service has been exceptional, it's quite acceptable to add a little more. Don't leave money on the bar counter after buying your drink. Amsterdammers will either think it a little vulgar, or take it for a tip. Taxi drivers expect 10 per cent—especially if they've helped with luggage.

Queuing at supermarket delicatessens, some banks and public institutions is controlled by an electronic ticketing system. You tear off a ticket as you enter and wait for your number to flash up on a screen. At cash machines and bank and post office counters, the rest of the queue keeps a polite metre or so's distance from the person transacting business. Sometimes there's a boundary line painted on the floor. Step over this mark (visible or otherwise) and the atmosphere turns icy.

English is spoken almost as a second mother-tongue in Amsterdam. Some Hollanders seem to resent this, but many (especially those working in restaurants, bars and shops) seem insulted if you ask 'Do you speak English?' One way round this is to open with a cheery dag! ('darhg'—good day) and then speak English. 'Dag'—called out with a friendly upward lilt in the voice—is used at all times of day or night, entering and leaving shops, when speaking to barmen, policemen, cabbies and tram drivers. When you meet a Dutch person for the first time, it's polite to shake hands and say your name clearly.

If you are used to slick New York service, or even to the slightly less brisk British style, then you are in for a sad surprise when you visit Amsterdam. Bring a bottle of Valium to help keep calm and a pack of cards to while away the time, or you will find your holiday intensely frustrating. It is not unknown for customers to sit for twenty minutes to half an hour in a café before there is even a whiff of a waiter, though when they do come they are so full of shiny-eyed friendliness that it is difficult to be angry. Expect to wait at least half an hour to forty minutes for your dinner to arrive once you have ordered it. The knowledge that everything is being prepared fresh rather than subjected to the microwave is scant consolation to a rumbling stomach. The maxim that the customer is always right does not hold true in the Netherlands. If you dare to complain, it will be pointed out to you in no uncertain terms that it is in fact you who is at fault. Inform the receptionist that something has been stolen from your room, and rather than an offer of sympathy you will be told off for not putting it in the hotel safe—and will probably have to pay for the phone call to the police. Dare to order a meal 15 minutes before the advertised closing time of the kitchen (usually astonishingly early anyway) and you'll have a strip torn off you for eating so late. Even situations where it seems self-evident that you are in the right—such as a complaint about the lack of a shower curtain—can lead to a brush-up with the management that leaves you feeling you are to blame. Paradoxically, service in Amsterdam is cheery, relaxed and friendly. Just be prepared to wait...and don't complain.

Toilets

Amsterdam is dotted with rather attractive, but foul-smelling, curved green metal **urinoirs**. These are right on the pavement, and blot out only the mid-torso from public gaze. All passers-by see is a pair of feet and a face trying desperately to look nonchalant. In the 1970s, feminists—less out of pissoir-envy than anger at the lack of facilities for women—bound up a few of the offending privies in swathes of pink ribbon. The protest had no effect. Apart from those at railway stations, there are still no normal public toilets in Amsterdam. For women, or men who balk at the idea of peeing al fresco, the best option is to duck into a café. This is perfectly acceptable practice, though bars in some of the busier tourist areas discourage it. The better hotel foyers provide classier options, but this takes a certain amount of poise, as you have to stroll through the lobby as if you're a resident, all the time darting your eyes about for the relevant sign—not easy if you're caught in a last-minute dash. Station loos—and sometimes those in larger cafés—are guarded by fierce women, who require you to drop at least 25c into a saucer before passing.

The **Amsterdam Tourist Board** has English-speaking staff who can change money and (for a ƒ3.50 fee) arrange hotel and theatre bookings. They sell a range of maps and brochures and can suggest tours and walks. The main Amsterdam branch is opposite Centraal Station at Stationsplein 10. There is another, less busy branch at Leidseplein 1, a small branch in Centraal Station and one in the south of town on the corner of Stadionplein and Van Tuyll van Serooskerkenweg (*all open Mon–Sat 9 to 5*). During the high season some offices may extend their hours, and open on Sunday. There is a **central information telephone number:** ✆ (0900) 400 4040, but it costs ƒ1 a minute and you are usually kept for ages in an electronic queue. There is also a nationwide tourist office at the airport, **Holland Tourist Information** (HTI, Schiphol Plaza, **open** *Mon–Sun 7am–10pm*). You can get information on the Internet at two official websites: *www.nbt.nl/nbt-amst-index.html* and *www.amsterdam.nl.*

Information about public transport is given by the **GVB** (Amsterdam Municipal Transport Authority), Stationsplein 15 (*open Mon–Fri 7–7, Sat and Sun 8–7*).

The AUB Uitburo (Leidseplein 26; ✆ 621 1211; *open Mon–Sat 10–6*) gives information and sells advance tickets (booking fee ƒ2) for the city's theatres and concert halls and for many other cultural events. It also distributes leaflets and listings magazines (*see* **Entertainment and Nightlife**, p.208). **Entertainment info** is also at the end of a phone line: Uitlijn ✆ (0900) 0191.

You can visit the website of the Amsterdam Promotion Foundation for business-orientated information on *www.amsterdampromotion.nl*

The **Netherlands Board of Tourism** offices can give you details of hotels and events:

UK: 25–28 Buckingham Gate, London SW1E 6LB
✆ (020) 7828 7900, ✆ (0891) 717 777 (recorded information)

USA: 355 Lexington Av, 21st Floor, New York, NY 10017
✆ (212) 370 7360

225 N. Michigan Av, Suite 1854, Chicago, IL 60601
✆ (312) 819 1500

605 Market Street, Room 401, San Francisco, CA 94105
✆ (415) 543 6772

Canada: 25 Adelaide Street E., Suite 710, Toronto, Ontario, M5C 1Y2
✆ (416) 363 1577

History

Watery Beginnings

A 17th-century English pamphleteer scoffed that the Dutch were 'bred and descended from a horse turd which was enclosed in a butter-box'. Our knowledge of the origins of the first Amsterdammers is only a shade more enlightened. For much of its early history Amsterdam was a swamp. The River Amstel petered out in the vast tidal flats of the IJ. There was a Roman settlement in the dunes near Leiden (Pliny was miserable there in AD 50), but they weren't too keen on the marshes to the north. The first inhabitants of the area we now call Amsterdam were probably intrepid adventurers who came floating down the Rhine in hollowed-out logs around AD 1000, looking for better land. Luck was certainly not on their side, but they made the best of a boggy lot, built huts on muddy mounds and drained the land around them, creating the first polders.

In the 12th century a local bigwig, **Gijsbrecht**, built himself a castle at the spot where the River Amstel was dammed (on the site of the present day Dam Square). He called himself the first Lord of Amstel and laid claim to the countryside emerging from the water around him. The Lords of Amstel were answerable to the **Bishops of Utrecht**, and rather resented it. In the late 13th century Gijsbrecht IV felt he was powerful enough to rebel, but he didn't reckon on his neighbour, **Floris V**, the **Count of Holland** joining in the fray. Floris had wooed popular support in 1275 by granting special **toll privileges** to the people who lived beside 'the Aemstelle Dam'. Floris defeated Gijsbrecht, but later Gijsbrecht murdered him. The Bishop of Utrecht took advantage of the confusion and confiscated Gijsbrecht's land. In 1300 he granted the town of 'Aemstelledamme' its **first charter**. When he died in 1317 he ceded Amsterdam and the surrounding countryside to his nephew, William III, the new Count of Holland. The people of Amsterdam took full advantage of their toll privileges and of William's wide influence and settled down to serious trading and money-making.

Growing Prosperity

The growth of Amsterdam as a trading post owes itself to **herring and beer**. In 1323 the Count of Holland granted Amsterdam the sole right to import beer from Hamburg—at that time northern Europe's largest brewing town and a prominent member of the powerful alliance of Baltic trading ports, the **Hanseatic League**. As most people drank beer rather than the poisonous local water, Amsterdam merchants began to get rich. Then in 1384 one **Willem Beukels** hit upon a way of preserving herring more efficiently—by gutting them before salting. This meant that ships could stay out at sea even longer and travel further afield. At about the same time, as if obeying some cosmic plan, the herring moved their spawning ground from the Baltic to the North Sea. The industry prospered. It needed salt (from Portugal) and wood for the barrels (from

Germany and Scandinavia). Amsterdam merchants had no qualms, as they moved further into the Baltic, about breaking in on the Hanseatic League's trade and developing new routes. Soon the city's ships were also carrying furs, iron ore, cloth, wine and grain to feed Europe's growing population (bread was still the staple diet). Wily merchants built warehouses all over the city to store goods until the best price could be fetched. Amsterdam became a thriving commercial centre and a nexus for European trade. It fought a bitter trade war with the Hanseatic towns, but, by the mid-15th century, was indomitable.

During medieval times the town remained small—a cosy cluster of wooden houses stretching along the banks of the Amstel. In 1300 Amsterdam had one church (the Oude Kerk) and two streets—the present day Warmoesstraat and Nieuwendijk. The town was razed by **great fires** in 1421 and 1452. Wooden buildings were forbidden after the second blaze, and only two remain today (*see* pp.95 and 139). By the 15th century the boundaries extended as far as Oudezijds Voorburgwal, Nieuwezijds Voorburgwal and Spui. There was a new church as well as a clump of monasteries, chapels and inns built to cope with pilgrims flocking to the scene of the **Amsterdam Miracle**. In 1345 a dying man had vomited up the host after his last communion. It was thrown on a fire but didn't burn. Later it developed healing powers, and would transport itself overnight between churches. A chapel of its own seemed to make it stay in one place and, though this burnt down, the host survived. It became an object of worship, and is still honoured today in the **Stille Omgang** (Silent Procession, *see* p.17). One of those healed by the magic wafer was **Maximilian I**, Emperor of Austria (later Holy Roman Emperor). Amsterdam had further earned his gratitude by supporting his faction, the Kabeljauwen (Codfish), against the conservative Hoeken (Hooks) in the struggle for domination of the Low Countries. In 1489 he upped Amsterdam's prestige by granting the city the right to use his royal insignia in its coat of arms. Trade flourished, and by 1500 Amsterdam bustled with 9,000 inhabitants.

Reformation and Revolt

At the beginning of the 16th century Europe was firmly in the grip of the Roman Catholic Church. But on 31 October 1517 **Martin Luther** calmly walked up to the chapel of Wittenberg Castle and nailed his '95 Theses' to the door. The 'Theses' condemned superstition in the Church and the practice of indulgences. Luther's act marked the beginning of the Reformation—theologians everywhere from **Erasmus** in Rotterdam and **Calvin** in Geneva became braver and more audible in their criticism. The Catholic Church responded swiftly and thousands were tried for heresy.

Trade ships carried new ideas quickly to Amsterdam. The revolutionary theology caught on, and there were many heresy trials, but the city fathers were-traditionally tolerant and didn't always carry out sentences they were obliged to impose. In fact Calvin's austere doctrines, and the notion of civil power, rather appealed to a number of wealthy merchant families. The city became ruffled only when the lower-class sect of **Anabaptists** began to jostle the status quo. In 1534 Melchior Hoffman became convinced that mankind was on the brink of a new world order. Münster in Germany was to be the New Jerusalem. He styled himself 'King of Münster' and sat back to await the Second Coming. Fervent crowds of believers joined him. Soon he was sending 'prophets' to Amsterdam, where people were easily convinced that they too lived in a chosen city. The city fathers were at first benign, but on 11 February 1535 a frenzied handful of Anabaptists stripped naked and cavorted about the Dam. Then, on 10 May, 40 members of the sect took advantage of the celebrations of the feast of the Guild of the Cross and occupied the town hall, while the councillors were 'far gone in drink'. It took the (probably inebriated) Civic Guard until the following morning to get them out. Heresy was bad enough, but civil unrest was intolerable. Normally mild Amsterdam came up with horrible death sentences for the usurpers: 'The chest is to be opened up while they are still alive, the heart removed and thrust into their faces, whereupon they are to be beheaded and quartered.' Pictures were commissioned of the Anabaptists' acts of 'raving insanity', and were hung in the town hall as a warning to anyone else. The lax city fathers were replaced.

At this time the Netherlands was ruled by **Philip II** of Spain (later husband of Mary Tudor). Philip was head of the mighty Austro-Spanish Catholic house of Habsburg which dominated much of Europe, owned most of South America and even laid claim to the English crown. Unlike his reassuringly named predecessors (Philip the Good, Charles the Bold and Philip the Fair), Philip II was a cruel and fanatical despot. He also took ages to reach decisions, so his subjects spent most of their lives in a terrified limbo. Action was dangerous, no orders came from above and political situations had the habit of deteriorating around the protagonists. This was particularly aggravating in territories as far flung as the Netherlands. Even Dutch Catholics, outraged by the Inquisition and this distant monarch's cruel repression, became antagonistic. Opposition to Philip began to grow along nationalist as well as religious lines. Philip took a quiet step back, leaving his sister, **Margaret of Parma**, to deal with any unpleasantness. Angry city regents persuaded her to sign the '**Moderation**', which implied some measure of religious tolerance. Calvinist preachers came to Amsterdam, where Protestant services were permitted outside the city walls. During the summer of 1566, hundreds of people left the city's churches to listen to these open-air '**hedge-sermons**'.

A crop failure the previous winter had caused a **famine** which gave an even sharper edge to the religious rancour being stirred up in the polders outside Amsterdam. On 30 August sailors brought back fragments of marble statues smashed by Puritans in Flemish churches. This sparked off a frenzy of destruction. The **iconoclasts** smashed the windows of the Oude Kerk and battered or burnt all popish treasures and artworks. A brave group of women encircled the chapel of the Heilige Stede (where the miraculous host was kept) and fended off furious attackers, but the violence spread. The rabble was diverted by the discovery of the wine cellars at the friary of the Friars Minor, but was only subdued when the city fathers offered up the Franciscan church for Protestant worship.

Even Protestant Amsterdammers, suddenly brought face to face with a wrathful populace, were shaken. Philip II was livid. He sent an army of 10,000 men under the **Duke of Alva**—the 'Iron Duke'—to punish the heretics. Most of the Protestant leaders, sensing what was coming, hastily left the country. He moved in style into a house on the prestigious but desolate Warmoesstraat and borrowed vast amounts of money to pay his army (including ƒ14,000 from his landlord). A reign of terror began. So many people were executed by his Council of Blood that the city was nicknamed 'Murderdam'. In 1568, the date taken as the beginning of the **Eighty Years' War** with Spain, the exiled **William of Orange** attempted a campaign against Alva. Terrified local Protestants gave him little support and the invasion was a failure. William didn't have enough money to pay his soldiers and had to creep away from them in the night. He wandered around France gathering another army, and by 1572 was meeting with a little more success. He was assisted by the **Sea-beggars**, a rough and ready bunch of quasi-pirates, who were later to form the basis of the Dutch navy. Soon William controlled all the towns around Amsterdam. Meanwhile, the populace was turning against Alva—less as a result of his vicious persecutions than because of the **10th penny tax** he had imposed (which diverted 10 per cent of all citizens' income into the Duke's coffers). Alva slipped away one night in 1573, just a few hours before he was due to face a meeting of angry creditors.

In the winter of 1575–6 William laid **siege** to the city. The town officials were so worried about infiltrators that they banned skating on the canals and even stood guard at important gates themselves. Priceless silver was melted down and minted into coins in an attempt to keep business ticking over. After a long siege, it became clear that William was going to win the war, so, in 1578, the city fathers judiciously swapped allegiance and made peace with William. This signalled the virtual end of Spanish dominion over the Netherlands (though they were to retain sovereignty for another 70 years). Exiles streamed back into the city and on 26 May all the Catholic officials and most of the clergy (who had expected retaliatory executions) were bundled into a boat and cast off to find their way to more hospitable climes. A Protestant city government was set up by members of leading Calvinist families. With characteristic Amsterdam grace, the events of 26 May were tactfully referred to as the 'Alteration'.

In 1579 the southern, Catholic and largely French-speaking provinces signed the **Union of Arras** and declared their allegiance to Spain. This gave Spain a base for attacks on the north (most notably the punishing **Siege of Antwerp** in 1584–5). Seven northern provinces responded with the **Union of Utrecht,** a Protestant military federation with The Hague as the centre of power. The Union upheld the 'freedom of religious belief': this meant that you could *be* a Roman Catholic, but still weren't allowed to worship openly. Amsterdam, however, turned a blind eye to the clandestine churches that opened up in attics and behind domestic façades all over town (*see* p.89).

Amsterdam was now by far the most economically powerful city in the federation. The siege of Antwerp had not only wiped out a major trade rival, but had despatched droves of refugees who made straight for the haven in the north. Amsterdam's tolerance paid off. The newcomers brought skills, like diamond-cutting, that fired the city's industries into a new life. Through much of its history Amsterdam seemed to operate on the principle that 'if we didn't supply the enemy, we couldn't afford to fight them'. Arms dealers would support entire wars all over Europe, and brokers of marine insurance (introduced in the late 15th century) had no qualms about insuring both sides in a battle. Amsterdammers excelled at making money. At the end of the 16th century they were on the brink of the most resplendent era of their history.

The Golden Age (17th Century)

A map worked into the floor of Amsterdam's 17th-century *Stadhuis* (town hall) places the city at the centre of the universe—and for much of the century that must have seemed true. Goods flowed into the port from around the world, guilds flourished, and even the lowliest workers earned nearly twice as much as their English counterparts. The **Bours** (Exchange) thronged with merchants from countries as far away as India and Turkey. Isaac le Maire had the idea of trading *in blanco*—dealing on paper with goods he didn't yet own—and the first futures market was begun. In 1609 the city council founded the **Amsterdam Wisselbank** (Bank of Exchange) in the cellar of the town hall. It drew up bank drafts to replace coins (which could be clipped, melted down or stolen), gave quick mortgages and lent at a good rate of interest (an encouraging 3½–4 per cent; England dragged behind at 6 per cent).

People flooded into the city and by 1650 the population had shot past the 200,000 mark. As early as 1613, far-sighted town planners had begun an extension of three new canals around the perimeter of the city. Initially the Herengracht (Gentlemen's Canal), Keizersgracht (Emperor's Canal) and Prinsengracht (Princes' Canal) went only as far as the present day Leidsegracht, but further construction in 1662 gave Amsterdam its familiar half-moon shape.

Malodorous industries and the poor were banished to the fields beyond, to the area now known as the Jordaan (see pp.126–8). Merchants built mansions along the new canals and the city built a *Stadhuis* that was proclaimed the eighth wonder of the world. The arts and intellectual life flourished. Rembrandt, Vermeer and Frans Hals kept busy, and lesser painters churned out 20 million pieces of work during the first part of the century. Books rolled off Amsterdam's uncensored presses—and in the cafés you might find Spinoza or Descartes.

The city's economy was solidly based on the Baltic grain trade (it filled four-fifths of the warehouses), but the spirit of the Golden Age shines clearest in the romance, daring and glamour of the trade with the East. Initially Amsterdam hadn't bothered to send ships further than Lisbon, relying on intrepid Portuguese sailors for booty from the Spice Islands. In 1580, however, Philip II conquered Portugal and closed its ports to his arch-enemy. It was clear that Amsterdam would have to send her own ships to the East. In 1595 **Cornelis Houtman** set off with four ships and 200 men on a voyage of discovery. Only 99 men limped back in battered ships on 23 August 1597, and investors just managed to break even, but the port buzzed with excitement. When a second voyage realized a profit of 400 per cent, merchants exploded into action. In 1597 the romantically named 'Compagnie van Verre' (Far Away Company) began direct trade with the East Indies. Everybody wanted to get in on the act. So many new companies were formed that they looked likely to put each other out of business before they'd really started. On 20 March 1602 they all united to form the **Verenigde Oostindische Compagnie** (United East India Company—VOC). All of Amsterdam seemed greedily caught up in the spirit of adventure. Domestic servants and seamstresses were among the thousands of early shareholders. The company had the monopoly of Dutch trade from the Cape of Good Hope to Cape Horn, and at the peak of its influence it had over 150 merchant vessels protected by 40 fighting ships and its own army of 10,000 soldiers. It sailed all over the East Indies and also to India, Ceylon, China, the South Pacific Islands and South Africa. For nearly two centuries it was the most powerful trade organization in the world. It could even establish colonies, sign treaties and declare war.

In 1624 the West India Company was formed, a smaller and less prosperouscopy-cat venture, which had the trade monopoly over the seas between Africa and the Americas. Its main claim to fame was that it administered the American colony of New Amsterdam—later captured by the British and renamed New York. The trading companies' economic clout gave Amsterdam tremendous sway over the rest of the Netherlands. Eight of the Chamber of Seventeen, the powerful governing body of the VOC, had to be Amsterdam citizens, and managers were appointed by the *burgemeester*. Power in the city itself was grasped by a handful of patrician families. The Catholic clique ousted during the Alteration was replaced by a Protestant oligarchy that became known as the **Magnificat**. Family names like Hooft, Pauw, Bicker, van Beuningen and Six can still raise an Amsterdammer's eyebrow. Wives and daughters sat on the boards of charities and almshouses (housed in confiscated monasteries) and sons would serve in the civil guard on their way up to becoming *burgemeesters* or magistrates. The city was ruled by the **Heren (Lords) XLVIII**, a council of four *burgemeesters*, a sheriff, seven jurists and 36 advisers. These 'regents' often came into conflict with national government. After the Union of Utrecht, the Netherlands was governed by the **States General**, a body of representatives that met at The Hague. Each province was headed by a *stadhouder* (an ancient title that was previously used for the king's deputy). In practice, *all* the provinces chose William of Orange as their *stadhouder*. Successive generations elected heirs to the House of Orange, so the title became all but hereditary. William's son, Maurits, was called 'Prince', and soon the family was grand enough for a match with an English princess.

The *stadhouder* was commander-in-chief of the country's armed forces, and this brought him into conflict with the regents. Peace was better for business than war and, after the final defeat of the Spanish in 1648, the Amsterdam merchants wanted to cut back on military spending. William II wanted to keep his armies. The traditional unease between Amsterdam and the House of Orange bristled into tension. On 23 June 1650 the *stadhouder* visited Amsterdam and demanded an official reception. The regents refused, and condescendingly invited him for dinner instead. 'If we are to wine and dine together,' sniffed William, 'then we would have to be better friends than we are at present.' He left the next day, gathered troops and sent them to take Amsterdam by surprise. Civil war was narrowly averted. The invading army had got lost in a fog and were spotted by a postman on his way over from Hamburg who warned the city. When William died of the pox, the States General passed a law forbidding anyone from the House of Orange ever to become *stadhouder* again—a resolution that only to lasted a few decades.

The Decline

In the first half of the 17th century Germany was battling through the Thirty Years War, the Roundheads and Cavaliers were roughing each other up in England, and France had been left rather limp by the war with Spain. Around 1650 the dust began to settle, and the pugnacious neighbours turned their attention to the prosperous little country in their midst. The conflicts of the late 17th and 18th centuries drained the United Provinces' (and especially Amsterdam's) coffers and gave the warfaring House of Orange a useful step-up back to power.

Squabbles over herring and punitive anti-Dutch import laws led to wars with England in 1652 and 1664. Rather unwillingly, the Provinces found themselves fighting France in the **War of the Spanish Succession** (1701–14). There was another war in 1780 when England discovered the Dutch had been trading with rebel American colonies. London and Hamburg began to take over as mercantile centres, while Amsterdam's old trade routes were threatened. England's increasing sea power began to erode the East Indies trade, and in 1791 the VOC went into liquidation. Antwerp was back on the map as an important port and trade became a less important part of the economy: while Amsterdam focused its attention on banking, the early industrial revolution passed it by.

As the money business boomed, the Amsterdam oligarchy became increasingly corrupt and complacent. The rich got ostentatious, and the poor got angry and subversive. On 24 June 1748 an Amsterdam merchant noticed a 'shameless slut' in the buttermarket who turned her back on a guard and 'several times raised her skirt, smacking her bare buttocks saying 'that's for you'. The guard shot her ('in her bare fundament') and she later died. This was all that was needed to spark off some well-organized street violence. Armed with lists of tax collectors' addresses, a mob stormed the grand canals and sacked the houses. The **Tax Farmers' Riot** was swiftly suppressed, but the civil guard had to beat drums below the scaffold to drown out the slogans shouted by the ringleaders as they went to the gallows.

Vociferous bands of volunteers, heady with Rousseau's ideas, began to roam the countryside spreading the gospel of democracy. They had the support of some patricians, such as Hendrik Hooft (affectionately known as 'Father Hooft'). Soon these Patriots had taken over the governments of many smaller towns, and on 27 April 1787 they staged a coup in Amsterdam. The Prince of Orange had had enough. With the armies of his brother-in-law, the King of Prussia, he sent the Patriots packing. Many fled to France, where they were just in time for the Revolution. In 1795 a French Republican army, with the support of exiled Patriots, crossed the frozen Rhine and advanced on Amsterdam. There was, by this time, strong pro-French feeling in the Netherlands. The invading armies were seen as liberators, and the Regents were bloodlessly deposed in what became known as **The Velvet Revolution**. A 'Freedom Tree' was erected on the Dam and Amsterdammers danced around it celebrating the newly declared **Batavian Republic** (the Batavians were the ancient tribe of the Netherlands). Amsterdam got its first elected city government, but the *liberté, égalité* and *fraternité* were not to last for long. In 1806 Napoleon appointed his younger brother, Louis Bonaparte, King of the Netherlands. Louis converted Amsterdam's *stadhuis* into a palace and demolished the ancient weighhouse on the Dam because it spoiled his view. The city wasn't consoled by the fact that it was now the new capital.

On his first day in the new job Louis announced to his ministers, in heavily accented Dutch, '*Ik ben uw Konijn*' ('I am your rabbit') rather than '*Ik ben uw Koning*' ('I am your king'). But though he started off on the wrong foot, Louis soon endeared himself by visiting the stricken during smallpox epidemics, actively supporting the arts and sciences and foolishly standing up to his older brother. (He allowed Dutch smugglers to break Napoleon's blockade of British ports.) Napoleon hadn't expected his young sibling to be such an upstart, so in 1810 he deposed him and incorporated the Netherlands into the French Empire. But Waterloo was just around the corner. Even before that battle, in 1813 (after Napoleon's retreat from Moscow) the French garrison withdrew from Amsterdam and the Netherlands was proclaimed a constitutional monarchy under the House of Orange. The 1814 **Congress of Vienna** united all the Netherlands provinces (north and south) for the first time—though this lasted only until 1831, when Belgium became an independent kingdom.

From Gloom to Light

Historian Jan Romein describes 19th-century Amsterdam as 'drabness piled on drabness'. After months of bickering with The Hague, Amsterdam had become the capital of the new Dutch Republic and home to the Netherlands Bank, but it was a stuffy and threadbare town. The city's coffers were empty. Napoleon's blockade of English ports and the British occupation of Dutch colonies during the Napoleonic wars had strangled trade, the money market had slipped across the channel to London, and Amsterdam's entrepreneurs had disdained the inventions of the Industrial Revolution. The trading companies' dainty sailboats were soon to be eclipsed by heavy steamships, too bulky to negotiate the Zuider Zee. In 1824 the North Holland Canal (between Amsterdam and Den Helde) was given a festive opening, but the bravado was misplaced: the bends and locks compelled such creeping progress that it was hardly worth the merchants' while.

The sagging city almost collapsed under the burden of a population that doubled in the last half of the century. Areas like the Jordaan and De Pijp became squalid, overcrowded slums, ravaged by cholera. Amsterdam had fallen far from the glory-days of the Golden Age. In 1838, with deft symbolism, the piles under the Stock Exchange gave way and the building collapsed.

As the disconsolate city limped through the early decades of the 19th century, a few valiant paladins of the new industries tried to revitalize her. The king set up the Nederlandse Handelsmaatschappij (Netherlands Trading Company) to perk up the drooping trade in tropical products. In 1825 **Paul van Vlissingen** started running regular steamship services to London and Hamburg and built an engineering works on Oostenburg island in east Amsterdam. Almost single-handedly he nudged the city into the industrial age. But the man most personally responsible for rousing Amsterdam from her torpor was the peppy doctor and philanthropist, **Samuel Sarphati**. With his motto *Amsterdam Vooruit!* (Amsterdam Advance!), he was bent on pushing the town headlong into another Golden Age. He founded a commercial college, several banks, a construction company, the city's first hygienic bread factory, the Amstel Hotel (still one of the best in town) and an efficient and profitable refuse disposal service (the city's stinking waste was shipped out in sealed barges, composted and sold to farmers). He founded the *Vereniging voor Volksvlijt* (Industrial Society) to knock new life into the city's manufacturers and to inject new technology into the factories. His sparkling glass Palace of Industry rose up on Frederiksplein and was home to countless displays, exhibitions and concerts until it burnt down in 1929.

Towards the end of the century Amsterdam began to thrive once more. New industries—even a motor car factory—flourished. The opening of the Suez Canal in 1869 meant easier access to the Orient, and in 1876 the North Sea Canal was cut through the dunes to give proper access to bigger ships. Amsterdam became the main supplier to a newly unified Germany, and manufacturing and ship-building industries revived. The discovery of diamonds in South Africa led to a boom in the diamond-cutting trade, with workers becoming deliriously rich overnight. In 1839 the first railway in the Netherlands ran from Amsterdam to Haarlem and fifty years later the city had a grand new railway station that obliterated the view of the harbour. During the 1880s the first trams and bicycles appeared. (Lady cyclists had to attend special riding schools, as it was thought undignified, if not lewd, for them to be seen wobbling along.) The Vondelpark was laid out on the edge of the city and the élite scurried to live around it. The arts blossomed. The Rijksmuseum, Concertgebouw, Carré Theatre, Amsterdamse Schouwburg and Stedelijk Museum sprang up in the last two decades of the century and in 1883 Amsterdam hosted the World Exhibition.

The 19th century saw an increase in parliamentary democracy in the Netherlands. The 1848 revolts in the rest of Europe made King William II nervous. Amsterdam was tense—the slum area of the Jordaan, in particular, regularly erupted into violence. In 1848 the king set up a reform committee under the liberal Rudolph Thorbecke and changes were hurried through after a mob stormed around the Dam in 1849, with the alarming proclamation that 'All men are brothers.' As the franchise was extended, support grew for the socialist movement. In 1902 Henri Polak took up the first seat for the **Social Democratic Labour Party** (SDAP) on the city council. By 1915 the SDAP was the largest party in Amsterdam, housing associations had been formed, a 1901 Housing Act had stipulated minimum living conditions, and council houses all over the city relieved the pressure on areas like De Pijp and the Jordaan.

Amsterdam entered the 20th century on the crest of a boom. The Netherlands remained neutral in the First World War. Amsterdam happily traded in arms with both sides, and emerged comparatively unscathed—though the rest of her trade had taken a blow and food shortages in 1917 had provoked the Jordaaners into riots. The city's population was again growing fast. Canals were filled in to cope with burgeoning road traffic and in 1920 two converted De Havillands, carrying two passengers apiece, began to fly regularly to London. The world's first air travel booking office opened at **Schiphol** in the following year. In 1928 Amsterdam hosted the Olympic Games, but the 1929 Wall Street crash slid the city into an economic depression. Gangs of unemployed were set to work creating the Amsterdamse Bos (Amsterdam Forest) outside the city, and when, in 1934, the council tried to lop 25c off the dole pay, the Jordaaners again rioted. The 1930s also saw the growth of a small but vociferous Dutch Nazi Party (NSB).

The Second World War

The Netherlands hoped to remain neutral in the Second World War, as they had in the first. But on 10 May 1940 the Germans attacked Dutch airports and military barracks. Queen Wilhelmina and the Dutch government skipped across the Channel to the relative safety of England. They left Supreme Commander Winkelman to deal with the advancing Germans. He held out for five days during which Rotterdam was mercilessly bombed from the air. On 15 May the German army occupied the Netherlands and Hitler declared the Austrian Nazi **Arthur Seyss-Inquart** *Rijkscommissaris* (State Commissioner).

At first life in Amsterdam carried on much the same as before, with citizens exercising their indefatigable capacity to turn a blind eye to anything that threatened to ruffle the smooth flow of daily business. However, when Seyss-Inquart's early softly-softly attempt to *nazificeren* ('nazify') Holland met with stolid Dutch inertia, he became more brutal. Jews, especially, were the butt of systematic oppressive decrees. The wearing of yellow stars was compulsory and Jews were banned from driving or from using trams. They had to hand in their bicycles, be indoors by 8 o'clock (not even out in their own gardens), were allowed to shop only in Jewish shops between 3 and 5 o'clock in the afternoon, and couldn't visit theatres, cinemas or sports grounds. Soon they were forbidden to visit Christians, had to go to separate schools and were fenced off in ghettos. On 22 February 1941 German trucks rumbled into the Jodenhoek (Jewish Quarter) and the **first round-up of Jews** began. In the years that followed nearly all of Amsterdam's Jews (10 per cent of the city's population) were transported, along with gypsies and homosexuals, to concentration camps in Germany. Hardly any survived.

The February *razzia* (raid on Jews) sparked off a spontaneous Amsterdam-wide strike that was viciously put down. Right through the occupation heroic Resistance fighters sabotaged German munitions and supplies stores, attempted to assassinate Nazi leaders, spawned batches of false documents and reeled off secret newspapers to keep the public properly informed. Nazi retaliation was diabolical. If they couldn't dig out the ringleaders, whole groups of innocent people would be shot in reprisal for any Resistance activity. Opposition also went on in quieter, but no less courageous ways. Many non-Jews wore yellow stars in sympathy and thousands gave shelter to *onderduikers* ('divers')—members of the Resistance, or Jews (like the Frank family), who went into hiding around the city. On Prince Bernhard's birthday, thousands imitated his habit of wearing a white carnation, much to the confusion of the Nazis who didn't know quite what to legislate against. Queen Wilhelmina broadcasted cheering messages to her people from the security of a BBC studio.

By the winter of 1944—'**Hunger Winter**'—the fabric of the city had collapsed. Everybody was starving (especially those sharing ration books with *onderduikers*), as the Germans had restricted the flow of food in retaliation for a Dutch railwaymen's strike. Walking was the only means of transport and rubbish bins and sewers overflowed. Fuel was impossible to come by, so Amsterdammers stole any wood they could lay their hands on. Sleepers were torn from the tram tracks, parks thinned out mysteriously overnight and any empty houses were stripped of furniture, beams and floorboards. The Jodenhoek began to crumble.

On 5 May 1945 the Netherlands was **liberated**. On 7 May jubilant crowds crammed the streets of Amsterdam to greet the Canadian liberation force. In a final lash of malice, German soldiers opened fire on the crowd, killing 22 people.

Post-war Amsterdam

The Netherlands was devastated by the war. Its transport system was paralysed, industrial production had slumped by 30 per cent and the Germans had broken dykes, flooding much of the countryside. Despite chronic shortages of almost everything, Amsterdammers bounced back with a lively resilience. They even managed city-wide street parties in 1948 to celebrate **Queen Juliana's coronation** and Dutch victories in the **Olympic Games**. Tropical trade declined, but Amsterdam soon got down to the more mundane business of keeping the hungry new Ruhr industries fed. After the widening of the North Sea Canal and construction of the new Amsterdam-Rhine Canal in 1952, **regeneration** was meteoric. Garden-city suburbs sprang up around Amsterdamand the 1960s vision of air, light and towering concrete gave birth to the Bijlmermeer (vast stretches of concrete dotted with towerblocks that nobody wanted to live in).

Old patterns began to emerge. The solid Calvinist burgers were still very much in control, but the city's traditional tolerance osoon made space for a new phenomenon of dreamy hippies and tatty youth. In the 1960s Amsterdam became a mecca for the blossoming youth culture. Troupes of long-haired young people hung out and slept around Centraal Station, the National Monument on the Dam and in Vondelpark. In 1969 John Lennon and Yoko Ono staged their week-long '**Bed-in**' for world peace in the Hilton Hotel. An old church near Leidseplein was converted into the Paradiso—a place to puff away on marijuana without fear of arrest, and have your ears blasted by the latest music. Homosexuals began to join the party, and soon Amsterdam was known as the **gay capital** of Europe.

At the centre of the Amsterdam counter-culture was a group of flamboyant jesters, the **Provos** (from *provocatie*—provocation: *see* pp.74–5). Philosophy student Roel van Duyn, and magician and one-time window cleaner Robert Jasper Grootveld, with a motley gang of accomplices staged 'happenings' on the Dam and around the statue of the *Lieverdje* ('Little Darling') on the Spui. The Provos were against capitalism, traffic and tobacco, and for free bicycles and free sex. However, when Crown Princess Beatrix married a German in 1966, the mood soured. The royal family was, to the Provos, the distillation of the Establishment. Not only the Provos were angry. Ratepayers resented having to foot the bill for the celebrations and the older generation—still raw from the Occupation—were appalled that their princess could marry a German. Demonstrators lined the route of the wedding procession waving banners demanding 'Republic' and 'Give me my bike back' (the Nazis had confiscated bicycles during the war). Although the day passed without serious incident, discontent bubbled on through the spring. One hot June day a minor industrial dispute over construction workers' holiday pay erupted into violence. During a scuffle with the police in the Jordaan (as always), one worker died of a heart attack. Rumour spread that the police had killed him, and a full-scale riot spread right across the city, sucking in Provos, Nozems (youth gangs) and anyone who enjoyed a fight. By nightfall the *burgemeester* was about to call in the army, but Chief Commissioner van der Molen of the Amsterdam Police took the matter in hand. He donned full dress uniform, called for his sword and strode out bravely into the midst of a bemused crowd. He didn't entirely defuse the situation, but the disruption fizzled out two days later.

Later that year, violence broke out again over proposals to build a huge bank on Frederiksplein. Amsterdammers felt that big money was destroying the heart of the city by denuding it of anything but banks and offices. Concerned burghers held a 'Teach-In' at the Hotel Krasnapolsky to debate the issue. In putting the case for the objectors, Dr W. F. Heinemeyer, a local academic, hit upon what, for many people, is Amsterdam's charm: '…most Amsterdammers want a closely mixed-up network of streets and squares…where there's a great variety of possibilities for doing things one doesn't have to do, shopping, going to films and plays, sitting on terraces, in cafés, looking around, wandering about…a place where one can be *out* and at the same time *at home*, where it's a pleasure simply to *be*…One can call it the "forum" nature of the inner city, and this is something so precious that no administration must be indifferent about it.' But three days later the city regents debated the proposal and voted in favour of the bank by 30 to 14. Meanwhile, the crowds camping out, especially those around the new National Monument (a war memorial), had begun to test the patience of upright citizens.

In 1967 off-duty Marines had descended on unsuspecting hippies outside the Centraal Station and cut off their hair. The mess left by the impromptu campsites was an affront to the obsessively neat Amsterdammers and a bye-law passed in 1969 banned sleeping around national monuments. In 1970, after violent clashes with the police had failed to oust the Dam dropouts, the Marines once again decided on unofficial unilateral action. Bands of strapping lads belted down the Damrak, and frightened the hippies away forever. Amsterdam's youth culture survived the attack, but was more formally accommodated in hostels and Sleep-Ins.

The Provos had broken up in 1967 'in order to avoid bloodshed', but Roel van Duyn went on to establish the **Kabouters** ('helpful gnomes')—a whimsical party of idealists with odd flashes of common sense. In May 1970 they gathered, wearing pixie hats, on the Dam, planted an orange tree and issued a proclamation. They declared an Orange Free State (with van Duyn as its ambassador) that would soon link up in a fairy circle with other socialist elf cities around the world. Theirs was no longer to be the 'socialism of the clenched fist, but of the intertwined fingers, the erect penis, the escaping butterfly'. They wanted more trees, fewer banks and polluting industries, a ban on traffic in central Amsterdam, free white bikes for all—and improved psychiatric services. In the summer election they polled 11 per cent of the vote and won five seats on the city council. As the decade wore on, they lost their appeal and were finally disbanded in 1981.

Though the Kabouters were on the wane, the late 1970s and early 1980s saw some spectacular battles. The council's plan to build a Metro—largely to serve the outer suburbs—met with outrage. It was expensive, and meant pulling down more houses in the inner city. Many refused to move and on 25 March 1975 '**Blue Monday**'—there were violent demonstrations when officials tried to clear the first houses for demolition. The ferocity of the opposition increased until 1978, when the council agreed to build new homes and renovate areas of the inner city. Skirmishes went on right up until the opening of the Metro in 1980.

In 1980 13 per cent of the city's population was on the housing list. Squatting had become a popular solution to the chronic shortages. A lot of work went into the renovation of squatter homes, and the building of accompanying studios and cafés. The network became highly organized, and, with 10,000 members by 1982, was a force to be reckoned with. Police attempts to evict squatters were heavy-handed (they used tanks on a squat in the Vondelstraat) and not always successful. But by 1984 the last of the big squats had fallen: on others a compromise had been reached—the council bought up the property, renovated it and let it back cheaply to the inhabitants.

Ed van Thijn, Amsterdam's (socialist) *burgemeester* for most of the 1980s and the early 1990s, was tough on squatters when he first came to office, but then initiated a strong programme of *stadsvernieuwing* (urban renewal) to help ease the severe housing crisis and to transform the city's image. Every few decades, the city fathers get it into their heads that Amsterdam is backward and old-fashioned and needs to be promoted as a modern metropolis. This usually leads to big new buildings in the centre of town. In the 1890s the Centraal Station, a temple to the new railways, blocked off Amsterdam's view of its harbour forever; in the 1920s the enormous Nederlandse Handelsmaatschappij (Chamber of Commerce) building pushed aside rows of historic gabled houses near Rembrandtplein; during the 1960s concrete and glass monstrosities appeared all over town, the most controversial being the Nederlandse Bank on Frederiksplein (*see* p.46). The 1970s and early 1980s saw the arrival, amidst violent protest, of the Metro and the 'Stopera', a combined city hall and opera house on Waterlooplein (*see* pp.69–71). In the 1990s *Burgemeester* Van Thijn began to emphasize Amsterdam's role as a tourist, banking and congress metropolis. (It is now Europe's fourth tourist city after London, Paris and Rome, and in the world's top ten as a congress venue.) Vast new development went on in the area around Centraal Station, a glittering casino complex was built alongside Leidseplein, and business parks bristling with skyscrapers appeared on the outskirts of town.

Van Thijn's successor, **Schelto Patijn**, assumed office in 1994. Amsterdam's mayors are not elected by the citizenry, but appointed (ostensibly by the Queen). Yet they wield extraordinary civic power. Patijn hails from The Hague, Amsterdam's arch-rival and it did not help his image at all when the news leaked out that he didn't even intend to live in Amsterdam—though this decision was hastily revoked. It is muttered that this outsider does not understand the city at all, and his efforts at giving Amsterdam a more upmarket, businesslike image have resulted in such moves as towing away some of the old houseboats (seen as illegal and messy), and attempting to close down a number of café terraces (thwarted by rousing local opposition).

Yet the city's notorious drugs problem does seem more under control. Heroin dealers have been cleared out of the tourist areas around Zeedijk and Nieuwmarkt and now hole out in the south of the city. The *stadswacht* (modern-day equivalents of the Civil Guards in the Old Masters' portraits) wander about, unarmed, in smart uniforms with red trimmings, keeping an eye on public behaviour and making sure that buskers don't sing too loudly. Tourist figures over the past few years have risen steadily. Amsterdam is enjoying a quiet, rather comfortable moment in its history, but its age-old tolerance of mischief remains the finest antidote to complacency. Amsterdam's flourishing gay community, the bustling red-light district, the newest wave of immigrants (from Turkey and Surinam), the Kabouters' legacy of environmental awareness and the Amsterdammers' nose for disruptive politics keep the cafés alive and the old port rough beneath its smooth veneer.

Art and Architecture

Sacheverell Sitwell wrote that painting and architecture are as endemic among the Dutch as poetry is among the English. During the 17th-century Golden Age (a high-water mark for painting, as well as an economic boom) an estimated 20 million paintings were executed. Even the humblest homes had the odd oil tacked up on the wall. A 17th-century English traveller observed that 'many times blacksmiths, cobblers etc. will have some picture or other by their forge or in their stall. Such is the general notion, inclination and delight that these country natives have to painting. These days Amsterdam is still the centre of a flourishing art trade, with nearly 150 commercial galleries that sell anything from Picasso to post-art-school hopefuls. There's an enormous annual art fair at the RAI Congress Centre (usually in June) and open-air art markets spring up around town in the summer. Here you often find inspired work nestling among more predictable ceramics and water-colours—but never the sort of kitsch and tat that's draped on the railings of London's Hyde Park on a Sunday afternoon. Artists' *ateliers* are everywhere: in the red-light district, on boats, stretched out in glass-walled grandeur in the posher parts of town. Clusters of studios in the same area have open days from time to time, when (clutching a rough, photocopied map) you can wander in and out, look at work in progress and chat with the artists. Sunday afternoons are the favoured time for 'openings'. These affairs seem less over-dressed, tense and poseur-ridden than is usual in other parts of the world.

And, of course, there are all the Old Masters in the Rijksmuseum, a whole building full of Van Goghs and the go-getting Stedelijk Museum. Even in the Stedelijk, how-ever, you're likely to find something by the latest American whizz-kid or the Dutch boy-next-door tucked in among the Chagalls and Mondriaans. In Amsterdam there's a feeling that art matters, is part of everyday life, and that even the zaniest of new painters belongs to a long continuum of artists working in Holland.

Before the Golden Age

It is important to draw a distinction between Dutch and Flemish art. In 1579 the Netherlands polarized into a Flemish, predominantly Roman Catholic south, and an alliance of seven Dutch, Protestant northern provinces. Eugène Fromentin, the 19th-century art critic, observed that 'Holland had never possessed many national painters… While she was blended with Flanders, it was Flanders that took upon herself to think, invent and paint for her.' Early Flemish art resounds with familiar names like Breughel, Bosch and van Eyck, while Holland musters Cornelis Ketel, a portrait painter who grew bored with his craft and, as a ruse to liven up his tech-nique, started painting with his toes, with no noticeable loss in quality. However, in the 17th century migrations of prominent painters to the Protestant north, a blossoming national confidence and snowballing economic prosperity stimulated a new Dutch School. This exclusively Dutch painting was influenced by Flemish artists, but also by Italians and a small heritage of local painters less disgruntled with their lot than Cornelis Ketel.

In his *Book of Famous Men*, the 15th-century humanist Barolemmo Fayio lists only two Flemish artists: Jan van Eyck and Rogier van der Weyden—painters we still consider pivots of the period. Both had a strong influence on later Dutch painting. **Jan van Eyck** (1385–1441) and his shadowy brother, Hubert (some say they collaborated, some say that Hubert never existed) are credited with the discovery of oil paint. In reality, they merely perfected a technique that northern European painters had been using for some time. Oil paints, which can be applied in layers, give a rich, deep tone which was much favoured by artists who were fascinated by *appearances*—the glowing colours of objects as they were touched by light. Italian artists, on the other hand, tended to be more concerned with *structure*, bodies and movement: they worked in tempera (egg-based paint) which rendered sharper, brighter colours—but soon latched on to the practical and artistic merits of oils.

Early Netherlandish art was mainly devotional. Static groups of bodies crowded pictures crammed with detail and heavily symbolic bric-a-brac. **Rogier van der Weyden** (1399–1464) swept the canvas clean. He focused tightly on a few figures and injected a passionate, authentic emotional intensity into his work. This was rare in religious art of the time, and had a powerful impact on later Dutch painters.

Albert Ouwater (active 1450–80) was the man who took these ideas north. He settled in Haarlem around the time that a book by the Florentine Leon Battista Alberti was being passed around painters' studios. Alberti argued that *historia* (narrative) was crucial to good art. Dutch painting became less static; small dramas and conflicts began to emerge from the canvas. **Geertgen tot Sint Jans** (*c.* 1460–95) was much influenced by Ouwater. He painted bright, beautiful pictures, still laden with symbolic references but with a much freer arrangement of figures. The figures themselves, however, were still rigid, with little real eloquence of human movement. **Lucas van Leyden** (1489–1553), a child prodigy who was already engraving in his native Leiden at the age of nine, burst on to the scene with sparkling, dynamic, densely peopled paintings that revolutionized Dutch art. As these various strands combine we can see, in the work of painters like Van Leyden and **Jan Mostaert** (1475–1555), the first signs of a separate Dutch school of painting.

In 1604 Karel van Mander, a painter and theorist working in Haarlem, published *Het Schilderboek*—a collection of biographies and a theoretical handbook for artists. It was the first full-scale work of art theory to delineate Dutch and Flemish traditions. Van Mander exalted Haarlem as the cradle of Dutch art. The school of painters working there was developing its own style of Italian Mannerism. The

Mannerists believed their work shouldn't slavishly imitate Nature, but improve upon it with imagination and Art. Paintings (even those with innocent titles like *John the Baptist Preaching*) swarm with lumpy nude musclemen and elongated female figures. They sport about in exotic settings in which piled-up fragments of Roman art, stylized plants and fabulous beasts abound.

The first Dutch painter to travel to Renaissance Italy (it later became *de rigueur* for any artist who wanted to be taken seriously) was **Jan van Scorel** (1495–1562). He passed through Germany and Venice on a pilgrimage to Jerusalem. On his way back he visited Rome, and was given the job of curator of the massive papal art collection by Hadrian VI, the only Dutch pope in history. This experience changed his painting style completely, and he returned to Haarlem (as Van Mander puts it) as 'the lantern-bearer and road-paver of the Arts in the Netherlands'. Others would claim that honour for Lucas van Leyden, but Van Mander thought that Van Leyden was a show-off—and, besides, he didn't come from Haarlem. Van Scorel's pupil **Martin van Heemskerck** (1498–1574) also travelled to Italy and was one of the main propagators of Mannerist ideas in Holland.

Mannerism made Dutch painting far more lively and flexible, but painters began to tire of its ornament. A move to greater realism and narrative clarity—more Nature, less Art—can be seen in the works of **Hendrik Goltzius** (1558–1616), another member of Van Mander's Haarlem mafia.

By the 1620s another school of painters had sprouted in Utrecht. Artists such as **Hendrick Terbrugghen** (*c.* 1588–1629) and **Gerrit van Honthorst** (*c.* 1590–1624) were followers of the Italian painter Caravaggio, whose *chiaroscuro* technique (strong contrasts of light and shadow) influenced successive waves of Dutch painters all the way through to Rembrandt and Vermeer. Terbrugghen was the first Dutch Caravaggist to return to Holland (after a ten-year stay in Italy), but he was self-effacing and a bit of a misfit—he wasn't even elected to office in the Utrecht guild. The flattering and flamboyant Van Honthorst, on the other hand, ran up impressive lists of patrons wherever he went and became the best known of the Dutch Caravaggists. His beautiful nocturnal scenes—candlelight and shadow playing over huddles of faces—earned him the nickname 'Gherardo delle Notti'.

The Golden Age

> France has shown a great deal of inventive genius, but little real faculty for painting. Holland has not imagined anything, but it has painted miraculously well.
>
> Eugène Fromentin, art critic, writing in 1875

In 1565 mobs stormed through the Netherlands breaking church windows and destroying religious paintings and statues. In their enthusiasm to eliminate idolatry, these iconoclasts wiped out much of the country's artistic heritage. There seemed little call to replace it. The austere Calvinists who took control of the northern provinces after 1579 whitewashed the insides of churches and had no time for papish decoration. Italy and its art went out of fashion. The rising merchant classes seemed suspicious of unprofitable aristocratic foibles like patronage of the arts. Artists were in a dilemma: what *were* they to paint, and who would pay them for it? Eugène Fromentin comes right to the point.

> The problem was this: given a bourgeois *people, practical, not inclined to dreams, very busy withal, by no means mystic, of anti-Latin tendency, with broken traditions, a worship without images, parsimonious habits—to find an art to please [them]...there remained nothing for such a people to propose to themselves but a very simple and daring thing...to paint its own portrait.*

And so the Dutch set about painting 'the portrait of Holland, its external image, faithful, exact, complete, life-like, without any adornment'. In the Golden Age that followed, you find few flamboyant devotional paintings or pompous, heroic battle scenes. Instead, you are given portraits of merchants, town squares, street scenes, glimpses of daily life, breakfast tables, brothels, taverns, the countryside, or moments in history. No other nation has managed a more intimate and beautifully executed chronicle of its life and times.

Genre Painting

Early English critics called the pictures of scenes from everyday life 'drolleries'—nowadays we refer to them as genre paintings. By the mid-17th century, genre was one of the most popular art forms in Holland, and the cheapest to buy. These were straightforward, unembellished paintings of taverns, brothels and family life, but they often contained a covert moral message. Sometimes the signal was crude—wildly copulating dogs in a doorway behind a flirting couple refer to the saying 'As with the woman, so with her dog'. Sometimes complex allegorical references and obscure symbols were knitted into the apparently simple pictures. Unravelling these was, for an educated 17th-century viewer, half the fun of genre paintings.

There are examples of genre work in the paintings of the Caravagists Hendrick Terbrugghen and Gerrit van Honthorst, and in the work of some Mannerists, but it was the writing and painting of **Willem Buytewech** (1591–1624) in Haarlem, and the short visit to the town of Flemish painter **Adriaen Brouwer** (1605–38), that really established the style in Holland. Brouwer was a disorderly bohemian and a popular painter. Both Rubens and Rembrandt went to great lengths to add his work to their collections, though Haarlem society took some time to recover from his high spirits. He was strongly influenced by his compatriots Breughel and Bosch, and would sit about in pothouses knocking off cruelly realistic sketches of the clientele. The grotesque portrayal of peasants appealed to his Haarlem pupil **Adriaen van Ostade** (1610–85), and became a feature of one strain of Dutch genre painting. (As Van Ostade grew older and richer, however, his work became calm, cosy and far more respectable.)

Another style of genre grew up in Leiden around the painter **Gerard Dou** (1613–75). His meticulous, highly finished, almost slick work was widely imitated and gave rise to the school of Leiden *fijnschilders* ('fine painters'). The paintings, often of genteel middle-class interiors, have subtle chiaroscuro lighting effects and some very abstruse symbolic references. Leiden seemed to enjoy especially difficult allusions, maybe because it was a university town. Dou's pupils **Gabriel Metsu** (1629–67) and **Frans van Mieris** (1635–81) excelled in elegant genre work.

In far-away Deventer **Gerard ter Borch** (1619–81) was developing his own style—highly attentive to detail and with an especially fine touch in painting fabrics. In Delft **Jan Vermeer** (1632–75) was painting the hushed, softly lit interiors that have earned him the reputation (with Rembrandt and Frans Hals) of being one of the three great painters of the age. Vermeer produced eleven children, and only three times that many paintings in his life. In the midst of his tumultuous household, he would lock himself away and work painstakingly on tranquil portraits of Dutch homes without a single child in sight. The reticent, and poor, painter would even hide from influential art dealers when they came to call.

The best recorder of riotous domestic uproar was tavern-keeper **Jan Steen** (1625–79). He paints the lewd, sozzled and wanton inhabitants of his sitting-rooms, taverns and brothels with such verve and good humour that it's difficult to judge just what his moral attitude really is. The paintings of **Pieter de Hooch** (1629–after 1688) and **Nicholaes Maes** (1629–93), on the other hand, are closer to the subdued interiors of Vermeer. De Hooch is especially known for his sensitive portrayals of mothers and children. His paintings of the dark interiors of burgher homes with, somewhere in the picture, a door opening on to the bright outdoors, set a pattern for many other genre painters.

Historical and Biblical Painting

The 16th-century Mannerists had used Biblical and historical subjects as a pretext for fanciful flights of imagination, an excuse to adorn paintings with naked bodies and elaborate ornamentation. As we have seen, there was no place for this in respectable 17th-century merchants' sitting rooms, and the austere Calvinists proscribed art in churches. Most artists were launched into an open market of more acceptable styles—portraits, landscapes and genre scenes—but a few soldiered on in the grand old style. Many of these painters were simply out of touch with the spirit of the new age, but others came up with an innovative, more realistic style of historical painting.

The Dutch Caravagists (*see* above) were prime movers in the new direction. Their bold realism appealed to painters in this Age of Reason. The new style of historical painting leant on experience, rather than invention, and had a much clearer narrative. Unlike the Mannerists, who had indulged themselves in flashy virtuoso performances without any deference to period, 17th-century painters painted scenes from the Bible or from history (especially banquet scenes or intimate group studies of Christ with the apostles), attempting to portray clothing, buildings and utensils with some sort of historical accuracy. (They were, however, usually quite spectacularly off the mark.)

The Amsterdam painter **Pieter Lastman** (1583–1633) was the spearhead of the new generation of history painters. It was to study as his pupil that **Rembrandt van Rijn** (1606–69, *see* pp.103) went to Amsterdam in 1624. Rembrandt clearly wanted to be part of the modern movement of realism. Kenneth Clark calls him 'the great poet of that need for truth and that appeal to experience which had begun with the Reformation'. His quest was for naturalness and authenticity. He used his neighbours in the Jewish Quarter for Biblical paintings, and infused his pictures with a powerful psychological realism. By the 1640s he was undoubtedly the best history painter in Holland, but it was a lonely mission, as the style remained unpopular during his lifetime. Only one of his pupils, the last, **Aert de Gelder** (1645–1627) concentrated exclusively on history painting. He worked in a lighter, more sentimental style than Rembrandt would ever have allowed himself to fall into.

Portraiture

Portraiture is the most conservative of all the categories of visual art. Painters commissioned to record the wealthy, pompous and important for posterity usually opt for well-tried, acceptable forms. The Golden Age brought some exciting innovators—especially with double and group portraits—but the changes were subtle and the style soon hardened once more into an emptier, more formalized genre.

Anthonie Mor (1519–74), who Italianized his name to Antonio Moro, spent some time in the court of Emperor Charles V, and introduced the fashionable classical style of Italian portraiture to the Netherlands. It was taken up by **Michiel Miereveld** (1567–1641). He had a comfortable job in the court of Frederick Henry in The Hague, churned out competent, formal pictures and became the leading portraitist of the early Dutch Republic.

It was **Frans Hals** (1585–1666) who brought verve to portrait-painting. His acute psychological perception, comic wickedness and lightness of touch give his portraits an unprecedented vibrancy. For the first time the sitters seem unconstricted, even friendly. Though his work became very dark towards the end of his life, his early group portraits are exuberantly stage-managed and really capture the high spirits and optimism of Holland's new-found freedom.

Rembrandt's portraits are more introspective, with subtle nuances of light and mood, but portraiture was, for him, primarily a source of income. The earlier 'jugs on a shelf' approach to sitters had been corrected by Hals, but it was Rembrandt who gave canvasses real vitality, particularly in larger works. His dynamic arrangement of the guardsmen in the *Night Watch* (1642; *see* p.101–2) revolutionized group portraiture. Although he brings his full artistic weight to the task, he reserves any radical experimentation for pictures of himself and his family.

Govert Flinck (1615–60) and **Ferdinand Bol** (1616–80), both students of Rembrandt, are admired as portraitists. Bol followed Rembrandt so slavishly that even art historians can't always tell them apart. Flinck had the awkward honour of being commissioned to paint for Amsterdam's new town hall after his teacher's preliminary sketches had been turned down. He died before completing his sketches, and Rembrandt was one of the painters employed to finish the job.

Frans Hals and Rembrandt gave portraiture a fresh burst of life, but by the middle of the century other artists were cementing their innovations into a new repertory of poses and gestures. Dutch society was becoming grander and more pompous, and the artists it commissioned to paint its picture—like **Bartholomeus van der Helst** (1613–70)—thought Hals' and Rembrandt's work too plain. Once again the portraits lost spontaneity and, though often stylish, became formalized and rhetorical.

Landscape, Still Life and Specialist Paintings

In his *Natural History*, Pliny marvels at the exactness with which some ancient painters could imitate Nature: birds would crash into a wall on which Zeuxis or Apelles had painted a still life. Early Netherlandish painters were impressed by this idea and paid loving attention to background landscapes—so much so that Sir Henry Wotton, a 17th-century English Ambassador to the Low Countries, could marvel at their 'Artificiall Miracles'. (Michelangelo, however, is reputed to have scoffed at the literalness of this Netherlandish style, saying it was fit only for young or very old women, monks, nuns and certain tone-deaf members of the aristocracy.) This interest in realism did mean that landscape established a sturdy niche for itself in Dutch art during the Golden Age.

The 16th-century Mannerists used natural scenery, laced with fantastical creatures, as an exotic backdrop to biblical and classical scenes. The well-travelled **Gillis van Coninxloo** (1544–1607) painted very much in the Mannerist style, but is generally regarded as the first Dutch landscapist. Mannerist pictures were usually painted from a high viewpoint. It was **Esaias van de Velde** (1591–1632) who, quite literally, brought things down to earth. He painted dry, rather matter-of-fact country scenes from a low, more naturalistic, viewpoint—a style which was adopted by practitioners of what became known as the **tonal phase** of Dutch landscape painting.

Paintings of the tonal phase, which lasted until the 1640s, are delicate, almost monochromatic and are animated by the atmosphere they create. The 17th-century poet and critic Constantijn Huygens praised the school for its ability to evoke 'the warmth of the sun and the movement caused by a cool breeze'. The first tonal painter was Esaias's pupil **Jan van Goyen** (1596–1656). Although he began painting in the bolder colours of his master, he was soon producing translucent worlds of hazy greens, browns and greys. **Salomon van Ruysdael** (1600–70) painted refined, spacious landscapes and is considered the second major tonal painter. **Hercules Seghers** (*b.*1590) painted some inspired and original scenes of waterfalls, valleys and stormy mountains. Although he worked at the same time as the tonal painters, his unique style evoked the power of a much grander Nature. He had a reputation for being drunk and depressed, and disappeared in 1633.

Rembrandt was a great admirer of Seghers, and owned eight of his paintings. His small *oeuvre* of landscapes strongly reflects Seghers' influence. From the 1650s a new generation of landscape painters started producing rugged, grandiose works with more solid forms and stronger contrasts of light and colour than the rather pale pictures of the tonal phase artists. Leaders of this new **classical phase** were **Jacob van Ruisdael** (1628–82; Salomon's nephew, though they spelled their names differently) and **Albert Cuyp** (1620–91). Ruisdael is acknowledged as the greatest Dutch landscapist and is especially admired for his stormy skies. Cuyp combined clarity and a firm classical structure with (especially in his late work) Italianate lighting that suffuses his pictures with a soft glow. Ruisdael's pupil **Meindert Hobbema** (1638–1709) produced paintings very much derivative of his master's work before marrying the *burgemeester's* kitchen maid and becoming a wine gauger in the Amsterdam customs house, abandoning painting almost entirely.

Cuyp, like many other Dutch landscapists, fell under the spell of Italy. Many Hollanders were drawn south by the warmth and shimmering light. Right from the beginning of the century **Italianate** landscapes existed alongside the more typically Dutch pictures. (The term, however, refers more to the subject matter than to the influence of Italian art.) The escapist, rather nostalgic paintings by artists like **Jan Both** (*c.* 1618–52) and **Nicolaes Berchem** (1620–83) were very popular with the Dutch public. By the 19th century the style was beginning to lose favour. The English painter John Constable, in a lecture in 1836, berated Both and Berchem as specious painters whose reputation was propped up by dealers demanding high prices. When, reeling from the vehemence of the attack, an avid collector remarked that he had better sell his Berchems, Constable replied: 'No sir, that will only continue the mischief, *burn them.*'

The English term '**still life**' comes from the Dutch '*stilleven*', the word that began to be used around the 1650s to describe a theme in Dutch painting that was very typical of the 17th-century taste for the domestic and realistic. The stylistic development of still life painting parallels that of landscapes. Early works are 'tonal'—suspended against a plain background, suffused by a transparent, dull light. The objects painted are simple everyday things. The *ontbijtje* (breakfast piece) with bread, cheese and pewter mug is a favourite subject. Later *Vanitas* still lifes, reminding us of the ephemerality of life and earthly pleasures, became popular. Fruit is seen at its *toppunt*, the point of ripeness just before it goes bad, and darker symbols like skulls and snuffed out candles make an appearance. As the Golden Age society prospered, the simple *ontbijtjes* were replaced by *pronkstilleven* (*pronk* means ostentation). The style of these luxurious pieces is similar to that of the classical phase of landscape painters. Colours are brighter and each object seems sharply picked out, as if by spotlight. Gold, silver, china, expensive seafood and exotic fruit replace the simpler fare of earlier work.

Paintings of flowers were a specialized branch of still life. Real blooms were often cripplingly expensive, and short-lived. The 17th-century Dutch preferred *pictures* of flowers in their houses. The paintings were often complete fantasies—exotic blooms from all over the world, that flowered at different times of the year, would all be arranged in one vase. They were painted with an exacting and extravagant realism. Samuel Pepys enthuses in his diary over a 'little flower pott' done by **Simon Verelst** (1644–1721), marvelling that it was 'the finest thing that ever I saw in my life—the drops of Dew hanging on the leaves, so as I was forced again and again to put my finger to it to feel whether my eyes were deceived or no'. (Verelst was asking ƒ70 for the painting. The notoriously mean Pepys 'had the vanity' to offer ƒ20, which wasn't accepted.) **Ambrosius Bosschaert the Elder** (1573–1621) and his three sons were the most prolific flower painters of the period. By the time he died, Bosschaert could command 1000 guilders a painting.

Sea, Buildings and Animals

Despite Holland's reliance on the sea, **marine painting** doesn't occupy an important position in its art. Early painters like **Jan Porcellis** (1584–1632) seem primarily concerned with atmosphere of the sea and sky, while later artists like **Willem van de Velde the Younger** (1633–1707) begin to reflect the nation's pride in the ships themselves. Of the **architectural paintings, Pieter Saenredam's** (1597–1695) exquisitely executed church interiors are the most pleasing—and so accurate that they are still used as blueprints for restoration work. The most interesting **animal painter** is **Paulus Potter** (1625–54) whose bulls and cows have an intense reality that is almost nightmarish.

The 18th and 19th Centuries

After decades of entrepreneurial adventure, Amsterdam settled back to enjoy its wealth, and seemed to lose the drive that had propelled it through the Golden Age.

Society began to look to France as a model of graceful living, and associations for the promotion of French ideas and culture sprang up.

With the deaths of Frans Hals (1666), Rembrandt (1669) and Vermeer (1675), the Golden Age of Dutch painting also came to an end. The achievements of the 17th century were so great that they seemed to haunt 18th-century painters, who didn't dare do anything new. Paintings became over-refined and uniform in their imitation of French styles and reworking of old ideas. Much 17th-century painting had reflected the stern ethics of Calvinism, but the 18th century began to shed the moral sobriety that had been the dominant humour of the previous age. The freshest painting of the period comes from the few artists who reflected this change in mood and worked playfully with the established Dutch styles. The most impressive of these lighter-hearted painters was **Cornelis Troost** (1697–1750), whose delicately composed satires have earned him the title of the 'Dutch Hogarth'.

Much work was to be had painting the ceilings of grand mansions and decorating the interiors of new public buildings. **Gerard de Lairesse** (1640–1711) was the market leader in this field. His somewhat over-enthusiastic admirers dubbed him the 'Dutch Raphael'. His successor, **Jacob de Wit** (1695–1754), excelled as a *trompe l'œil* artist and a decorator of churches. Protestant churches were still bare, but Catholicism was tolerated provided that (a 1730 decree cautioned) care was taken 'that the meeting places of the Catholics do not have the appearance of churches or public buildings, nor should they strike the public eye'. There were no such restrictions, however, on interiors, and De Wit made his fortune on commissions from wealthy parishes.

During the 19th century, painting became more documentary—any allegorical meaning or high moral purpose disappeared entirely. Romantic painters such as **Jozef Israëls** (1824–1911) and **A. H. Bakker Korff** (1824–82) did imbue their work with emotion, but it was of the sober, cosy Dutch variety rather than anything explosive or passionate. Landscapists ploughed on in a neoclassical or grand Romantic manner, though in the world of **A. G. Bilders** (1838–65) you can *see* the beginnings of a simpler naturalism. In place of the distant, artificially constructed views found in previous paintings, the landscape is seen from close to. This radical change, which gave paintings the sort of perspectives seen in photographs, characterized much work later in the century. (This is particularly evident in the city scenes of the Amsterdam Impressionist **G. H. Breitner** (1857–1923). The landscapes and seascapes of **Johann Barthold Jongkind** (1819–91), drawn from the 17th-century tonal tradition, influenced later French Impressionists and Dutch artists of the Hague School.

The Hague School was active between 1870 and 1890, an Art for Art's Sake movement made up of an enthusiastic group of Impressionistic painters. They became famous for their grey skies, and paintings of the long flat beaches and rainswept polders (reclaimed land) around The Hague. Subject matter was less important than personal feelings and style. **Anton Mauve's** (1838–88) gently coloured landscapes are the best known. **Hendrik Mesdag** (1831–1915) was a skilled seascapist, and painted the impressive Panorama in The Hague. The brothers **Maris**—**Jacob** (1837–99), **Matthijs** (1839–1917) and **Willem** (1844–1910)—contributed fine landscapes and nature studies to the movement.

Undoubtedly the greatest painter of the century was the man that a director of the Stedelijk Museum called 'the lowliest, most human', **Vincent Van Gogh** (1853–90). During his short, troubled painting career, Van Gogh produced work quite unlike any other Dutch artist; his work also takes its own individual course in the stream of Post-Impressionist painting in general (see **Walk VI**, pp.164–9).

Jan Toorop (1858–1928) trailed along with the stylistic changes of the century, from Pointillism to Expressionism. His best work, like that of his contemporary **Johan Thorn Prikker** (1868–1932), was in a delicate, almost fairytale Symbolist style that begins to point towards Art Nouveau.

The 20th Century

The individualism of the late 19th century undermined the supportive strength of the great painting traditions of the past. Twentieth-century Dutch artists were left not only with the question that had dogged their 17th-century forebears (*what* to paint), but also by a new problem: *how* to paint. There was no longer a framework of assumptions within which they could make their decisions. Twentieth-century art fragments into splinter-groups trying to find their way through the dilemma.

The artists of *De Stijl* ('Style', or 'The Way') came up with a new set of assumptions, a theory they believed would take the place of the old traditions. This theory was propounded in a series of polemical articles in the periodical from which they got their name (published from June 1917 to January 1932). They claimed that they were getting rid of all the inaccuracies, obscurity and casual accidents of individualism, and had discovered the essence of art—a Platonic ideal that the world could understand. The best known visual expression of this great universal principle is the straight black lines and blocks of primary colours in the work of **Piet Mondriaan** (1872–1944). (He dropped the second 'a' in his name in order to appear more French—a pretension that most Dutch Museums ignore.) Mondriaan gives us a one-man lesson in the development of abstract art. Even in early, recognizable landscapes you can see the germs of his fascination with horizontal and vertical lines. Gradually the figurative images dissolve and you're left with the dashes and criss-cross lines of what is aptly known as his 'plus-minus' period. Then the lines get straighter and bolder, and the colours resolve into bright, flat reds, yellows and blues. Mondriaan claimed he was aiming for the 'lucid tidiness' that the new age demanded. In this he is, paradoxically, very much part of a Dutch tradition of stillness and quiet, careful composition. As Kenneth Clark suggests: Mondriaan is Vermeer without the light.

The prime motivator of *De Stijl*, and editor of the periodical, was **Theo van Doesburg** (1883–1931). His paintings were more dynamic than Mondriaan's, and caused the final rift between the two artists (*see* p.152). The work of a third member of the group, **Bart van der Leck** (1876–1958), is instantly recognizable—coloured triangles scattered on a white canvas. Van Doesburg was the real energy behind the movement. When he died, the magazine ceased publication and formal contacts between members dissolved. Though *De Stijl* lasted only fifteen years, its impact was felt all over the world, not only in painting, but also in architecture, interior design, typography and even literature and music. The images are still plagiarized by trendy designers for company logos, coffee mugs and T-shirts.

Most of the major art movements of the early 20th century seemed to pass Holland by. There were, however, two Dutch schools of Expressionists active before the Second World War. The **Bergen School** centred on the recalcitrant work of **Charley Toorop** (1891–1955; daughter of the 19th-century painter Jan Toorop). **De Ploeg** ('The Plough') was led by **Jan Wiegers** (1893–1959) and influenced by Van Gogh and the German Expressionists. They painted angular and explosively coloured pictures, often of the countryside around Groningen.

The hard, nightmarish quality of the Dutch **Magic Realists** is reminiscent of Salvador Dali's Surrealism, but their scenes are not as hallucinatory. **Pyke Koch** (b. 1901) paints alluring, pithy works with awe-inspiring prowess. He is shamefully little known outside Holland. **Carel Willink** (1900–83) and **Raoul Hynckes** (b. 1893) are two other prominent Magic Realist painters, if not quite as inspired.

The most exciting movement to emerge after the war was **COBRA** (made up of artists from **CO**penhagen, **BR**ussels and **A**msterdam). These painters were inspired by primitive art and children's paintings to develop a *volwassen kinderstijl* (grown-up child style). Their keywords were vitality and spontaneity. **Karel Appel** (b. 1921) remarked 'I just mess about' and 'I paint like a barbarian in a barbarous age.' The gaudy, vibrant and topsy-turvey paintings of COBRA appear to represent a purposeful effort to wipe out any vestige of classical tradition.

During the 1960s minimalistic monochrome canvasses and white reliefs made an appearance. Work by **Jan Schoonhoven** (b. 1914) was influenced by the German **Zero/Nul** movement, which was trying to create a new beginning for art by reducing individual influence to nothing. **Ad Dekkers** (1938–74) and **Edgar Fernhout** (1912–74; Charley Toorop's son) produced similar work, but were more in the abstract geometrical tradition of Mondriaan.

The technological revolution has had its impact on Dutch art. **Peter Struycken** (b . 1939) began very much in the vein of Dekkers, but since 1968 has been using a computer to generate the colour and patterns of his work. **Jan Dibbets** (b. 1941) uses montages of photographs geometrically arranged on clean white canvases, in a way that seems to link him to Mondriaan and Saenredam (the 17th-century painter of church interiors). Nowadays, the club scene and the computer revolution is spawning exciting multi-media art—Conscious Dreams gallery (Kerkstraat 117) is where to find it. Colourful pieces by **Dadara**, rather in the manner of Keith Haring, are proving commercially very popular, and finding their way on to T-shirts and mouse pads. The **Stedelijk Museum Bureau** (*see* p.182) keeps tabs on the local art scene. Among contemporary artists, keep an eye open for witty sculptures by **Servaas**, innovative painting by **Aldert Mantje** and **Ger van Elk**, **Gijs Bakker's** poised mixed-media pieces, **Arjan Lancel's** inspired installations and sculpture, and beautifully shaped ceramics by **Wouter Dam**. In the early 1990s **Seymour Likely** made an appearance on the art scene. Likely was the creation of three Amsterdam artists. He berated gallery directors and collectors in long letters, and produced works that tweaked at the Art Establishment with a refreshingly cheeky iconoclasm. Before his demise he lent his name to a trendy Amsterdam bar, which continues to top up the original artists' coffers.

Architecture

The delights of Amsterdam's architecture are small-scale, domestic ones. It's a city of little corners and quiet surprises. Wealthy merchants over the centuries have built some grand mansions, but they're not gargantuan. Though you're unlikely to be bowled over by the sheer magnificence of some glittering edifice, you're sure to be stopped in your tracks, suddenly captivated by an ornamented gable, a witty façade decoration or a neat, perfectly poised little house.

Amsterdam is built on treacherously soft soil. Buildings are prevented from gracelessly subsiding into the bog by a centuries-old method, perfected around 1700 and little changed since. Rows of piles are sunk, in twos, along the line of a proposed wall, right down to one of two hard sand levels (at 12m or 20m below the surface).

Nowadays concrete piles are used in preference to wood, and some skyscrapers have piles that reach down to a third hard layer, 50m underground. Planks are fastened to the piles, and the walls are built on top. As old piles rot or sink, so buildings lean, bulge, crack or collapse. You can see houses listing at precarious angles, propped up by wooden beams. Over the gap left by the demise of one structure, two others will incline towards each other until they're stoutly pushed apart (by more wooden beams). There are a few sad cases where owners have had to make do with propping up the first floor and amputating the rest.

In the Beginning...

The first houses in Amsterdam were made of wood, but after fires nearly destroyed the city (in 1421 and 1452), people began building in brick. At first this only applied to the lower walls; the gables (which formed the outer walls of attics and were often shaped to give more interesting definition to steep triangular roofs) were still wooden. The shapes of early brick gables, called **spout gables**, are a direct reflection of their wooden ancestry. Wooden constructions were built with each successive storey sticking out a little further than the previous one, so that rainwater would drip on to the street and not seep back into the body of the building. Early brick gables leant over for the same reason, which is another contributing factor to Amsterdam's cityscape of tilting façades. Only two wooden buildings remain in the centre of Amsterdam (*see* pp.95and 139). Most of the pre-17th-century buildings still standing belonged to the city fortifications, built in stone in the 15th century to deflect the impact of newly invented gunpowder. These include the Schreierstoren (*see* p.139–40), the Munttoren (*see* p.124) and St Antoniespoort (*see* p.141). Amsterdam's oldest building is the Oude Kerk, (*see* p.88) dating back to 1300 but now a hotchpotch of styles covering three centuries.

New Ideas

Towards the end of the 16th century, architectural pattern books from Italy made an appearance in Amsterdam. The Dutch architects who pored over translations of these books were inspired both by the classical system of proportion, and by the ornamental designs. In the buildings these architects subsequently produced, the simple **spout gable** gave way to the more decorative **step gable**, and red-brick façades were lavishly decorated with plaster scrolls, escutcheons, vases and masks. The ornamentation reached a high point in the playful work of **Hendrick de Keyser** (1565–1621). It took until the end of the 17th century for people to stop building in the Renaissance style, but the adventurous were already experimenting with a purer form of classicism in the 1620s. This new wave reacted against lavish ornament, and were far more intrigued by the strict lines and proportions of classical design. Fruit, flowers, animals and human figures do join the line-up of gable adornments, but not in such profusion. The larger houses begin to resemble temple fronts, with garlands and festoons under windows. Smaller buildings sport **neck gables**. Simpler and more suitably classicist than the cascading step gables, neck gables are often topped off with a purely classical fronton and are a compromise between a vision of architecture that imitates the buildings of Greek and Roman antiquity, and the practicalities of building for a rainy climate. (The tall 'necks' mask steep roofs, something a conventionally classical straight cornice could not do. It was only in the 19th century that reliably leak-proof flat roofs could be built, and straight cornices became more widespread.) Notable architects of the period

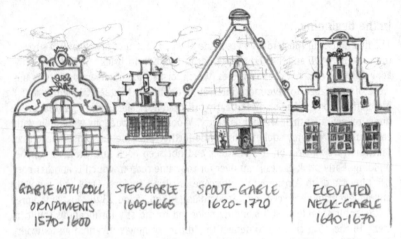

GABLE WITH SCROLL
ORNAMENTS
1570-1600

STEP-GABLE
1600-1665

SPOUT-GABLE
1620-1720

ELEVATED
NECK-GABLE
1640-1670

are **Jacob van Campen** (1595–1657), who built the town hall on the Dam (*see* pp.92–x3 and **Philips Vingboons** (1607–78) and his brother **Justus** (1620–98), famed for their domestic architecture.

Decoration and Decline

Towards the end of the 17th century austerity set in, and architects began to emphasize simplicity and harmony. **Adriaan Dortsman** (1625–82) is the master of the school of 'Restrained Dutch Classicism'. Windows were made larger and façades became simpler and more rhythmical in design. In the 18th century, as the economy picked up, many merchant families gave their homes a facelift during which brick façades were plastered over or replaced by sandstone. But more money to spend also meant more decoration. The century is marked by a fascination with things French. Gables became draped with acanthus leaves (Louis XIV), encrusted with asymmetrical fripperies (Louis XV) or strung with modest garlands (Louis XVI). Sometimes buildings were crowned with excessively ornate balustrades—a nifty way of hiding a steep roof with what appeared to be a classical straight cornice. The 18th century also saw the advent of the standardized, pre-fabricated gable—a sort of architectural mix-and-match. Unfortunately, plot widths were inconveniently irregular, so little disguises to hide the shortfall in the gable width—like vases on corners—were introduced.

Public Pomp

Amsterdam was a poor and sorry city for most of the 1800s. Little building went on until money began to dribble back into the coffers in the last decades of the century. The city's first social housing estates went up in areas like De Pijp and the Jordaan, but the period is remembered more for public buildings than domestic.

NECK-GABLE 1640-1770 | BELL-GABLE 1660-1790 | FAÇADE WITH CORNICE 17TH-19TH C. | FAÇADE WITH ELEVATED CORNICE 18TH C.

The driving force behind 19th-century Dutch architectural innovation was **P. J. H. Cuypers** (1827–1921), the designer of the Centraal Station and Rijksmuseum (*see* pp.84 and 100). He based his work on indigenous brick and wood architecture, but was easily lured towards neo-Gothic extravagance. His belief that the entire building, from basic structure to the smallest detail of decoration, should be governed by a single coherent principle became the basis for modern Dutch architecture. Two other styles dominated 19th-century building: the upstarts of the **Architectura et Amicitia** society went in for idiosyncratic fantasies that outdid even Cuypers' ornamentation, while the more conservative members of the **Maatschappij ter Bevordering der Bouwkunst** (Society of Architects) favoured an eclectic approach, resulting in a mixture of diluted styles. Most of the interesting 19th-century buildings in Amsterdam today come from the boom period of the latter part of the century, and reflect this divergence of taste. On the one hand you'll see buildings like A. N. Godefroy's Adventskerk (Keizersgracht 676), which manages to lump together a classical rusticated base, Romanesque arches, Lombardian moulding on the façade and imitation 17th-century lanterns. On the other hand, there are also wildly ornamented buildings like J. L. Springer's Stadsschouwburg (*see* pp.172–3). In the last decades of the century architects began to reject eclecticism and work in a neo-Renaissance style. This led to a revival of indigenous Dutch brick architecture.

Modern Times

H. P. Berlage (1856–1934), the designer of the Beurs (*see* p. 86), is known as the father of modern Dutch architecture. Like Cuypers, he used traditional Dutch materials. He relished displaying a building's structure with graceful brickwork, but was never tempted into frivolous ornamentation. The most exciting 20th-century school of Dutch architecture arose as a reaction to Berlage's homespun, rational buildings. Younger architects, many of them in the employ of the city's housing department, began experimenting with decorative folds and turrets of brickwork shaped around a more solid inner skeleton of concrete. These modern, quirky brick fantasies of the **Amsterdam School** (active from around 1912 to 1924, *see* pp.154–5) have, until recently, been neglected, but an exhibition of photographs and architects' drawings at the Stedelijk Museum in the 1980s shot them back into fashion.

But the work of the Amsterdam School stands beside the mainstream Dutch architecture. A second modern movement, which emerged as an extension of rather than a reaction to Berlage's work, was to prove more influential. Under the influence of *De Stijl* (*see* p.58), Bauhaus in Germany, Frank Lloyd Wright in the USA and Le Corbusier in France, a new style of building emerged—all sharp edges, concrete, steel and glass. Like Berlage, the architects of what became known in the Netherlands as **Nieuwe Zakelijkheid** (New Functionalism), believed that they should use their materials to emphasize, not disguise, the basic structure of their buildings. Nieuwe Zakelijkheid dominated the middle decades of the century. Though it produced some neat and attractive buildings such as the Round Blue Teahouse (1937; *see* pp.162 and 170) and some fine domestic architecture by Gerrit Rietveld, it must also take the blame for the thinking behind high-rise 1960s horrors, such as the estates at Bijlmermeer.

Amsterdam has suffered more than its fair share of architectural atrocities in recent years—tacky façades of insensitively used modern materials and buildings hugely out of scale. Notable exceptions are the colourful Moederhuis (built in 1981 by the imaginative modernist, Aldo van Eyck, winner of the 1990 Royal Gold Medal for Architecture—the world's most prestigious architectural award), the monumental new Muziektheater (1985; *see* p160) and the NMB Bank Headquarters (1987). This extraordinary brick building in Bijlmermeer has hardly a right-angle in sight, mineral water fountains instead of air-conditioning, a system that warms the building by recycling the heat generated by computers, and installations of mirrors and stone that play light tricks at the solstices. (It's sometimes possible to be taken on a guided tour: *see* Archivisie in **Travel**, 'Guided Tours', p.10.)

Amsterdam's most impressive contemporary architecture is in the **business parks** sprouting around the edges of town, most notably in Sloterdijk and Amsterdam South East. Dutch architects are encouraged to take chances, and the result is a series of sparkling high-rise blocks—many of them European headquarters of multinationals—that show bravura and flair. Foreign architects invited to work on projects in the city have also made their mark—especially in new housing estates such as the **Oranje Nassau Kazerna** (converted 19th-century barracks combined with a row of new buildings commissioned from various architects), and on **KNSM Eiland** (a rejuvenation of derelict islands in the eastern docks). The most exciting addition to the city's skyline in the 1990s has been the **New Metropolis Science & Technology Center**, designed by Renzo Piano (architect of the Pompidou Centre in Paris). Shaped like the prow of a giant ship, it thrusts out into the harbour beside Centraal Station.

A Short Glossary of Architectural Terms

attiek: (stress the second syllable—'teak'), not the same as English 'attic', but the line of ornaments above a cornice (*q.v.*) that hides the roof from the street.

bel-étage: (rhymes with massage), the floor above the souterrain (*q.v.*), reached by a short flight of steps, but functionally the ground floor.

cartouche: elaborate sandstone ornamentation often seen around small oval windows or hoist beams (*q.v.*).

claw-piece: the ornamentation that fills in the right-angled step made by the side of a neck-gable and the wall below.

console: a supporting bracket (rather like a shelf bracket), often ornamented and supporting a cornice (*q.v.*).

cornice: a moulded projection which crowns a façade and runs the width of the building. It may be simple and flat, or ornamented.

festoon: ornament in the form of a garland—usually with fruit or flower motifs.

fronton: triangular (though sometimes rounded) piece that crowns a façade. It runs the width of the gable only (not the whole building, like a cornice). In some classical designs the fronton is very large, often supported by pillars and running almost the full width of the building—this is called a **tympan**.

gable: the Dutch word *gevel* refers to the whole façade, but technically this is just the part of the wall that covers the triangular end of the roof.

gable stone: stone tablet, with a picture or symbol carved on it, embedded in the façade. In the 17th century it acted as a house number.

hoist beam: beam sticking out from the top of a façade. It has a hook on the end through which a block and tackle can be hung to hoist goods to the upper floors.

œil-de-bœuf: ('bull's eye') small oval windows, often with an elaborate sandstone framing, seen in the tops of façades.

pilaster: flattened pillar that projects slightly from a façade. May be decorative or have a structural function.

pothouse: an extension of the kitchen with a separate entrance slightly below street level. (Originally used to store pots, later as workshops for craftsmen.)

souterrain: the part of the house below street level. Because of Amsterdam's high ground water level, the souterrain is not as low as a conventional cellar, and is usually reached by a door under the stoop (*q.v.*).

stoop: the steps leading up the front of a building to the front door (which is usually a little above street level). In most houses the steps rise across the façade, rather than extending frontally from the door down to the street. The landing is sometimes big enough for a few chairs, and there is occasionally a small bench built into the railings.

volute: scroll-like whorls which form part of claw–pieces (*q.v.*), or fill in the 'shoulder' of a gable.

Where Cows Wear Coats and Other Stories

Cleanness

Seventeenth-century travellers used to slopping through the ordure and dodging flying sewage in other European cities were impressed by Amsterdam's pristine pathways. 'The beauty and cleanliness of the streets,' marvelled one passing Englishman, 'are so extraordinary, that Persons of all ranks do not scruple, but seem to take pleasure in walking them.' Jets of water from special spray devices regularly washed down the houses, roads were 'paved with brick and as clean as any chamber floor' and flotillas of maids and housewives scrubbed, buffed, swept and polished until (according to an astonished Owen Feltham, one of Cromwell's henchmen, so not generally known for his pro-Dutch sentiments) 'every door seems studded with diamonds. The nails and hinges keep a constant brightness as if there were not a quality incident to iron.' As early as the 15th century, Emperor Charles V's quartermaster—who had plundered the kitchens of Europe—thought that there was none to equal the neatness of Dutch housekeeping.

As time wore on, the Dutch became even more scrupulous. By the end of the 19th century canny Dr Samuel Sarphati was sealing up household waste in barges, shipping it out to the countryside and selling it to farmers as compost. In 1874 the writer Henry James was riveted by the sight of an Amsterdam house-maid compulsively scouring an apparently spotless stoop:

> Where could the speck or two possibly have come from unless pro-
> duced by spontaneous generation: there are no specks on the
> road—nor on the trees whose trunks are to all appearances carefully
> sponged every morning. The speck exists evidently only as a sort of
> mathematical point, capable only of extension in the good woman's
> Batavian brain... It is a necessity, not as regards the house, but as
> regards her own temperament.

This ablutionary temperament was not to the liking of all. Some visitors complained of the excessive neatness, of trees all clipped to look the same and of 'the endless avenues and stiff parterres' which seemed like 'the embroidery of an old-maid's work-bag'. A supperless Abbé Sartre opined that the Dutch would die of hunger surrounded by their glittering cauldrons and sparkling crockery 'rather than prepare any dish that might conceivably disarrange this perfect symmetry'. Sir William Temple, British ambassador to the Netherlands in the 17th century, was much tickled by the story of an English magistrate who dared go visiting in muddy shoes. A forthright Amsterdam housemaid plonked him down on the stoop, plucked off the offending footwear, and carried him across the shining hall floor to her mistress's parlour.

Nowadays you're in little danger of being manhandled, but the scrubbing and polishing go on. Windows have a transparency rare in big cities, the humblest bed-and-breakfast (if it's owned by a Hollander) will be spotless, and battalions of street-sweepers work right through the day (joined in the early hours of the morning by spraying and scrubbing machines). In country towns Virginia Woolf's description, written in 1935, still holds true: 'Oh but the carved doors, the curved white façades...the air of swept and garnished prosperity, antiquity, air, cleanliness.' Amsterdam can often appear grimy and litter-strewn, but its ring of smart canals is as spruce as ever.

Opera and Stopera

The early Calvinist Church regarded opera with horror. It was not only an invention of the devil, but (perhaps even more damning) was most extravagantly un-Dutch. Conventional drama was bad enough. In 1655 one Reverend Witterwrongel railed against stage performances 'because they are generally lecherous and wanton, full of indecency, cruel, bloody, usually taken from the heathen comedies and tragedies which are filled with superstitions, shameful idolatry, blasphemy and embellished fables and lies'. Anything so solely committed to entertainment as the *opera*, which added profane music and 'enjoyable dancing' to this list of wrongs, was intolerable. Amsterdam's first opera house survived just 53 weeks.

Dirk Strijker was the son of the Consul of Holland in Venice. He grew up feeling more Italian than Dutch, changed his name to Theodoro, and returned to Amsterdam around 1679 filled with a missionary zeal. Opera was the driving passion of his life, and he was determined that his fellow Hollanders should see the light. Despite the disapproval of the Church elders, the general populace of Amsterdam was already developing a taste for opera. Amsterdam did have a theatre, on the Keizersgracht. The Calvinist Church (which seemed to have learned accounting practice from its Roman Catholic predecessor) was willing to turn a blind eye to the existence of this house of sin, provided that certain 'charity levies' were made to Church concerns. Almost the entire box-office receipts from the theatre on the Keizersgracht went to the Orphans' Home and the Men's Home for the Aged. On the evenings when nothing was scheduled, itinerant Italian and French opera companies would sometimes stage performances. These met with wild success—they were even more popular than the theatre's conventional fare.

Strijker, however, was determined that the city should have a purpose-built opera house. In 1680, after complex negotiations with the Church and the city fathers, and substantial donations to the orphans and aged men, he was finally granted permission to build a theatre on the Leidsegracht for (in the words of the uninitiated council secretary) 'silent performances and fine music'. But this was the beginning rather than the end of the battle. The building of the new theatre took longer and proved more expensive than Strijker had anticipated. The musicians he had contracted sat around, twiddled their thumbs, and collected their pay packets. When he finally set the opening night for Saturday 28 December 1680, the Church objected that it was the night before a Holy Communion celebration and would brook no competition. The opera house eventually opened on New Year's Eve. Over the next few months, audiences flocked over from the theatre on the Keizersgracht, and its box office takings dropped to such a sad level that the Orphans' Home and Men's Home for the Aged began to complain. The large chunk of Strijker's profits that was destined to placate these worthy concerns never materialized. Opera is an expensive business, and his theatre ran at a loss. Deprived of this income, the Church began to exert pressure for the closure of the opera house. Strijker got no help from a blandiloquent city council, and after a year and a week he was forced to abandon his venture and retreat '*in slechten en miserabelen stand*' ('in a sorry and deplorable state') into obscurity. Today there is no sign of the old opera house on Leidsegracht. No one even knows what happened to it and not a single picture of the building exists. The Church must have been determined to obliterate every trace.

Strijker's audience, however, had had their appetites whetted. They streamed to French and Italian operas given in theatres outside the city's boundaries—in Overtoom and in Buiksloot across the IJ. Gradually the Church's attitude began to soften. The theatre on the Keizersgracht, which had been churning out moralistic dramas, began to stage operas again, and the first *Stadsschouwburg* (Municipal Theatre) opened on Leidseplein in 1774. Here you were subjected to operas of a rather questionable standard—good singers were thin on the ground and all the female leads were taken by the director's wife. Towards the end of the 18th century performances of a rather better quality could be seen at the German Opera House and the French Opera House (now the Kleine Komedie) which opened on the Amstel. The middle years of the 19th century were boom years, with a good local opera company resident at the *Stadsschouwburg*, but by the turn of the century interest had dwindled dismally. A plan in the 1920s to build a national opera house across from the Concertgebouw on Museumplein was vetoed by the city council.

After the Second World War, however, there were murmurings in the corridors of power about the need for a national opera house. Plans for a building on the Museumplein, and for one further to the south on Allbéplein (where a Hilton hotel was later built), were abandoned when someone suggested Frederiksplein. This large site, closer to the city centre than the other two, had been derelict since Amsterdam's Crystal Palace—the glittering *Paleis voor Volksvlijt* or Palace of Industry, built to house international exhibitions—had burned down in 1929.

At just the same time, the council committee responsible for the building of a new city hall was also attracted to the idea of Frederiksplein. There followed a sort of architectural musical chairs, during which opera house and city hall pursued each other about Amsterdam, claiming for themselves in turn the few choice sites available and preventing each other's plans from materializing.

By 1969 the council had decided to build the new city hall on Waterlooplein. An Austrian architect, Wilhelm Holzbauer, won the competition to design the new *Stadhuis*, but in 1972 the provincial authority vetoed the funding because his building was going to be too expensive to run. One afternoon in 1979, with the authorities still locked in negotiation, Holzbauer was standing on the Blue Bridge, looking glumly over Waterlooplein, when he had the brilliant idea of *combining* the *Stadhuis* and opera house into one complex. This seemed to solve everyone's problems. Within weeks the Prime Minister had approved a 230 million guilder budget and a combined plan by Holzbauer and local architect Cees Dam had been passed. But the idea caused a furore among the burghers of Amsterdam.

Many of the objections seemed to follow the old Calvinist pattern. Opera was unnecessary. Amsterdam didn't need an opera house, especially not in the centre of town. Those who really felt the urge could indulge themselves in theatres on the outskirts. But it was the choice of the site that caused the greatest ill-feeling. Waterlooplein had been the heart of Amsterdam's large Jewish neighbourhood, and had been a sad and derelict scar since the Nazis had all but obliterated the Jewish population. Many people thought an opera house to be an inappropriate building to occupy a location with such poignant associations. The few people still living on Waterlooplein after the war had already been evicted in the 1960s to make way for the proposed *Stadhuis*; they had then looked on as their empty homes were occupied by squatters while the council dithered over the cost of the proposals. When plans for the combined *Stadhuis* and *Muziektheater* were mooted, the by then long-established squatter communities had no intention of giving up their homes to what they saw as a temple of élitist entertainment. The complex was nicknamed the Stopera (from *St*adhuis and *opera*) and a vociferous 'Stop the Stopera' campaign erupted. Police attempts to evict squatters met with the strongest public resistance the city had seen since the street fighting of the 1960s and 1970s. Opposition raged, with little success, right up until the day the *Muziektheater* opened in 1986. (At the opening ceremony Queen Beatrix and Prince Claus had to be smuggled in through the stage door to avoid the angry throngs around the main entrance.)

Today the dust has settled, and though few people like the austere, bland *Stadhuis*, most Amsterdammers will admit that the elegant *Muziektheater*, with its coliseum of white marble, has become an attractive city landmark.

Flowers are everywhere in Amsterdam. The tattiest houses sprout window-boxes, you'll see neat little posies on the counters of bars and fetching bouquets on bank clerks' desks. People give flowers for the flimsiest reasons. Bunches hurriedly bought from canal-side barrows pass between friends like pecks on the cheek. Everyone has favourite blooms and nose-curling aversions, and to forget your loved-ones' floral preferences is like not remembering whether they take milk in their coffee.

Flowers are a national obsession. In the 17th century, when the blossoms were stratospherically pricey, painters made a comfortable living churning out floral still lifes as a substitute. Though these cost as much as the blooms themselves, the (at times regrettable) permanence of the paintings justified the expense. More recently, carnations were the vehicle for a subtle national rebellion. In the early months of the Nazi occupation, thousands of Amsterdammers wearing white carnation buttonholes suddenly appeared on the streets one morning. The Germans were taken by surprise and hadn't the faintest idea what was going on, but any Hollander knew: it was the birthday of their exiled Prince Bernhard, who always wore a carnation in his lapel. When the war ended and Queen Wilhelmina returned, people flocked spontaneously to Noordeinde Palace in The Hague and left so many offerings of bouquets that the lawn in front of the palace was completely covered in flowers. Ever since then, the reigning monarch has had to emerge on her birthday to accept thousands of posies and shake the hands of adoring subjects as they file past.

Tulips—homely, suburban and pure—have become a national cliché. Yet behind these apparently innocent blooms lurks a past of envy, greed and intemperance almost unparalleled in Dutch history. Tulips were first spotted in Adrianople, Turkey, by Dutch diplomats at the Ottoman court. In the early 17th century the flowers made a spring début in some of French and Dutch society's best gardens. Soon, Johan van Hooghelande, a Leiden botanist, had found out how to vary the colour and shape of the blooms. Connoisseurs queued up, money pouches bulging, for the latest varieties and by the 1620s the tulip was *the* flower of fashionable aristocracy. This alchemical combination of scientific research, visual allure and the chance of profit—three great Dutch enthusiasms—incited the Great Tulip Mania. At first, the bulbs were seen as exotic rarities. The Calvinist Church even regarded them as dangerous—perhaps because the flamed petals reminded them of the ribbons, ruffs and other vanities that ministers railed against from the pulpits. The bulbs were swapped and grown by a handful of aristocratic connoisseurs who, as was their wont, imposed a strict hierarchy on the tulip world. The noblest were the roses (red and pink on white), then came the violets (lilac and purples on white) and finally *bizarden* (red or violet on yellow). Humble plain colours barely merited an estate. It was the irregular, flamed and striped varieties, like the red and white Semper Augustus and the Viceroy, that mattered. (The democratically minded Dutch, however, preferred to call their nobler varieties 'Admiral' or 'General' followed by the name of the grower.)

Gradually the hoi polloi began to edge in on the scene. Tulips were easily reproducible for a wider market. Delftware, an imitation of expensive Chinese porcelain, was already decorating more modest homes. The Flemish carpet industry had its foundations in copying Turkish rugs. Tulips copied themselves, so by the mid-1630s weavers, blacksmiths and bakers were able to buy the bulbs at village fairs. The fashion spread and a tulip fever gripped the nation. Prices took off, then went into orbit. An Admiral de Maan that sold for ƒ15 in 1634 went for ƒ175 three years later. At the height of the boom an ƒ800 Scipio changed hands after a few weeks for ƒ2200. People went to any lengths for a prized bulb. One farmer met the ƒ2500 demanded for a single Viceroy by payment in kind: two *last* of wheat, four of rye, four fat oxen, eight pigs, a dozen sheep, two oxheads of wine, four tons of butter, 1000 pounds of cheese, a bed, a suit of fine clothes and a silver beaker.

The rocketing prices were fuelled not only by demand, but by the growth of a futures market. In 1634 one bright dealer had the idea of buying in the winter for future delivery, and then selling to a new buyer before he actually possessed the stock. Soon deals were being done on negotiable pieces of paper, with the time of delivery as an expiry date. A quick turnover meant a quick paper profit. Dealers were selling bulbs they didn't yet possess, for amounts they couldn't possibly raise. As the delivery date drew closer, the danger that you would actually have to pay up increased, but so did the possibility of making an intoxicating profit as prices rose by the hour. At the bottom of the pile, and in danger of ending up with a heap of worthless bulbs if the market collapsed, were the growers. (The actual tulips would be the last thing on the mind of a merchant facing bankruptcy and trying to settle his paper debts.)

And collapse it did. By 1636 this *windhandel* (literally 'trading in the wind') was beginning to worry the city magistrates and outrage the Church. Whether it was the rumour of intervention that caused the panic, or the panic that caused the intervention, is unclear. But on 2 or 3 February 1637 a warning whisper shot round Haarlem and dealers went all-out to sell. Prices plummeted, the bubble burst and the magistrates had to intervene with special legislation to rescue the innocent growers from the debris of bankrupts. It wasn't until the spring of 1638 that the market found a normal level, but the passion for tulips was there to stay. As the scandal subsided they quietly assumed their place alongside clogs, cheese and blue and white china as part of the nation's iconography.

Provos and Kabouters

If you walk from the Maritime Museum, along the avenue that now links the eastern islands, towards central Amsterdam's last remaining windmill, you'll notice a floating forest of scrap metal and brightly painted wood moored alongside a canalboat in the dock. These crumbling heaps of 1960s flotsam are the vestiges of water-borne sculptures by Robert Jasper Grootveld, one-time window cleaner and self-proclaimed 'anti-smoke sorcerer and medicine man of the Western asphalt jungle'.

Grootveld and his fellow Provos were the fire beneath the cauldron of the Dutch youth revolution; their antics in the mid-1960s were to influence the course of Dutch politics for decades to come. The Provos (from the Dutch *provocatie*—provocation) began as a literary and philosophical group, but soon became a political expression of the youthful rethinking that was going on across Western Europe and the USA. In their chaotic way they captured the attention and sympathy of older Amsterdammers, and shook up the rigid structures of the Establishment. The groundwork done by the provos, and their successors the Kabouters—especially in such areas as environmental awareness, drugs advice and squatters' housing problems—went far towards establishing the liberal attitudes prevalent in Holland today.

On Saturday nights, the Provos would gather around the *Lieverdje* on the Spui for a 'Happening'. In 1960 a tobacco company had donated the *Lieverdje* ('Little Darling'—a diminutive statue of a little boy) to the city, and it was becoming something of a landmark. Grootveld branded the statue a symbol of 'tomorrow's addicted consumer'. He and his band would subtly provoke the police with faintly ludicrous performances—like handing out raisins to passers-by while shouting out anti-smoking slogans. The police invariably rose to the bait and would bash a few heads with truncheons and make some arrests. But the Provos were nothing if not master showmen. By the time the police took action, the protesters would have a sympathetic audience on the café terraces around the Spui. At best the police appeared fools, at worst bullies.

The campaign wasn't confined to Saturday nights at the Spui. The Provos frequently met at the 'K-temple', a derelict garage near the Leidseplein, to sing the *Ugge-ugge-song* (a 'psalm to the smoker's cough'), listen to cryptic addresses on the cigarette industry and submerge themselves in the 'post-sexual electric jesus pandemonium-language' of Arnhem poet Johnny the Selfkicker. They also daubed the letter *K* (for *kanker*— 'cancer') on cigarette advertisements all over town. Later the words *Gnot* and *Klaas kom* ('Klaas is coming') also appeared. *Gnot* was an amalgam of God and genot ('delight')—nobody was ever really able to fathom out what it meant. Nor was anyone sure just who Klaas was. Perhaps it was Sint Nicolaas, Amsterdam's patron saint. Perhaps it was an oblique reference to Nicolaas Kroese, restaurateur of the famous De Vijff Vlieghen, who wanted to link the towers of Amsterdam's churches with gold chains to form a shield against the destructive forces of the universe.

But the Provos also had a serious side. It was they who fomented the street riots of the mid 1960s and produced the famous White Plans for a better city. Many of these were frivolous or naive, but some—like the provision of 20,000 free White Bicycles to replace cars in the city centre—were seriously considered by the sitting city council. In the 1966 council elections, the Provos polled 2.5 per cent of the vote and won a seat on the council. By 1967, however, the Provos had lost impetus and disbanded.

In 1970 they emerged again as the Kabouters ('Gnomes'—named after a helpful character in Dutch folklore). The leading light this time was sociologist Roel van Duyn, who held the Provo (or ex-Provo) seat on the city council. The Kabouters had a lot of the playful pottiness of the Provos, but with a jot more common sense and pragmatism. In a ceremony on the Dam they proclaimed an Orange Free State, and inaugurated their own ministers. The Minister of Public Works, for example, was to preside over the planting of more vegetables and the breaking up of motorways; the Minister of Environment and Hygiene would battle against pollution and for 'biological balance'. The White Bicycles idea became a plan for electric White Cars that was later (unsuccessfully) piloted. They expressed widespread concern that information gathered in a forthcoming census would be correlated on computer, and were chary of the growing powers of corporate industry. The movement caught on around the country, and in the 1970 June elections the Kabouters polled 11 per cent of Amsterdammers' votes, and sent five members to the city council.

Although they have now also largely faded from view (they were officially disbanded in 1981), you can still find the odd ex-Kabouter on neighbourhood committees, or agitating against another Amsterdam architectural ravishment. The Provos and Kabouters have had their day, but the effects of the shake-up that they gave post-war Dutch politics still remain. 'Amsterdam is known as a difficult city, and Amsterdammers are difficult people,' said the *burgemeester* in the midst of the 1965 riots. The Provos were the essence of Amsterdam: at once tolerant and far-sighted, cheeky and difficult.

Gezelligheid

Dictionaries translate the Dutch word *gezellig* as 'convivial' or 'cosy'. A 1970s historian defined it, in the idiom of his time, as 'partly a sort of cosiness and partly a living togetherness'. *Gezelligheid* is the stuff of the Dutch temperament, and Amsterdammers pride themselves that their town bulges with it.

A café with nicotine-stained walls and scuffed leather chairs is *gezellig*; when you move into a new apartment you hang a few pictures, buy in some pot plants, adjust the lighting and make the flat *gezellig*; the mood in a neighbourhood bar on a cold winter's afternoon is *gezellig*; the behaviour of British lager louts in the bars of Leidseplein is definitely not. Sometimes *gezelligheid* seems subconscious. During the street riots of the 1960s the police were equipped, not with aggressive-looking anti-riot gear, but with large round wicker shields. It must have been almost impossible to hurl a missile at a policeman who was sheltering behind something resembling a dog basket. In its extreme forms *gezelligheid* becomes oppressive—the lace window screens, shelves of knick-knacks and safe respectability of a stolid burgher sitting-room. At worst *gezelligheid* inhabits a trim, embroidered world somewhere between kitsch and twee. A nice, *gezellig* family hotel in a small seaside town would probably be the *last* place you'd choose to spend your summer holiday.

The up-side of *gezelligheid* is to be felt in the warm conviviality that suffuses Amsterdam cafés, and even markets and town squares. Living in cramped houses in a small-scale city has honed Amsterdammers' social behaviour to a fine edge. They seem to have discovered that the best way of getting on when your neighbours are at such close quarters is by developing a frank, easy-going tolerance—a subtle decorum. Rules are clear, universally understood and sometimes broken if the occasion demands. In 17th-century Calvinist Amsterdam, Roman Catholics were allowed to worship freely, provided that their churches were discreetly hidden behind domestic house-fronts. Today Amsterdam authorities turn a blind eye to the sale and smoking of marijuana (technically still illegal) in certain cafés. Centuries of reasonableness have produced a culture that, perhaps more than any other in Europe, deserves the epithet 'civilized', and at its core are the virtues of *gezelligheid*.

Tesselschade

One rough night, towards the end of the 16th century, a small trading ship ran aground on one of the treacherous sandbanks around the island of Texel off the coast of North Holland. The young Dutch merchant and man of letters, Roemer Visscher, was one of the few survivors. That very night his wife (snug in their house on the Engelsekaai in Amsterdam) gave birth to a daughter. Although she was christened Maria, her father felt compelled to mark the coincidence and celebrate his survival by burdening her with the sobriquet 'Tesselschade' (literally Tessel/Texel-damage, but with gentler connotations of mischief).

Despite her nickname (and an accident involving a spark from a blacksmith's anvil) Tesselschade went on to become the one-eyed doyenne of Amsterdam salon culture. Her father made sure that Maria and her sister Anne got a sound classical education (a younger daughter, Geertruid, seemed content with embroidery) and that they picked up all the subsidiary skills required to sparkle in erudite society. By the time she was a young woman the handsome (if slightly imperfect) Tesselschade could supply fluent translations of the most complex Latin, Greek or Italian texts, was an accomplished poetess, would entertain delightfully on harpsichord, lute and viol and had a singing voice of high repute. When some of the older Chambers of Rhetoric (medieval literary societies) joined forces in 1630, it was Tesselschade who won the competition to write a poem celebrating the union.

In the first two decades of the 17th century, the house on the Engelsekaai became Amsterdam's foremost literary and philosophical salon. When their father died, the daughters were snapped up by the poet Pieter Cornelisz. Hooft to join his famous literary circle at Muiden Castle, just outside Amsterdam, where they held court until their respective marriages. The list of Tesselschade's suitors had read like a *Who's Who* of Dutch letters—men like Vondel, Bredero, Constantijn Huygens and P. C. Hooft plied her with eulogistic verses. But she finally married a sea captain from Alkmaar. Anne fulfilled her merchant family's social ambitions by marrying a minor nobleman. Tesselschade returned to Amsterdam as a widow in 1640 to resume her position as a literary *Grande Dame* and when she died in 1649, Huygens compared her to the sun. Yet despite their obvious attributes and the frantic praises heaped upon them, the sisters never appear in any of the group portraits of the Muiden circle, and seem to have been regarded as prodigious ornaments. It took a 19th-century painter, J. C. Kruseman, to give the Visscher sisters pride of place among the male luminaries of the Muidenkring and today (if the painting's not in storage in the cellars) you can see the portrait hanging in the Rijksmuseum.

Where Cows wear Coats...

Holland is a dream. A dream in a haze of smoke and gold,
in the daylight more of smoke, but golden in the evening.

Albert Camus, 1956

If you look at the manners of everyday life, there is no race more open to
humanity and kindness or less given to wildness or ferocious behaviour.

Erasmus, 16th-century Dutch humanist

The women are not particularly engaging. One sees few slim waists,
they do have pale complexion, but are devoid of personality. Excessive
coffee and tea drinking ruins their teeth completely.

Marquis de Sade, 1769

The Dutch landscape has all the qualities that make geometry so delightful. A tour in Holland is a tour through the first books of Euclid.

Aldous Huxley, 1925

Holland, that scarce deserves the name of land,
As but the off-scouring of the British sand—
This indigested vomit of the sea
Fell to the Dutch by just propriety.

Andrew Marvell, 1653

A Dutchman is a lusty Fat, Two-Legged Cheeseworm. A Creature that is so addicted to eating Butter, Drinking Fat Drink and Sliding (skating) that all the world knows him for a slippery fellow.

Dutch Boare dissected; or, a Description of Hogg-land
(1664 English pamphlet)

Physically, even spiritually (the Dutch) are nearer to the English than any other nation—Calais Pier is a hundred times more remote from our shores than the Hook of Holland.

Sacheverell Sitwell

It is the peculiar genius of the Dutch to seem, at the same time, familiar and incomprehensible.

Simon Schama, historian, 1986

If I knew that the end of the world was imminent, I would take myself to Holland; for everything there happens ten minutes later.

Attributed both to Dr Johnson and Heinrich Heine

As for Holland: in the first place the cows wear coats; then the cyclists go in flocks like starlings, gathering together, skimming in and out. Driving is dangerous.

Virginia Woolf, 1935

Amsterdam is a practised but subtle temptress. Her gentle charms begin to work the moment you arrive, as they have for generations of travellers before you. These walks help you to succumb. There are six walks, each with a dominant motif. The first two are biased towards the Golden Age, taking in the best 17th-century architecture, rooms of Old Masters and grand stretches of canal. If your time is limited, **Walks I and II**, with a quick visit to the Van Gogh Museum, will reveal the essential Amsterdam. **Walk II** is a good walk for the late afternoon and early evening, especially in summer when the bridges and canal houses are lit up and look their best.

The Walks

Walk III takes its cue from the Anne Frank House, and leads you through what remains of Jewish Amsterdam, then introduces you to the vibrant city sub-culture of the Jordaan. Amsterdam's maritime past, and the all-but-forgotten old port, are the main focus of **Walk IV**, which is most enjoyable on a Sunday, when much of Amsterdam is closed. You can go to a morning coffee-concert then wander about evocatively deserted ship-yards. **Walk V** bounces you into the 20th century with modern art at the Stedelijk Museum and a visit to some intriguing architecture, and **Walk VI** starts at the Van Gogh Museum, then takes you through Amsterdam's antique markets and to some of its quirkier shops. **Walks I and II** cover the northern and central parts of town, **Walks III and IV** traverse east and west, and **Walks V and VI** are largely in the south (*see* map on inside front cover).

Pick of Amsterdam

Canals:	Brouwersgracht (**II, IV**); Egelantiersgracht (**III**); Reguliersgracht (**V**); Prinsengracht between Amstelveld and the Amstel (**II, V**).
Secrets:	The Hollandse Manege (**VI**); the Amstelkring (**I**); Buiksloterweg; a little patch of country life across the IJ (**IV**).
Oases of calm:	Begijnhof (**I**); Koepelkwartier (**IV**); Amstelveld (**V**).
Architectural eccentricities:	The Scheepvaarthuis (**IV**); De Dageraad (**V**); Roemer Visscherstraat (**VI**).
Stunning: interiors:	The Royal Palace (**I**); the glass-box concert hall at the Beurs (**I**); Museum Van Loon (**II**).
Views:	From the glass dome of the Metz (**VI**); from the Westertoren; and from the bridge on Jodenbreestraat up towards the New Metropolis (**III**); across the Amstel to the Muziektheater at night (**V**).
Rides:	Under your own steam on the canals (*see* **Travel**); on an antique tram to the Amsterdamse Bos (*see* **Day Trips**).
Undeservedly neglected painters:	Jan Steen (17th century, Rijksmuseum); Pyke Koch (20th century, Stedelijk Museum).
Neighbourhoods:	The Jordaan (**III**); Western Islands (**IV**); Spiegelkwartier (**VI**).
Museum interludes:	Cafés at the Stedelijk (**V**) and Film Museum (**VI**); gardens at the Theatre Museum (**III**).

Walk I: Central Amsterdam

Start: *Metro or tram to Centraal Station*
(nos. 1, 2, 4, 5, 9, 13, 16, 17, 24, 25)

Walking time: *1½–2 hours for visiting the*
churches and museums

This is a short walk, yet it takes in the major landmarks of the city's Golden Age and gives you a taste of the variety and piquancy of modern Amsterdam life. Here is quintessential Amsterdam: compact, vibrant and full of contradictions. Turn the corner of a dark alley and you're blinded by the light reflected off a canal. Slip through a stone gateway, and the fluorescent glitz of a crowded shopping mall yields to a quiet 17th-century courtyard. Brothels surround the city's oldest church; sweaty nightclubs thump away beside the gliding waiters and clinking champagne glasses of the Hotel Krasnapolsky Winter Garden. The railway station is palatial; the Palace looks like a post office.

You can start off with a slap-up breakfast in the sombre elegance of the Centraal Station's First Class restaurant, then whizz past the tourist razzmatazz of the Damrak and into the red-light district. Here, apart from the expected allures, you can visit a secret church in an attic and potter about canals and alleys little changed since the 17th century. After braving the crush and lethal traffic on the Dam, you can visit the Royal Palace, then ring one of the city's oldest carillons before finishing up with a coffee in a trendy café on the Spui.

It's best to start early (in Amsterdam this means 10am) to avoid the crowds. On Mondays the museums are closed, and you'll have to be in Amsterdam at the height of the season to be sure of getting into the Palace without an appointment.

Lunch and Cafés

1 Grand Café Restaurant le (Eerste) Klas, Platform 2b, Centraal Station. Recently restored First Class dining room, now open to all. It's timeless railway camp. You wouldn't bat an eyelid if you saw women in cloche hats whispering in the corner or an Edwardian touring party march through the door. Coffee, snacks and also much grander meals (*from around f25 for a main course*).

2 Het Karbeel, Warmoesstraat 58. An upmarket café on the edge of the red-light district. It started life in 1534 as an inn and is still connected to the Damrak by a secret smugglers' passage. Good sandwiches, snacks and fondues.

3 Lunchlokaal, Pijlsteeg 35. Tucked behind the Hotel Krasnapolsky, and reached through a narrow alley, is a quiet courtyard garden. Chairs are set out between the trees and you can enjoy sandwiches and homemade soup (*around f6*) in calm obliviousness of the seething Dam.

4 Ricky's Koffiehuis, Oudezijds Voorburwal 206, in the red-light district. Starts early as a workers' café and changes clientele as the day progresses. Accordions hang from the walls, sugar is served from zinc

Het IJ

Centraal Station

PRINS HENDRIKKADE

STATIONSPLEIN

❶

START

DAMRAK

Damrak

HEKELVELD

SPUISTRAAT

NIEUWEZIJDS VOORBURGWAL

NIEUWENDIJK

Herengracht

Singel

Beurs van Berlage

Amstelkring Museum Ⓜ

LANGE NIEZEL

ZEEDIJK

Geldersekade

BEURS-PLEIN

WARMOESSTRAAT

OUDEZIJDS VOORBURGWAL

PAPENBURGSTG

STANNENSTR

❿

GRAVEENSTR.

❾

Nieuwe Kerk

De Bijenkorf

DAMRAK STG

Oude Kerk

Ⓜ

Koninklijk Paleis (Stadhuis)

DAM

Grand Hotel Krasnapolsky

Ⓗ

❹

Voorburgwal

Achterburgwal

NIEUW MARKT

Madame Tussaud's Ⓜ

Nationaal Monument

DAMSTR.

❽

❸

Oudezijds

OUDE Oudezijds

KOESTRAAT

Post Office

SPUISTRAAT

ROKIN

NES

DOELEN STR.

Kloveniersburgwal

Oude Schans

Bank van Lening

Gate to Spinhuis

OUDE HOOGSTRAAT

❼

Huis op de Drie Grachten

RUSLAND

❶

Amsterdam Historical Museum

Ⓜ

SCHE BEGG STG

GRIMBURGWAL

❻ ❺

Gate to Oudemanhuis

⓯

Begijnhof

⓮

⓬

SPUI

⓭

Gate to Gasthuis

WATERLOOPLEIN

KALVERSTRAAT

HEILIGEWEG

HANDBOOGSTRAAT

NIEUWEZIJDS VOORBURGWAL

FINISH Gate to Rasphuis

ROKIN

Zwanenburgwal

Singel

AMSTEL

Binnenamstel

Stopera

N

REMBRANDT-PLEIN

250 metres

250 yards

buckets and there's a large, cheery communal table in a nook at the back.

5 Crea Café, Grimburgwal, at the end of Oudezijds Voorburgwal. Spacious student café with tatty pool tables, earnest groups arguing in corners and tired-eyed academics.

6 Upstairs Pannekoekhuis, Grimburgwal 2 (*open Tues–Sun 11–7*). Home-made pancakes up an almost vertical stairway, in a tiny room overhanging the street, with space for about ten customers. The owner's collection of teapots outnumbers clients 10:1. Pancakes around ƒ10.

7 Kaptein Zeppos, Gebed Zonder End 5 (*open Mon–Fri 11am–1am, Sat and Sun 4pm–2pm*). The street-name means 'prayer without end'—the narrow alley used to wind through ten different cloisters and was always crammed with muttering clerics. The restaurant serves simple, well prepared food in an airy, relaxed environment. On some afternoons you'll find a gipsy violinist or jazz band.

8 Hotel Krasnapolsky Winter Garden, Dam 9. Careful redecoration in the early 1990s gave the Krasnapolsky back some the old elegance that an insensitive 1970s job had destroyed. In the Winter Garden you can sit surrounded by palms and flattering mirrors and enjoy a genteel lunch. Breakfast (*6.30am–10.30am*) ƒ30, buffet lunch (*12–2pm*) ƒ42.50.

9 't Nieuwe Café Restaurant, Eggertstraat 8, next door to the Nieuwe Kerk. A noisy terrace, but quieter interior. Set breakfasts, snacks and fuller meals.

10 De Drie Fleschjes, Gravenstraat 18. *Proeflokaal* behind the Nieuwe Kerk that dates from 1650.

11 David and Goliath, Kalverstraat 92, at the entrance to the Amsterdam Historical Museum. After visiting the museum, the best place to relax and ponder the delights within is at the feet of a life-sized wooden David and an enormous Goliath, rescued from a 17th-century pleasure garden.

12 Café Esprit, Spui 10 (*closed Sun*). Trendy aluminium-box café on the Spui.

13 Lasalle, Spui 15. At the sharp end of Amsterdam dining chic, and good for lunches too. Waiters with epaulettes, like stewards on a 1930s liner. Good fish and fancy salads.

14 Café Luxembourg, Spui 22–24. Grand café that becomes crammed with young professionals on the way home from work.

15 Café Hoppe, Spui 18–20. Dates from 1670, also popular with local office workers. On summer evenings there's standing room only on the terrace, and it looks a bit like a cocktail party.

The **Centraal Station,** built between 1884 and 1889 atop thousands of wooden piles on an artificial island, is such an elaborate and sustained exercise in 19th-century ornament that it can almost be forgiven for screening off Amsterdam's view of the old harbour. The architect P. J. H. Cuypers (also responsible for the Rijksmuseum) succumbed to every temptation to gild bits of his red-brick extravaganza, so that it sparkles in the sunlight like a Walt Disney palace. Its twin towers are adorned not only by a clock, but also by a wind-rose, a delightfully superfluous instrument that rotates languidly showing the frequency of winds blowing from the various leading points of the compass. The roof bristles with stone and iron spikes and the central section sports classically inspired reliefs showing allegories of sailing, trade and industry. There's a large section over the entrance depicting the peoples of the world paying homage to the maiden Amsterdam. The building seems very much in the tradition of the triumphal arch or elaborate city gate and is indeed a grand place to arrive in Amsterdam. The city is laid out like a semi-circular spider's web with the Centraal Station in the middle. As you step out of the main entrance you get the full impression, across the shapeless open space of **Stationsplein**, of the spires, gables and cupolas of Amsterdam's delicate skyline.

Stationsplein itself is wildly and happily chaotic. Traditional Dutch barrel organs compete bravely with ten-piece South American bands and the 1970s rock music repertoires of buskers with portable amplifiers. Pedestrians stream in all directions, oblivious of the battalions of trams which, bells clanging, seem intent on converging on one particular spot in the centre. Rent-boys eye you from the arches, junkies and alcoholics droop against the walls, smart businessmen and paradigms of fashion stride purposefully past and backpackers picnic on the concrete, propped up against their rucksacks.

> *Head straight across the square for **Damrak**, once a busy port built along the Amstel, but these days a street lined with the fast food joints, rip-off bureaux de change, tacky restaurants and tackier hotels that usually cluster around tourist inlets. The only remaining patch of water is a tiny dock filled with the glass-covered boats that bus you around on hour-long canal trips (for details, see p.8).*

The original settlement of Amsterdam grew up in the early 13th century along Kerkstraat (Church Street, later renamed Warmoesstraat) on the left (east) side of the river. Towards the end of the last century the village expanded along Windmolenstraat (Windmill Street) on the right (west) bank. The Church Side and the Windmill Side soon became known as Oude Zijd (Old Side) and Nieuwe Zijd (New Side) and the corresponding sides of Damrak are still called that today.

> *Hurry past the gaudy signboards and flashing neon lights, but keep an eye open for the four baboons and twenty-two owls that stare down at you from the façade of Nos.28–30. They're the work of expressionist sculptor J. Mendes da Costa. He was lodging opposite the zoo when he submitted the design. At No.62 is Albert de Lange, one of Amsterdam's best bookshops and the outlet for German refugee writers like Max Brod and Bertolt Brecht during the 1930s. Halfway up Damrak, on the left-hand side, you come to the **Beurs van Berlage** (museum open Tues–Sun 10–4, basic adm f6, includes visit to tower).*

The first Beurs (Exchange) was built by the prolific 17th-century architect Hendrick de Keyser in 1608. The city council thought it necessary to confine all the outdoor wheeling and dealing that took place along Damrak and around the Oude Kerk to one (warmer and drier) venue. The result was deafening. As international trade expanded, Turks, Indians and Hungarians joined the locals packed around the pillars and arcades of the small hall on the Rokin, bargaining madly for silks, shares, tobacco and tulips—or anything the boats brought in. De Keyser's Beurs held out for two hundred years. The building that replaced it (on the site of the present Bijenkorf department store) was universally unpopular and in 1874 the city held a competition for a new design. When it was revealed that the winner had cribbed the façade from a French town hall, H. P. Berlage (who had come third) smartened up his original plans and landed the prize. Many revisions later (he was still at the drawing board while the builders were at work), he came up with a building that has become an Amsterdam landmark and earned him the reputation of being the father of modern Dutch architecture.

The Beurs van Berlage (completed in 1903) is all clean lines and functional shapes. Berlage allows himself some gently patterned brickwork, but there's not one extraneous twirly bit nor a glimmer of 19th-century gothic fantasy. The pillars and arcades inside are an echo of the original Beurs. The clock tower (also a quote from De Keyser's building) displays the mottoes '*Duur uw uur*' and '*Beidt uw tijd*' ('Last your hour' and 'Bide your time'), apt maxims given the seven years Berlage took to come up with a final design. These days part of the Beurs is used for concerts, while the rest is a museum (comprising a modest display on the history and design of the building) and exhibition hall. A visit to the museum gives you access to the clock tower and a view over the oldest part of town. In the smaller of two concert halls you sit and listen to the music in an enormous glass box which has solved the problem of abysmal acoustics without defacing the original interior. You can get a glimpse inside without buying a concert or a museum ticket by popping into the café at the south end.

The café opens out on to Beursplein. To the right the traffic on Damrak hurtles past. The dainty neoclassical Effectenbeurs (Commodities Exchange) on the left is the place where the real trading now happens. Across the square, a row of silently chewing, blank faces stare out at you from behind a sheet of plate-glass. These are exhausted shoppers propped up along a snackbar in the back window of De Bijenkorf, though they look as if they're for sale.

> *Leave Beursplein by Papenburgsteeg at the far left-hand corner. In the days before telex, runners bearing the latest prices from the Beurs would thunder down this narrow alley to the press agency building on Warmoesstraat where, to save time, the despatch would be reeled up to the relevant floor using a fishing rod. At the end of Papenbrugsteeg, turn left into* **Warmoesstraat**.

Warmoesstraat is Amsterdam's oldest street. Originally a cluster of wattle and daub cottages, it was by the 16th century a row of prosperous merchants' houses and powerful banks. The Duke of Alva lived here in 1574 during his reign of terror (the rest of the street was understandably empty at the time) and left without paying his rent. Vondel (the 'Dutch Shakespeare') had a small hosiery business at the Dam end before he became a famous poet (*see* p.170); and Sir Thomas Nugent, a seasoned 17th-century traveller, recommended it as the only street where you'd find English inns and so avoid being cheated by wily Dutchmen. In 1766 Mozart senior held court in the tavern of De Goude Leeuw and sold tickets for his son's recitals at *f*2 apiece; and a century later Karl Marx pondered and scribbled away in the inn next door. These days Warmoesstraat is the first layer of the red-light district, and a strange mixture of past respectability and the seediness which lies beyond. You arrive directly opposite the Condomerie (condom as consumer item—everything you could imagine). Next door is W139, an enormous gallery, set up by squatters, where you're sure to catch the very latest (though not always the best) of what's going on in Amsterdam art. Further up, past a string of leather fetish bars, you'll find Amsterdam's best tea and coffee specialists (Geels & Co at No.67). Just around the corner a butcher's shop lays out its trays of chops and drumsticks right next door to a display of enormous dildos and little plain-covered books with titles like 'Pent-up Pleasure' and 'Mom's Donkey Urge'. It's a grubby, dishevelled street, but no one seems to take it seriously enough for it to be sordid.

> *When you've seen what you want to in Warmoesstraat, turn off into St Annenstraat, past the Hotel Winston where the bar comes to life after midnight as a favourite drinking spot for local scruffs and wannabe artists. St Annenstraat takes you right into the **red-light district**, known to Amsterdammers as 'de walletjes' (the little walls).*

A 1629 law closed all taverns between St Annenstraat and the Oude Kerk because of the 'great acts of insolence and wantonness' going on there. The taverns have since reopened, though little else has changed. In those days the women nailed up romanticized portraits of themselves outside the doors. Nowadays they display themselves live, barely clad and deeply bored, perched on bar stools in the windows. Catch someone's eye and immediately there's a bright smile and a sparkle which disappears the moment you look away. If business is bad, or if you walk with eyes downcast, you'll hear the windows being rapped noisily. The rooms are functional cubicles, though from time to time you'll see one decked out in lace, knick-knacks and potted plants—a quaint parody of a Dutch bourgeois sitting-room. In the mornings the little alleys, some narrower than a doorway, are inhabited only by the desperate (on both sides of the glass) and the area has a feeling of secrecy and expectancy, rather like an empty theatre. Off-duty prostitutes join friends to go out shopping, or wander off in groups to the clinic for a check-up. In the afternoons it all seems too blatant and seedy, but later a wild festivity sets in as the lanes fill with the merry, the lecherous and the plain curious. Phalanxes of Japanese businessmen troop about aching to take photographs, drunken schoolboys gawp and try to pluck up courage, tight clutches of Dutch families from the provinces ooh and aah and snicker at all the wickedness.

> *A left turn down St Annendwarsstraat takes you to the Oudekerksplein, a peaceful square almost entirely taken up by Amsterdam's oldest building, the **Oude Kerk** (Old Church; open summer Mon–Sat 11–5, Sun 1–5; entrance f5).*

Only the tower of the Oude Kerk actually dates from 1300. The original basilica disappeared behind an increasingly haphazard outgrowth of side chapels, transepts and clerestories. Most of what you see today is lofty early 16th-century Renaissance, but even that has a crust of warden's offices, choir rooms and houses, built over a period of three centuries. The interior has survived frequent bouts of heavy-handed restoration, an engulfing coat of Prussian blue paint in the 18th century and violent attacks by iconoclasts. In August 1566, roused by the sight of fragments of statuary from smashed-up churches in Antwerp, Protestant mobs stormed the church, breaking windows and destroying all graven images. A local girl, Lange Weyn, threw her shoe at a picture of the Virgin Mary in the excitement, and was later drowned in a barrel on the Dam for the outrage.

After what is discreetly called the 'Alteration' of 1578, when the Protestants finally took control of the city, the new Calvinist city fathers stripped the church of its dedication to St Nicholas (patron saint of sailors and so, aptly, of Amsterdam) and the popular title of Oude Kerk became official. They also set about turning it into a more sombre place of worship. It had become a hearty communal gathering place. Dossers and travellers slept in the corners, pedlars set up stalls in the aisles, merchants clinched deals on the square outside and dog-owners crowded the entrance. (Only certain classes of Amsterdam society were allowed big dogs, and if your mutt couldn't squeeze through the special iron hoop at the church door, its days were numbered.) These days the church plays host to travelling exhibitions and the occasional concert. Inside you can see the tomb of Rembrandt's wife, Saskia van Uylenburgh (near the Weitkoperskapel on the north side); some beautifully restored and remade stained glass (especially the windows depicting the Annunciation in the Mariakapel); and the secret door (once covered by plaster, 5m above the ground in St Sebastiaanskapel) to the IJzeren Kapel (Iron Chapel), a hiding place for important city documents until 1892.

*Walk around the Oude Kerk to the other side of the square and turn left up the nearside of Oudezijds Voorburgwal. You come almost immediately to the **Amstelkring Museum** (Oudezijds Voorburgwal 40), one of Amsterdam's most charming small museums (open Mon–Sat 10–5, Sun 1–5; adm f7.50).*

The Amstelkring Museum, also known as *Ons Lieve Heer op Solder* (Our Lord in the Attic), was a '*schuilkerk*'—a clandestine church. During the 17th and 18th centuries Roman Catholic services were illegal, but ever-tolerant Amsterdam turned a blind eye to what was going on behind domestic façades. The attic of the little spout-gabled house joins up with two others in the houses behind and was consecrated as a church in 1663. Inside the museum you can wander about an 18th-century reception room, into a classic 17th-century Dutch '*sael*' (living-room) with symmetrical black and white marble flooring and a monumentally grand walnut fireplace, up through bedrooms with quaint box-shaped cupboard beds, higher and higher to a small wooden staircase. Turn the corner at the top of the stairs and suddenly you're in what seems an enormous church with two galleries, light streaming in, an abundance of carving and painting and a voluptuous organ that *must* have been audible throughout the neighbourhood. The church is filled with treasures and mementoes of oppressed Catholicism (you can get an explanatory pamphlet downstairs). Try to get there early in the day, when you can appreciate the dream-like atmosphere in relative solitude.

*Turn right out of the museum and double back along the right-hand side of **Oudezijds Voorburgwal.***

Oudezijds Voorburgwal was the canal immediately inside (*voor*, 'in front of') the first city wall. Today it's a brash, brazen strip of porn shops, video booths and peep-shows, though some stylish gables and façades poke out above the lurid layer at street-level. Look out for: the diving dolphins opposite the Amstelkring; a mask- and bust-encrusted house by Hendrick de Keyser opposite the Oude Kerk; Africans and Indians relaxing on tobacco bales on the neck-gable at No.187; and an elegant neoclassical building by one of the three great 17th-century domestic architects, Philips Vingboons, at No.316.

Halfway down the canal the sleaze shops suddenly come to an end and you find yourself in a leafy nook of old Amsterdam. At No.300 is the Municipal Pawn Broker—the **Bank van Lening**, euphemized as '*Ome Jan*' (Uncle John's). For the past three hundred years it has been a more sympathetic alternative to professional moneylenders—interest is fixed at a rate that corresponds to your ability to pay. Vondel, bankrupted by his playboy son, spent his septuagenarian years here as a clerk, going to work each day through a gateway that had one of his own poems inscribed in the arch. (It's still there, advising the rich to hurry past, as they have no business inside.)

On the opposite side of the canal is the **Agnietenkapel** (*open Mon–Fri 9–5, though phone © 525 3341 first to check; adm f3.50*), a 15th-century convent church that houses a specialized and not particularly captivating collection of prints, photographs and ephemera centering on academic life.

> *Turn left into Grimburgwal, past the **Huis op de Drie Grachten** (House of the Three Canals—the only one in the city with this qualification), and left again up the right-hand side of Oudezijds Achterburgwal, the canal that was just outside (achter, 'behind') the first city boundary.*

Most of the buildings in this area are now part of the University of Amsterdam, but they were once (in the words of a 17th-century visitor) a collection of 'almshouses which look like princes' houses, hospitals for fools and houses where beggars, frequenters of taphouses, women who feign great bellies and men who pretend they have been taken by Turks' were confined and set to hard work.

These institutions, a product of prosperous and Calvinistic Amsterdam, were considered far-sighted and revolutionary by the rest of Europe. The gateway on the corner, copied from a Michelangelo design, led to the **Gasthuis** (hospital). A little further down you come to another elaborate arch, the entrance to the **Oudemanhuis**, an old men's almshouse. These days glass doors slide back as you approach and you find yourself in a dim arcade of second-hand bookstalls with medieval-looking proprietors. A shaft of light halfway along comes from a door that leads to the elegant almshouse courtyard. It's a private court belonging to the university, but nobody will stop you if you want to have a look.

> *Continue down Oudezijds Achterburgwal; turn right into Spinhuissteeg. On the left you'll see the entrance to the **Spinhuis**.*

The Spinhuis was a place where 'incorrigible and lewd women' were made to spin cloth for the poor. A rather alarming relief above the door shows the poor women being whipped with a cat-o'-nine-tails. Underneath is the not entirely convincing inscription:

> *Schrik niet, ik wreek geen quaat maar dwing tot goet.*
> *Straf is mijn hand, maar Lieflijk mijn gemoed.*

> Cry not for I exact no vengeance for wrong, but force you to be good.
> My hand is stern but my heart is kind.

The altruism of successive custodians seems to have been directed more towards passing gentlemen. For a small fee they were given access to the wicked inmates.

Turn left into Spinhuisdwarsstraat and back along Korte Spinhuissteeg to Oudezijds Achterburgwal. Turn right and walk up to Oude Doelenstraat, where you turn left again. As you cross the canal you'll see the **Hash and Marijuana Museum** *on the corner and, a little further along, the* **Tattoo Museum** *(see p.181). At the end of Damstraat you come to the* **Dam.**

Riots, garrottings, camping hippies—the **Dam** has seen it all. Reputedly the site of the original dam across the Amstel, it hit its zenith as city centre in the 17th century. Pragmatic Amsterdam merchants wouldn't stand for any decorative open space at the heart of the city and the Dam bustled with a fishmarket, a public weighing house, a communal crane and a dock that allowed ships to sail right up into the middle of town to offload. Popular tunes rang out from the Stadhuis carillon and, above all the racket, the town crier's horn would from time to time blast out (once for good news, twice for bad). When you needed to go home, you could ring a bell to summon a taxi. After a brief wait for the drivers to throw dice to decide who should take you, you'd set off at reckless speed in a slide carriage (wheels presented a problem on the hump-backed bridges), accompanied by packs of sprinting boys throwing water and greased rags under the runners to make the carriage go faster, or straw to make it stop. You'd have to drop out coins at intervals to ensure your rapid progress, and a few more at the humpy bridges to the stalwart lads who hung around to give a much needed extra push.

Traffic on the Dam these days is just as frantic, but the square has lost all its verve. It's still the city centre and the carillon still peals out pop tunes, but the Dam is soulless, spiritless and dull. The eastern end is dominated by the towering, phallic **National Monument**, erected in 1956 as a memorial to the people killed in the Second World War. In the 1960s it became a sort of hippie totem pole and hundreds of people would sleep around it in the summer. Police attempts to put a stop to this (such as washing it down with firehoses) led to protest riots, but in 1970 a marauding group of off-duty marines chased away the campers forever.

Walking anti-clockwise around the Dam you pass the **Grand Hotel Krasnapolsky,** *where the Winter Garden has been a chic gathering place for over a century, and* **De Bijenkorf,** *a run-of-the-mill department store with a grand reputation and arty window displays. The view from the roof of De Bijenkorf was filmed for montage shots of the fictive capital of Tomania for Charlie Chaplin's* The Great Dictator. *On the other side of the square you reach the* **Nieuwe Kerk** *(New Church; open daily 11–5).*

The construction of the Nieuwe Kerk actually began nearly 600 years ago. It's a soaring Gothic heap without a steeple. (In the 17th century, Oude Kerk parishioners, who had always been jealous of the flash rival church, were delighted when the city council stopped construction of the tower because it was going to be higher than the town hall.) Until 1890 all the city's clocks were set weekly by the church's sundial. Like most of Amsterdam's large churches, the Nieuwe Kerk is now used mainly for exhibitions and concerts. Even if you can't catch a recital on the sumptuous Great Organ, the instrument itself, fluttering with angels and cherubs and surrounded by soft-painted shutters, is worth a visit. Admiral de Ruyter, the Dutch naval hero, is buried in the choir. (His invasion of the River Medway in England caused Sir William Batten, Surveyor of the British Navy, to explode to Samuel Pepys: 'I think the devil shits Dutchmen.') There's a memorial to the poet Vondel near the west door. Before you leave, have a look also at the richly carved pulpit and ornate copper choir screen.

> *Next door to the Nieuwe Kerk, taking up the entire western end of the square is the* **Koninklijk Paleis** *(Royal Palace; opening times vary, in summer generally daily 11am-5.30pm, sometimes closed for state functions; information on © 620 4060).*

The Koninklijk Paleis was the Stadhuis (City Hall) until Louis Bonaparte decided he wanted to live there in 1808. It's been a royal palace ever since, though Queen Beatrix prefers the leafier groves of Huis ten Bosch in The Hague and never spends the night here. The area in front of the Stadhuis was a favourite spot for theatrical public executions. On the right, above the entrance arches, you can still see the blocks where the scaffold slotted into the wall. The ornate street lamps along the front were commissioned by King Willem Frederik in 1840. They were the city's first gas lamps, but were so expensive to run that the council secretly turned them off whenever the king was out of town.

When the Stadhuis was built in the mid-17th century, only St Peter's, the Escorial and Venice's Palazzo Ducale rivalled it in grandeur. The poet Constantijn Huygens dubbed it 'the eighth wonder of the world', and a passing Englishman wrote of 'a most neat and splendid pile of a building'. But Sir William Temple, the British Ambassador to the Netherlands, harrumphed that it was '*una gran piccola cosa*' ('a big little thing'—he was quoting someone else's remark about the Louvre).

The architect, Jacob van Campen (designer of the ill-fated Nieuwe Kerk tower), had produced a grandiose celebration of Amsterdam's mercantile supremacy and civic might—a classicist heap of windows, pilasters and relief carving. On the front pediment, collected water deities worship an allegorical Maid of Amsterdam; at the back of the building the trading nations of the world grovel to her. Peace stands high under the dumpy dome (a cornucopia overflowing at her feet) holding not only an olive branch, but also Mercury's staff (a symbol of commerce). Atlas buckles under a copper globe so heavy that it needs iron rods to prop it up. Despite all this confident symbolism, there's no grand entrance (the eight little arches along the front look more like tradesmen's gates or the way into the stables) and nowadays you are more likely to agree with Sir William Temple than Constantijn Huygens: the rather grimy palace in a busy city centre has as much architectural impact as a main post office or magistrates court.

However, if you're passing during the rather restricted opening hours, don't miss the chance of popping inside to be dazzled by the Burgerzaal (Citizens' Hall). It's a vast space encrusted with marble carving that glints in the light pouring in from all sides. Rows of chandeliers drip from the distant ceiling, and brass inlaid maps on the floor show the heavenly and terrestrial worlds (with Amsterdam very much at the centre of things and the enthroned maid of Amsterdam proudly surveying it all). The few chairs around the edges, even a grand piano for the inevitable recital, look like doll's house furniture. Scattered throughout the building are delicate and often witty marble reliefs (Icarus takes a tumble outside the Bankrupts' Court, caryatids look bored with holding up the cross-beams). Most of them are by Artus Quellinus, the noted Golden Age sculptor who also carved the pediments outside. The city fathers, however, blundered when it came to commissioning the wall paintings: they sent Rembrandt packing after he had presented his preliminary sketches.

The Empire furniture dispersed around the building was left behind by Louis Bonaparte. When he took over the Stadhuis he carpeted the marble floors, boarded up the galleries, turned the virtually empty upper storey into living accommodation and also had the weighing house on the Dam demolished because it spoiled his view. When the bored and wayward Queen Hortens granted a royal pension to a foundling abandoned at the palace door, he forestalled an inundation of hapless infants by surrounding the entrance with cobble stones and appointing guards to prevent anyone from stepping on them. His wooden-partitioned upstairs apartments lasted well into this century and were such a fire risk that whenever Queen Wilhelmina used the palace everyone was instructed not to smoke and to sleep with the doors open. A fireman in gym shoes would creep about at night to catch offenders.

*Carry on in an anti-clockwise direction around the square. Before leaving the Dam you might like to visit **Madame Tussaud's** waxwork museum in the Peek & Cloppenburg department store (open daily 10–5.30, July and Aug 10–7.30; adm ƒ17.50, under 15s ƒ15, under 5s free, family ticket ƒ57.50).*

Here you can see some rather good reconstructions of 17th-century life and a perfectly horrible personified Europe (in a frock made of national flags) who rises from the centre of a tulip to the strains of Beethoven's 'Ode to Joy'. Madame Tussaud disdainfully floats away from it all on a painted cloud.

> *To leave the Dam, turn down Kalverstraat, a pedestrianized shopping street where shoulder-to-shoulder consumers push in and out of Euro-high street stores, scrabble about in the sales baskets and devour pungent fast food. A little way down, on the right, you can seek sanctuary behind the lost-looking Gothic door of **De Pappegaai** (the Parrot), a 19th-century Catholic church which gets its name from the fierce-looking polly carved into the archway. Walk on down to No.92 and up the yellow cobbled path to a rather lopsided gateway. At one time all houses on public roads had such cobbles in front of them to stop night-time travellers veering off the highway into the gutter. The gate, by Joost Jansz. Bilhamer (who designed the main extensions to the Oude Kerk) leads you in to the old **Burgerweeshuis**, a home founded in 1520 for orphans from the top ranks of Amsterdam society.*

You find yourself immediately in the quiet loggia and courtyard of the boys' section, now the terrace of In de Oude Goliath café, but with the boys' wooden lockers still visible in the wall. Through the next arch, the girls' courtyard is even quieter and emptier. It's a sober red brick court with sensible Ionic pilasters. Occasionally an itinerant lutist or string quartet plays something suitably restrained in one corner, while beyond the walls the oblivious crush in Kalverstraat pushes past. The girls had their own gate, on the right side of the courtyard. The thrifty governors transferred it stone by stone from a building that was being demolished nearby and had a mason carefully alter the date stone from 1571 to 1634. Boys and girls were effectively kept separate by an open sewer that ran between their respective dormitories. The sewer has been covered and the resulting passageway converted into a promenade gallery for civic guard portraits which are too big to hang anywhere else, but they don't make particularly riveting viewing.

> *On the far side of the court is the door to the **Amsterdam Historical Museum** (open Mon–Fri 10–5, Sat and Sun 11–5; adm ƒ11, under 16s ƒ5.50), a compact and accessible introduction to the city's history.*

The exhibition is arranged chronologically from Amsterdam's foundation right up to the 20th century and, armed with a file of English explanations of all the exhibits (free from the ticket desk), you can skim round quickly or stop to pick up details about periods that interest you. A map on the ground floor lights up in sections showing different phases of Amsterdam's growth. There's a sudden expansion in the Golden Age and an even bigger one in the late 20th century, after which all the lights go out with an alarming thud. You can get a bird's eye view of early Amsterdam from a medieval painting (quite a feat of imagination for an artist who had never been higher than the top of the Oude Kerk tower); see a collection of the surprisingly basic navigational instruments that guided the Dutch East Indiamen all over the world; and push buttons that make period music come out from behind models and paintings. There's a whole room of paintings, banners and relics connected with Amsterdam's 'miracle' (*see* p.33). Up a spiral staircase at the top of the building you can listen to recordings of the city's various carillons and even have a go at playing the one taken from the medieval Munttoren (*see* p.124)—though if you get too carried away an attendant clambers up to glower at you. The museum also stages excellent temporary exhibitions on specialist aspects of Amsterdam's history.

> *Turn right out of the museum and leave the girls' court by the door in the far corner. Turn left and walk through the gates to Gedempte Begijnensloot, where you turn right. Where this alley is joined by Begijnsteeg, you'll see a stone gateway on your right. This opens into the* **Begijnhof**.

The Begijnhof has the atmosphere of a quiet village square. You can hardly believe, in the leafy calm walled in by its neat gables, that the busiest parts of the city are only a few metres away. The Béguines were an order of lay nuns, founded in the 15th century, who, through self-effacement and powerful family connections, remained undisturbed by the religious upheavals of the following centuries. Sister Antonia, the last of the order, died in the house at No.26 in 1971. The small mound near the gate (covered by flowers in the spring) is the grave of another Béguine, Sister Cornelia Arens. When she died in 1654 she was buried, at her own request, in the gutter. Most of the houses were rebuilt in the 17th and 18th centuries, but at No.34 you can see the last remaining original façade, one of only two medieval wooden houses left in Amsterdam. Next door is an old clandestine church which still holds weekly mass. The church across the pathway was the original **Begijnkerk**, consecrated in 1419 and the only medieval church in the city with the tower in its original state. After a period of disuse during the Reformation, it was offered to Protestant dissenters fleeing England in 1607 and became known as the English Church. A plaque on the tower and stained glass in the chancel commemorate the fact that this group formed the core of the Pilgrim Fathers who sailed for America in 1620.

> *Leave the Begijnhof through an arch in the red brick house on the far left of the courtyard, along a short passage lined with Delft wall tiles, and out on to the* **Spui**.

Some of Amsterdam's most enduringly popular cafés skirt the **Spui**. At the southern end, the diminutive statue of *Het Lieverdje* ('The Little Darling', an impish Amsterdam rascal) was the focal point of provocative 'happenings' in the 1960s (*see* pp.45). You can end your walk with a quiet coffee, or nip down Voetboogstraat for a look at the outrageous gate of the old **Rasphuis**, the male equivalent of the Spinhuis, where men had to saw wood into a fine powder used for dye. Carved figures are tied down by real chains. A castigating Amsterdam raises her hand high, but someone has pinched her flail. The Calvinist custodians of the Rasphuis thought up a most ingenious method of compelling the inmates to good soul-saving work. A 17th-century British consul in Amsterdam was much impressed: 'They are beaten with a bull's pissel (penis) and if yet they rebel and won't work, are set in a tub, where if they do not pump, the water will swell over their heads.'

When it's time to go home, trams 1, 2 and 5 will set you on your way.

Walk II: Essential Amsterdam

Start: *Take Tram 6, 7 or 10 to Weteringschans.*

Walking time: *1½ hours, though this depends on the time you spend in cafés or museums. You're unlikely to need more than half an hour for the Willet-Holthuysen, but the Rijksmuseum is the sort of place where you could spend the whole day. Allow at least an hour for the Dutch collection, and another to skim through the rest and whet your appetite or a return visit. The Willet-Holthuysen Museum is closed on Mondays.*

For most people, Amsterdam means old paintings and charming canals. The most hallowed artworks are in the Rijksmuseum, and the Herengracht is the most splendid of the waterways. This walk guides you through the warren of Old Masters, reveals treasure-troves of antiquities and then leads you out for a leisurely stroll around the Golden Bend, a curve of Amsterdam's smartest canal houses. You'll see Rembrandt's Night Watch, Vermeer's exquisitely poised interiors and Jan Steen's riotous family scenes. There's a Delft-china violin and a portable altar, jewellery to make your knees weak and four-poster beds that will make you want to collapse entirely. Back in the open air, you can visit one of the city's most eccentric coffee shops, wander around a Golden Age mansion and, if you're not careful, be undone by some curiously named local liqueurs.

The canals look their best in the early evening. On summer nights the stateliest stretches are floodlit, and the bridges twinkle with fairy-lights. You might like to set off on this walk in the mid-afternoon, then take your time walking along the Herengracht once the museums have closed.

You'll pass some excellent restaurants; stop for an early dinner or choose somewhere and make a reservation for later.

Lunch and Cafés

The Rijksmuseum café has got you where it wants you. It's the only convenient place for a coffee, and they know it. Use it for a (vital) break, but have your lunch somewhere else.

1 Backstage Boutique, Utrechtse-dwarsstraat 65–67 (*closes 6pm*). Teas, coffee and home-made cakes in a coffeeshop that doubles as a boutique for fluorescent knitwear, tarot-reading parlour and local gossip shop. Sit among the gaudy jerseys and tea-cosy hats and enjoy your tea with the transvestites, busy mums, pretty young men and local lads who come in for the owner's infectious humour and good food.

2 Huyschkamer, Utrechtsestraat 137. The name means 'living-room', but there's little sign of comfy sofas or cosy firesides here, nor of the building's dubious past as a male brothel. Instead you find a tastefully designed and studiously hip Café that sells good food.

3 De Magere Brug, Amstel 81. On the banks of the Amstel near the 'Skinny Bridge', hence the name. One of the few brown cafés on the walk.

4 Villa Zeezicht, corner of Singel and Torensteeg. Lively sandwich bar where you can get tasty snacks and cakes. The canalside terrace is a great place to sun yourself in good weather.

5 De Admiraal, Herengracht 319. Proeflokaal for Amsterdam's last remaining

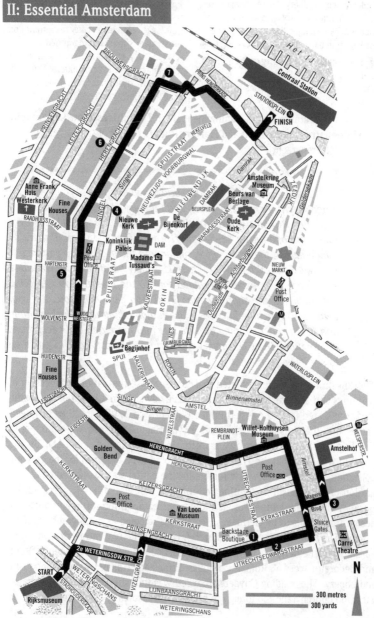

independent distillery, De Ooiyevaar. Here you will find soft sofas, and also potent liqueurs like 'Hempje ligt op' and 'Pruimpje prik in' (the names translate obscenely).

6 **Beiaard,** **Herengracht** **90**. Reproduction Art Deco lamps, snooker tables and numerous varieties of Belgian beer.

7 **De Belhamel, Brouwersgracht 60** (*open daily 12–12; lunch served 12–2.30 pm*). Art Nouveau café/restaurant on Amsterdam's most photographed canal. A relaxed, arty crowd eat snacks or meals with imaginative sauces (like saffron tagliatelle with oysters, cream, blue cheese, wine and sunflower seeds).

The best restaurants for an evening meal are in **Utrechtsestraat**, **Leliegracht**, or **Huidenstraat**, **Runstraat** and **Hartenstraat** (a cluster of side-streets halfway along the Herengracht).

*The tram stops right at the bridge which takes you over the Singelgracht. Across the canal, and the busy Stadhouderskade, you'll see the **Rijksmuseum** (National Museum, pronounced 'reyks-museum'; open daily 10–5, adm f15, with free floor plan. If there's a long queue at the ticket office, nip around the back to the entrance to the new South Wing, where there is usually hardly anyone waiting at all). There is an excellent guided tour to the museum on CD-ROM, obtainable on the shop level for f7.50. You can walk around at your own pace, punching in codes to learn more about individual paintings and, if you wish, tapping ever deeper into more detailed background information. The CD comes with a printed suggestion of 15 paintings to see if you're in a hurry.*

The Rijksmuseum was completed in 1885 to house the national collection of paintings and sculpture. The collection has evolved from a hoard of 200 paintings confiscated from the exiled Prince William V in 1798. First they had been gathered in the Huis ten Bosch palace in The Hague, and later were brought to the Trip brothers' 17th-century mansion in Amsterdam (see p.141). By the 1860s it was clear that the Trippenhuis was going to be too small for the growing collection. The quest for a new temple for the nation's art sparked off a conflagration of chauvinism, in-fighting and intrigue that would have impressed the Borgias. When the winners of an anonymous competition for a new museum design turned out to be German, the plan was rejected as 'non-Dutch'. Once a suitable Dutch architect was found in P. J. H. Cuypers (of Centraal Station fame) a new scandal emerged. The architect, project co-ordinator, government advisor and decorator were all Roman Catholics. Protestant Holland scented nepotism and popery. The building Cuypers produced was thought altogether too extravagant, too churchy and too foreign to house the treasures of Dutch culture. What made it worse was that Cuypers, having had a more sober Romanesque plan accepted, managed, while building was in progress, to slip in more fantastical bits of a previously rejected Gothic plan. Good patriotic Calvinists found this mish-mash of foreign styles deplorable. One critic railed: 'For two million guilders we now have the most sorry spectacle of a building that anyone could have thought to call a museum.' In response to the gilding and plethora of sculptures, portraits and tiling depicting Dutch artists that adorns the outside walls, another critic compared the museum to 'a garishly decorated house of a rich parvenu'. Even the king pleaded a prior engagement on the day of the opening ceremony.

Ironically, Cuypers thought his red-brick and wood building with its clean, simple lines to be quintessentially Dutch, and today one would be inclined to agree with him. Though not as magical as the Centraal Station, 'De Rijks' is one of Amsterdam's most conspicuous landmarks, and has become a cultural icon. When it reopened after the Second World War the waiting queue of pallid, underfed Amsterdammers in slightly shabby formal dress stretched all the way down Stadhouderskade.

In the years following the completion of the Rijksmuseum in 1885 so many people left their complete collections to the museum that it had, almost immediately, to embark on a programme of expansion. Not all the additions have been happy ones. In 1906 a committee of artists and architects spent months fiddling about in a life-sized model of a hall intended to show off Rembrandt's Night Watch. They finally decided that light from the left, tempered by carefully placed curtains, would be ideal. It wasn't. The room was a disaster, ended up being used for minor exhibitions and earned the monicker 'De Puist' (the pimple). All of Cuypers' ornate interior decorations have been removed and today the museum is a maze of white-washed rooms. Prince William V's modest collection has become: 5000 paintings, 30,000 sculptures and works of applied art, 17,000 historical objects, 3000 works of Asiatic art and a million prints and drawings.

> Like the Centraal Station on the other side of town, the Rijksmuseum was designed as a grand entrance to the city. (When it was built there were only fields beyond it.) A walkway through the middle of the building has bright bathroom acoustics that attract anything from opera-singing accordionists to steel bands. Because of this tunnel, the museum's important halls are on the first floor. If you climb the stairs to the museum shop on the first floor you'll see an archway leading to the **Gallery of Honour.** If your time is really tight, this is the one place to visit. It gives a good introduction to Golden Age painting, and houses the Rembrandt for which the museum is famous. At the far end, taking up the full wall, is Rembrandt's **Night Watch.**

The *Night Watch* was commissioned in 1642 by the militiamen of the Kloveniersdoelen (the Arquebusiers' Guildhall) to hang in their banqueting room alongside five other portraits of companies of the civic guard. It's officially called *The Company of Captain Frans Banning Cocq and Lieutenant Willem van Ruytenburch* and got its present title in the 19th century because ageing layers of varnish made it dim and murky. For years it's had the reputation of being the work that signalled Rembrandt's decline. This is ill-deserved—he still had some of his most important commissions ahead of him. It is true though, that the 17th-century public didn't like it very much, and when it was moved to the Town Hall in 1715 the city fathers thought nothing of lopping a bit off the left-hand side so that it would fit on the wall: two of Captain Cocq's militiamen disappeared forever.

Today, together with *The Syndics*, it's considered the prize of the Rijksmuseum's collection. It was usual to paint group portraits in fairly static compositions, giving each member equal prominence. Rembrandt, however, paints the company in a flurry of movement, as if about to set off on a march. Rich clothes and a wonderful collection of plumed and pointed hats all add to the sense of grandeur and motion (this is all pure invention—the guards' uniforms were in reality rather dull, and they never marched). A little girl in a luminous gold dress, possibly the company mascot, looks bewildered by all the activity. (The rather surreal touch of a dead chicken tied to her waist is an allusion to the militia's coat of arms.) The captain and his lieutenant, in fine clothes, dominate the scene. The rest of the company look far less important—which is possibly why the painting was initially unpopular: they had after all each paid their ƒ100, and deserved the same billing.

When the controllers of the Drapers' Guild (the 'Staalmeesters', or 'Syndics') commissioned Rembrandt to paint their portrait in 1662, they were determined not to make a similar mistake, and stipulated a more traditional composition. Rembrandt obeyed, yet still managed to create a work that brims with life. The Syndics look up from their table, and the viewer has the odd sensation of having just walked into the room and disturbed them at work. It's one of the finest group portraits ever painted—Kenneth Clark goes as far as acclaiming it 'one of the summits of European painting'—and seems to be the image picture librarians most reach for to evoke old Holland.

As you wander through the Gallery of Honour, keep an eye open for three more of Rembrandt's paintings: *The Jewish Bride* (1667), a glowing, tender portrait of a couple, no longer all that youthful, but very much in love; a rather depressed, world-weary *Self-portrait as the Apostle Paul* (1661); and St Peter's Denial (1660), showing a very troubled, down-to-earth apostle. Other paintings in the

Rembrandt

Rembrandt Harmensz. van Rijn (1606–69) was the son of a Leiden miller. When the poet Constantijn Huygens, who was also something of an art critic, visited Leiden in 1628, he went into raptures over Rembrandt's paintings (though he reprimanded the then unknown youth for his puniness and lack of manly exercise). A few years later Rembrandt upped sticks for the big city. He had made his mark in Leiden, and as the burgemeester wryly remarked: 'His portraits and other pictures pleased the citizens of Amsterdam, who paid him well for them.'
And indeed they did. Wealthy burghers, trades guilds and companies of the civic guard all spent handsome sums to be painted by the fashionable young artist. His unromanticized portraits hit just the right note in rationalistic, post-reformation Holland. Even his biblical and historical paintings have a truth and psychological rigour, especially in the faces, that seem to suggest direct experience of the world he's depicting. In 1634, already a rich and celebrated painter, he married heiress Saskia van Uylenburgh and five years later felt confident about paying a swinging *f*13,000 for a house in the Jewish quarter. (This was where he had always wanted to live—he found Hebrew culture fascinating and preferred Jewish models for his religious painting.)

Saskia died in 1642, having just changed her will to leave everything to their infant son Titus, with the estate to be held in usufruct by Rembrandt for as long as he didn't remarry. The painter got round this by having a clandestine affair with Titus' nurse, Geertghe Dircx. Then, in 1649, he fell in love with a younger servant, Hendrickje Stoffels. Geertghe sued successfully for breach of contract. This came at a bad time. Rembrandt was receiving fewer commissions now—perhaps because of gossip about his domestic affairs, perhaps because he was becoming increasingly uncompromising in his work, or maybe he was just going out of fashion. He'd also spent far too much on paintings and the house. In 1656 he was declared bankrupt. The property that had been his home for some 20 years was sold, and he moved out to live on the Rozengracht with Hendrickje and Titus. They were going to try to revive his flagging fortune by working as his agents, but Hendrickje died within two years, followed by Titus in 1669, only months after he had married. Rembrandt was so hard up that he had to sell Saskia's tomb to pay for Hendrickje's funeral. When he himself died, he was buried in an unmarked grave in the Westerkerk.

Gallery of Honour may change from time to time, but you can probably see Nicholas Maes's delicately detailed *Old Woman at Prayer* and work by one of Rembrandt's better-known pupils—Ferdinand Bol. Massive *penschilderijen* ('pen paintings', rather like etchings) of naval battle scenes by Willem van de Velde I are also on show.

Make your way back to the entrance hall where, if you turn through the door on the right, you can set off on a chronological journey through Dutch painting. In Rooms 201–6 you'll find works from the Middle Ages and the Renaissance (which reached the Netherlands a century later than Italy).

You'll probably want to save your energy for the Golden Age, but as you pass through the early rooms have a look at Geertgen tot Sint Jans' brightly detailed *Holy Kinship* (1485), crammed with emblems and symbolic references and his *Adoration of the Magi* (1490), set against an intricate backdrop of ruined landscapes, processions and misty forests. *The Seven Works of Charity* (1504), instructive panels by the Master of Alkmaar, have survived attacks by iconoclasts and creeping damp, and still preach their catalogue of worthy acts. Lucas van Leyden's *Adoration of the Golden Calf* (1530) is suitably riotous and a good example of the way Dutch Renaissance painters introduced realistic landscape settings for mythological scenes. The youth trying hard not to break the egg on the tavern floor in Pieter Aertsen's *Egg Dance* (1557) prefigures the scenes of everyday life that were to be such a feature of the Golden Age. The Dutch Mannerists, who worked in Haarlem between 1580 and the 1620s, get a good showing, Cornelis Cornelisz.'s enormous *Fall of Man* (1592) teems with animals mythical and domestic. In Karel van Mander's *The Magnanimity of Scipio* (1600), the 3rd-century BC Roman hero nobly refuses the offer of a beautiful captive for his slave and returns her to her betrothed.

*Rooms 207–236 are filled with paintings from the 17th century, the '**Golden Age**' not only of Dutch art but of the Netherlands' political and economic might.*

Intense realism and the naturalistic rendering of domestic and everyday life are the hallmarks of the Golden Age. There are precise, calm interiors, minutely detailed still lifes, wild taverns and salacious brothel scenes. Homely Dutch mothers and their *onnozele schaapjes* (innocent lambs) take the place of the Madonna and Child, and you'll see businessmen and civic guards rather than generals and fantastical battle scenes. As you walk around the collection you'll see more of Rembrandt and his pupils, but there are a number of other artists particularly worth searching out.

Frans Hals' happy and rather cheeky-looking *Wedding Portrait of Isaac Abrahamsz. Massa and Beatrix van der Laen* (1622), and the florid *Merry Drinker* (1628–30), seemingly dashed off with swift brushstokes and scratches in the wet paint, testify to his greatness as a portrait-painter. Pieter Saenredam's church interiors are so still, and he pays such close attention to architectural shapes, that they seem almost abstract. Pieter de Hooch—especially in *Woman and Child in a Pantry* (1658) and *Women beside a Linen Chest* (1663)—is a master of quiet family scenes. Light from the busy outside world streams in through a door or window in the background, while in the spotless rooms with their symmetrical black and white floor tiles all is order and calm—though the impish children seem just on the verge of disrupting it.

A somewhat sadder schaapje can be seen in Gabriel Metsu's touching, yet unsentimental *Sick Child*. Jan Steen gives quite another idea of family life. He used his experiences as a tavern-keeper to create scenes of such jolly domestic upheaval—as in *The Merry Family* (1670)—that the Dutch still use the expression 'a Jan Steen household' for any chaotic but cheerful home. You'll also find still lifes which, at the beginning of the century, are sober arrangements of herring, bread and cheese, but later overflow with ornate tableware, full-blown flowers and juicy fruit at its *toppunt* (literally: top-point)—the last moment of perfection before decay. Abraham van Beyeren's 1665 painting shows fat peaches, seafood, leaking melons and a toppled silver candlestick in meticulous detail. Look out also for Gerard ter Borch's exquisite fabrics—poor little Helena van der Schalke (1648) is weighed down by her fine silk dress and in *Gallant Conversation* the young woman's silver gown shimmers. (The conversation wasn't really that gallant—the man holding up his hand in gentle admonition was originally offering her a coin. A pious owner painted it out.)

Skim as fast as you like through the rest of the collection, but don't miss the **Vermeers** (Room 221a). Only thirty works by Johannes Vermeer (1632–75) exist; the Rijksmuseum has four of them. He had a passion for light and his paintings seem translucent. Light from a window reflects off a white wall, a jug, or softly glowing fabric. The tranquil *Kitchen Maid* (1658) and *Woman Reading a Letter* (1662/3) are totally without stylistic artifice, yet come close to perfection. In quiet, everyday scenes, Vermeer captures a sense of eternity.

> *If you walk through the rooms in numerical order you'll end up back in the Gallery of Honour. From here you can totter downstairs for a coffee. Before you do, have a look in Room 248, tucked away behind the film hall. Here you'll find the small* **Italian Collection** *with some chubby pink Rubens, Carlo Crivelli's elegant tempera* Mary Magdalene *(1485/90) and Piero di Cosimo's warts-and-all portraits of a Florentine architect and his cauliflower-eared father (1485).*

*It's probably a better idea to come back another day to see the rest of the museum, but if time is short refresh yourself as best you can in the museum café and head back up the stairs, this time to the right wing of the building, devoted to **sculpture and applied art**.*

The museum's collection of sculpture and applied art includes ceramics, china, glass, furniture, costumes, lace, tapestries, jewellery and silver from the Middle Ages to the 20th century, and can be utterly overwhelming. On a first visit the best idea is to give yourself a gentle overview. In the rooms leading off the entrance hall (Rooms 238–42), you'll find some of the best pieces in the collection. Ten 15th-century bronze figures, poised in graceful attitudes of mourning, have been filched from the tomb of Isabella de Bourbon in Antwerp. There's a tiny portable altar, carved in gold and encrusted with enamel, that some lucky nun used for her private devotion in the Abbey de Chocques in France in the 16th century. Look out also for Adriaen van Wesel's busy and energetic oak carving of *The Meeting of the Three Magi* (1475–7). A little further on, in Room 245, you can see Late Gothic German carvings of *Christ and the Last Supper*, still with some original polychrome and gilding.

If you have a taste for camp, head straight for Room 251A and Wenzel Jamnitzer's extraordinary *Table Ornament*, made for the city of Nuremberg in 1549. Mother Earth stands, one hip cocked, in a rockery of flowers, lizards and shrimps (all silver casts of real specimens) and supports on her head an enormous birdbath of cherubs rampant, scrolls, snakes and more flowers. All this is surmounted by yet another posy of enamelled silver foliage. Its ornate gilded wood and leather carrying case is displayed alongside.

The collection of Delftware (Rooms 255–57) has some prize polychrome as well as more traditional blue and white pieces. The people of Delft started making cheaper imitations of the Chinese porcelain brought back by the Dutch East India Company in the 17th century. (Things have turned full circle. Now souvenir shops sell imitation Delftware made in Taiwan.) Among the usual plates and cups you can see a functioning Delftware violin and towering tulip pagodas with space for forty stems (which, in the 17th century, would have cost a fortune to fill).

A blue staircase off Room 260 will take you back to the ground floor.

Back downstairs (in Room 164) you can see two exquisite early 18th-century dolls' houses—collectors' pieces assembled by the lady of the house, rather than toys. The museum is full of choice life-size furniture too, but it's rather coldly presented and, unless you have a specialist interest, the canal-house museums later in the walk will probably appeal to you more—though do keep an eye open for the rich Gobelin tapestries (Room 165) and an ornate oak table-leaf veneered with tortoiseshell and inlaid with a mass of birds, monkeys, fruit and putti worked in copper, brass and mother-of-pearl. If you appreciate good porcelain, the Meissen collection (Rooms 170–71) is one of the best in the world. An alchemist in the German town of Meissen, near Dresden, discovered the secret of Chinese porcelain manufacture while trying to make gold for the king, and the pieces subsequently produced in the area have been collectors' items for centuries.

A covered walkway leads from Room 166 to the restored South Wing.

The South Wing houses a small but carefully selected **costume and textile collection** (in Room 15, near the door to the walkway) and **18th- and 19th-century art**, including bright, ethereal pastels by the Swiss artist Jean-Etienne Liotard (1702–89)—mostly of aristocrats and socialites. The best 19th-century work is by painters of two movements from the second half of the century. The three Maris brothers were leading artists of the Hague School (nicknamed the 'grey' school after its heavy, cloudy skies). Jacob painted beaches and townscapes, Matthijs portrayed romantic fairy-tale scenes and Willem seemed preoccupied with ducks. Anton Mauve's pearly grey *Morning Ride along a Beach* (1876) is characteristic of the movement. The Amsterdam Impressionists are well represented by George Breitner, who liked to paint Amsterdam in the rain, and Isaac Isradls, whose brighter pictures are closer to the work of the French Impressionists.

*Downstairs you'll find **The Asiatic Art Collection.***

Three hundred years of Dutch trade connections have resulted in a glittering stash of treasures from the East. You can see lacquerwork, ceramics and textiles from Japan, Javanese sculptures, and religious works from China and India. A small, bronze dancing Lord Shiva (the Hindu god of creation) from the 12th century and an elegantly relaxed Chinese Buddhist saint, the **Bodhisattva Avalokitesharva**, from the same period, make the trip across to the South Wing worthwhile.

*Make your way back along the walkway to the main building. As you work your way back to the central staircase you pass a series of four-poster beds: the first is peppermint-green with embroidered birds, the second hung with rich tapestries, the third sparkling gold and silver—each is more alluring and sumptuous than the last, like the temptations in a fairy-tale. A door off the staircase (near the café entrance) leads to the **Rijksprentenkabinet** (Printroom) exhibition hall where you can see temporary exhibitions from a vast collection of prints, drawings and watercolours by the likes of Rembrandt, Dürer, Goya and Canaletto. To see works from the collection not on view, you need written permission (from the Director, Jan Luykenstraat 1A).*

On the ground floor of the left wing of the main building, you'll find the
Dutch History Collection.

The history collection comprises paintings, documents and memorabilia dating
from the Middle Ages to the Second World War. There's an understandable
emphasis on ships and sea battles, but the presentation is not very exciting. The
Amsterdam Historical Museum (*see* p.94) will give you a far more interesting
and accessible introduction to Dutch history. If you have the time, pop in for a
look at some of the more amusing curiosities—like a deceptively gorgeous
copper crown with glass jewels sent as a trade bribe to an African king by the
17th-century Duke of York (via the Dutch naval hero Admiral de Ruyter), or the
grand but diminutive jackets worn by the toddler Prince William V.

Before leaving the museum, have a quick look at the divinely noncha-
lant statue of Apollo in the small sculpture garden at the back. Then
cross the busy Stadhouderskade, which runs in front of the building,
and go over the Singelgracht and Lijnbaansgracht. Turn right along
Tweede Weteringsdwarsstraat, where at No.40 you can peek into the
78rpm Society's den. Old horned gramophones are stacked up against
the walls and a row of enthusiasts concentrate intensely under their
headphones.

At the end of the street turn left into Vijzelgracht, then right up the
right-hand side of Prinsengracht. This brings you to the **River Amstel**.
On your way you'll cross Utrechtsestraat. This is a good street for
restaurants, and your chance to duck down to Utrechtsedwarsstraat
and visit the Backstage Boutique (see 'Lunch and Cafés' above).

Across the river is a lively classical building with a cornice of jesters and grinning
clowns. This is the **Carré** theatre, built as a circus for Oscar Carré in 1887. Until
1875, Amsterdam had held an annual fair every September. It was a three-week
beanfeast that engulfed the entire city with celebrity performances, balls,
sideshows and circuses. One of these was Carré's, which King Willem III had
granted the honorary title of 'Royal Dutch'—the equivalent of a 'By
Appointment' stamp. But the revels had grown a little too unleashed for the
tastes of the Protestant patricians, and the city council declared that the 'Kermis'
of 1875 was to be the last. Despite rioting in the streets (which destroyed much
of the original mauve 17th-century glass in canal-house windows), their edict
was carried out and Amsterdam lost its annual wassail. But Carré decided he was
going to stay. He built a 'temporary' wooden circus tent beside the Amstel, and
when the council wasn't looking, erected a stone façade. Outraged city fathers
declared that he should take it down, but Carré fought on tenaciously

throughout the 1880s, and eventually got his way. The striking building you see today was built within months as the circus's permanent home. Now it hosts mainly musicals, but the best time to see its circular plush interior is when it reverts to being a circus over the Christmas holiday.

In the river is a barrier of **sluice gates**. Every night between 7 and 8.30 two hefty men turn the wooden wheels that close them. Far to the east of the city, on the island of Zeeburg, a pumping station starts up and forces 600,000 cubic metres of water into the canals, forcing the old water out through sluices in the west. This helps stop the pong, which at one time was quite overpowering. Even when Amsterdammers stopped tipping their sewage into the canals and sent it off in covered wagons to be sold as field manure, the stagnating water still presented a problem. Not everyone seemed to mind. When in 1765 plans for better water circulation were proposed, 33,000 domestic maids petitoned against the idea as they felt that a reduction in the vile emanations from the canal would lose them cleaning work.

A little way up the river you can see the **Magere Brug** ('Skinny Bridge'). It was built in the 17th century for two spoilt young maidens who were too lazy to walk the long way round from their house in Kerkstraat to their stables across the river. A public outcry prevented its being replaced by a steel bridge in 1929, but the old structure was rotting and today's delicate white wooden swing bridge is a replica. The long, rather austere two-storey brick building on the far side of the river, just beyond the Magere Brug is the **Amstelhof**, a 17th-century almshouse. The severe walls enclose a luscious garden courtyard with fountains, arbours and choruses of birds, where you can sit and rest if you're discreet.

> *Walk up the Amstel and turn left on to the **Herengracht**, keeping to the right-hand side.*

Amsterdam's population increased tenfold between 1550 and 1650. In the early 17th century the far-sighted city fathers were already planning to push the city boundaries outwards with three grand concentric canals. The Prinsengracht (Princes' Canal), Keizersgracht (Emperor's Canal) and Herengracht (Gentlemen's Canal—rather than Kings', a nice move by bourgeois Amsterdam) were intended for rentiers and rich merchants who wanted to live away from the smells and noise of the harbour. The shops and industries there were banished to poorer parts of town. The city hall parcelled out the land in 30ft, rather than the usual 20ft lots (though wily speculators would buy up two adjacent plots and split them into three and the really opulent merchants would combine two into a single house). Fashion has claimed each canal, at one time or another, as Amsterdam's best address, but it was the Herengracht that was really built to impress. It's more grand than pretty, a little ravaged by centuries of ostentation. Subsequent occupiers have (until recently) thought nothing of pulling down old buildings to make way for bigger and better displays of wealth, but the survivors have an endearing, if worn, panache. Some extraordinary gables poke up out of the trees that line the canal.

Space was at a premium in Amsterdam and you were taxed on the width of your house, so height often became an expression of wealth and the boastful decoration was applied to the inside, or to the gables. Even the rear façades got special attention. ('Our Lord finished off a canary's behind as neatly as its front,' remarked one contemporary architect.) Narrow houses mean winding stairways, uncongenial to four-poster beds and heavy carved dressers, hence most Amsterdam buildings have a hoist beam poking out from the gable so you can winch your furniture up the outside. Many lean dangerously over the street, not necessarily because they're about to subside into the city's soggy soil, but because this shows off the gables to passing pedestrians and makes the building more imposing. It also stops rising furniture from crashing into the wall. Angles became so alarming that a bye-law was introduced in 1565 to put a stop to the more adventurous tilts.

A short way along the Herengracht, at No.605, you'll come to the **Willet-Holthuysen Museum** *(open Mon–Fri 10–5, Sat and Sun 11–5; adm f7.50).*

The Willet-Holthuysen Museum is a 17th-century canal house. For two centuries it was occupied by a succession of Amsterdam glitterati. The last, Sandrina Holthuysen, had spent most of her life married to Abraham Willet, an avid collector of paintings, art books, glass, ceramics and silver. When she died in 1895, alone, riddled with cancer and surrounded by cats, she left the house and contents to Amsterdam as a museum. The city then filled it with pickings from a number of similar bequests. Most of the rooms are now reconstructed as 18th-century period pieces, with the different collections scattered about the house, mainly in rather stiff salons and boudoirs; there's also a crisp formal garden. Everything seems in its Sunday best—including the surreal headless mannequins that stand strategically about, sporting 18th-century costume. It's a good place to get an insider's view of one of the more stately canal houses, but if you'd prefer something that feels a little more lived-in, try to get to the **Van Loon Museum** just around the corner in Keizersgracht (*open Fri–Mon 11–5; adm f7.50*).

Turn right out of the museum to begin a stroll along the canal. You'll probably want to criss-cross it as you walk, but the best views are generally to be had from the right-hand side.

Monumental sandstone frontages seem to push aside the traditional dainty gabled brick façades. Cornices curled with acanthus leaves, strung with garlands and surmounted by urns lord it over the modest step-gables, though the odd defiant bell or neck-gable might reply with an extravagant claw-piece. At No.502, though, you'll find an austere, late 18th-century building with only the slightest flutter of exuberance in the three raised œils-de-bœuf along the roof-line. This has been the official residence of Amsterdam *burgemeesters* since 1927. Nearby (Nos.504–10) is a little stretch of wildly decorative claw-pieces. Tigers, dolphins and seagods curl about the gables and for once upstage the grander buildings.

> *The bit of the canal between Vijzelstraat and Leidsestraat is known as the **Golden Bend**, perhaps more for the wealth of the inhabitants than the refinement of the architecture. There are two clusters of more gorgeous and more graceful dwellings further up the canal that better deserve the epithet, though the elegant Louis XIV building with curved balustrades at No.475 does have the reputation of being Amsterdam's most beautiful house. You'll find the first of these more impressive constellations on the corner just beyond the Leidsegracht.*

On the right-hand side of the canal, No.401 manages to lean in three different directions at once. Across the canal is a pretty little 17th-century house with a simple festooned neck-gable (No.394). The outrageous confection at Nos.380–2 is a late 19th-century imitation of a French Renaissance château scrunched down to city mansion size. The more dignified row of four houses (Nos.364–70) with clean lines, stately neck-gables and quieter decoration are by the famous 17th-century domestic architect, Philips Vingboons. The house at No.366 is now the **Bijbels Museum** (Bible Museum, *partially closed for restoration until late 2000, open Mon–Sat 10–5, Sun 1–5; adm f5*) worth a visit only if you are interested in models of Solomon's temple and the history of the Dutch Bible over the past millennium—though the interior does preserve ceiling paintings by the 18th-century design supremo Jacob de Wit.

> *The next notable group of houses is on the sharp curve in the canal, just after you cross **Raadhuisstraat**.*

The Bartolotti House at Nos.170–2 was built in 1617 by Hendrick de Keyser (who designed most of Amsterdam's spiky towers) for West India Company director Van den Heuvel. (It was paid for by Van den Heuvel's mother-in-law who stipulated the house be called after her late husband.) Its enormous neck-gable is all but invisible under the encrustation of pilasters, pinnacles and decorative reliefs. These days part of it houses the **Theatre Museum** (*see* p.125). The white sandstone house next door (known as the White House), built in 1668, was Philips Vingboons' first.

As you walk up to the end of the Herengracht, you'll pass (at No.120) one of the few smaller 17th-century houses to have kept its façade free of later additions and amendments. The Herengracht flows into the Brouwersgracht, a quiet, pretty, picture-book canal (see p.134.

You could end your walk with coffee or a meal at the Belhamel (see 'Lunch and Cafés', p.100), or wander back along the other side of the Herengracht (quite a different experience) or along one of the other canals to a restaurant you might have found earlier. If you'd prefer to head home, cut across to Centraal Station, where you'll find trams to take you to virtually any part of the city.

Walk III: Jewish Amsterdam & Jordaan

Start: *Take Tram 7, 9, 14
to Plantage Kerklaan.*

Walking time: *1½–2 hours.
The museums are all fairly
small. Another two hours should
be quite enough browsing
and shopping time.*

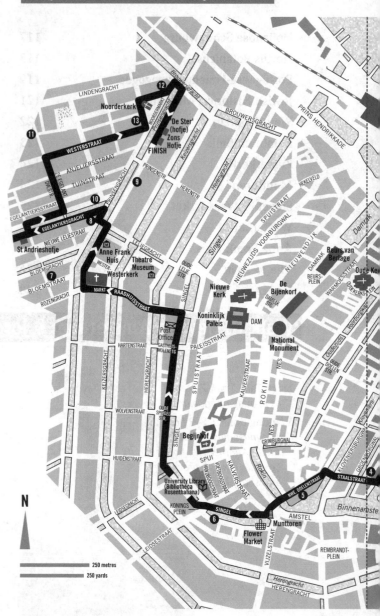

III: Jewish Amsterdam & Jordaan

LINDENGRACHT

12

Noorderkerk

13

'De Ster' (hofje)
Zons Hofje

FINISH

11

WESTERSTRAAT

ANJELIERSSTRAAT

TUINSTRAAT

9

PRINSENSTR

EGELANTIERSGRACHT

10

8

St Andrieshofje

NIEUWE LELIESTRAAT

Anne Frank
Huis
Westerkerk

Theatre
Museum

7

BLOEMGRACHT

BLOEMSTRAAT

MARKT RAADHUISSTRAAT

ROZENGRACHT

BROUWERSGRACHT

PRINSENGRACHT

KEIZERSGRACHT

HERENSTR

LELIEGRACHT

OUDE
LELIE
STR

Nieuwe
Kerk

Koninklijk
Paleis

Post
Office

GASTHUIS
MOLENST.

HARTENSTRAAT

KEIZERSGRACHT

HERENGRACHT

WOLVENSTRAAT

HUIDENSTRAAT

LEIDSEGRACHT

PALEISSTRAAT

SPUISTRAAT

KALVERSTRAAT

OUDE
SPIEGEL
STR

Begijnhof

University Library
(Bibliotheca
Rosenthaliana)

KONINGS
PLEIN

SPUI

HANDBOOGSTR

VOETBOOGSTR

6

SINGEL

Munttoren

Flower
Market

VIJZELSTRAAT

HERENGRACHT
HERENGRACHT

PRINS HENDRIKKADE

BROUWERSGRACHT

HEKELVELD

SPUISTRAAT

NIEUWEZIJDS VOORBURGWAL

Singel

NIEUWENDIJK

Damrak

Beurs van
Berlage

BEURS
PLEIN

DAMRAK

DAMRAK
STR

Oude Ker

WARMOESSTRAAT

DUIFJESSTEEG

De
Bijenkorf

DAM

National
Monument

NES

ROKIN

NES

ROKIN

GRIMBURGWAL

NWE. DOELENSTRAAT

STAALSTRAAT

AMSTEL

Binnenamste

REMBRANDT-
PLEIN

OUDEZIJDS VOORBURGWAL

OUDE
DOELEN
STR

KLOVENIERSBURGWAL

GROENBURGWAL

4

5

N

250 metres
250 yards

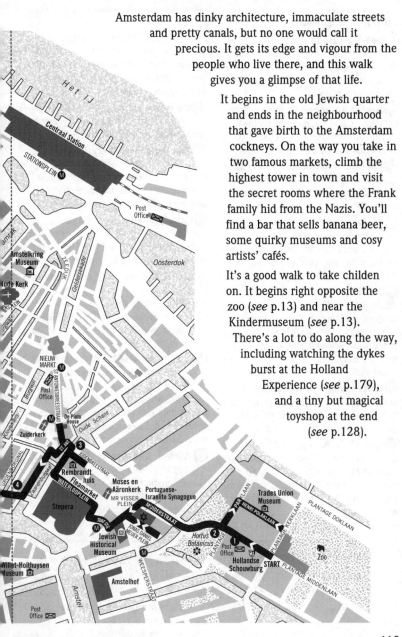

Amsterdam has dinky architecture, immaculate streets and pretty canals, but no one would call it precious. It gets its edge and vigour from the people who live there, and this walk gives you a glimpse of that life.

It begins in the old Jewish quarter and ends in the neighbourhood that gave birth to the Amsterdam cockneys. On the way you take in two famous markets, climb the highest tower in town and visit the secret rooms where the Frank family hid from the Nazis. You'll find a bar that sells banana beer, some quirky museums and cosy artists' cafés.

It's a good walk to take childen on. It begins right opposite the zoo (*see* p.13) and near the Kindermuseum (*see* p.13). There's a lot to do along the way, including watching the dykes burst at the Holland Experience (*see* p.179), and a tiny but magical toyshop at the end (*see* p.128).

Map labels:
Het IJ
Centraal Station
STATIONSPLEIN
Amrak
Post Office
Amstelkring Museum
Oude Kerk
Oosterdok
TEEDIJK
Geldersekade
NIEUW MARKT
ST ANTONIESBREESTRAAT
Post Office
Borgwal
Kloveniersburgwal
De Pinto House
Oude Schans
Zuiderkerk
JODENBREESTRAAT
ST ANT
Rembrandt huis
Fleamarket
WATERLOOPLEIN
Moses en Aäronkerk
MR VISSER PLEIN
Portuguese-Israelite Synagogue
MUIDERSTRAAT
PLANTAGE DOKLAAN
PLANTAGE KERKLAAN
PLAN
HENRI POLAKLAAN
Trades Union Museum
Stopera
TURF STG
JONAS DANIEL MEIJER PLEIN
Jewish Historical Museum
Hortus Botanicus
Post Office
PLANTAGE MIDDENLAAN
START
Zoo
Hollandse Schouwburg
Willet-Holthuysen Museum
WEESPERSTRAAT
Amstelhof
Amstel
Post Office

115

Lunch and Cafés

❶ De Eik en Linde, Plantage Middenlaan 22, next to the Hollandse Schouwburg. Brown café with diverse local crowd. It was once connected by an upstairs corridor to the theatre next door.

❷ Hortus Botanicus Orangery, Hortus Botanicus. Cakes and coffee under the trees or behind hothouse glass—though you'll need a ticket to the gardens to get in.

❸ Café de Sluiswacht, St Antoniessluis 1. Quaint café in a 17th-century lock-keeper's house, which these days rivals the tower at Pisa for tilt.

❹ Puccini, Staalstraat 21 (*closed Mon*). Classy modern café with delicious cakes. The air is filled with the aroma of chocolate steaming in the vats of the adjoining 'Dessert Shop'.

❺ De Jaren, Nieuwe Doelenstraat 20. Amsterdam's most spacious Grand Café, right on the Amstel. Comfortable chairs, high ceilings, newspapers in all languages, and anyone who's anyone in Amsterdam arts. Sandwiches and light meals *f*5.50–*f*25.

❻ Coffeeshop Divertimento, Singel 480, in the flowermarket. A fragrant café that serves enormous ice creams as well as inexpensive sandwiches and snacks.

❼ Café Chris, Bloemstraat 42, across the canal from the Westerkerk. A taphouse since 1624, it predates the bar that calls itself 'Amsterdam's oldest' by five years. The workers who built the Westerkerk received (and spent) their wages here. It's so small there's no room for a cistern in the

men's loo; you flush it from a handle on the wall once you're back in the bar. On Sunday afternoons and evenings the café reverberates, in traditional Jordaan style, to a rousing opera singalong.

❽ De Prins, Prinsengracht 124. Trendy café with a sunny canalside terrace. Serves good sandwiches and snacks (*f*5–*f*20).

❾ The Pancake Bakery, Prinsengracht 191, near the Anne Frank Huis. A low-beamed cellar that boasts the best pancakes in town. They could well be right. Sweet and savoury pancakes from *f*8.50 to *f*18.

❿ Café 't Smalle, Egelantiersgracht 12. Restored *proeflokaal* of Pieter Hoppe's 18th-century liqueur distillery. Now sells a wider range of drinks and snacks.

⓫ De Blaffende Vis (The Barking Fish), Westerstraat 118, and **'t Monumentje**, Westerstraat 120. Two busy Jordaan cafés frequented by traditional Jordaaners and the new generation of young artists.

⓬ Café 't Papeneiland, Prinsengracht 2, just up from the Noorderkerk. Full of pink-faced old men. A 17th-century café with a shady past. It was originally a funeral parlour that sold beer on the side. There's an unexplained secret passage running from the cellar to the house over the canal.

⓭ Winkel Lunchcafé, Noordermarkt 43, opposite Noorderkerk. Good salads. Gets its produce (much of it organic) fresh from the farm, though the standard of service often spoils the lunch.

*If you've arrived on Tram 7, double back a few yards along Plantage Kerklaan and turn right into Plantage Middenlaan. The other trams drop you off right on Plantage Middenlaan, which, if you follow it westwards, takes you into what was the heart of **Jewish Amsterdam**.*

Amsterdammers nickname their city 'Mokum', from the Yiddish 'Mokum aleph', 'the best city of all', and they'll often leave you with a cheery 'de mazzel'—'good luck'. As early as the 16th century, Amsterdam's religious tolerance was attracting Jews fleeing persecution in other European countries. This tolerance stemmed less from the milk of Christian kindness than from sound commercial reasoning. The Sephardic Jews, who came from Spain and Portugal in the 16th and 17th centuries, brought good inside information on the opposition's colonies and trade routes. Even the poorer Ashkenazim (from central and eastern Europe) had skills that fuelled the Golden Age boom. The city's trade guilds, however, refused to admit Jews and so Jews could only find work in fields that did not present direct competition to locals. Many were physicians or apothecaries, or worked in high-risk finance and in the new trades associated with the cotton or diamond industries. But they could retain their religion and didn't have to live in ghettos or wear distinguishing badges. The city soon became known as the 'Jerusalem of the West'. Jewish prayers rang out above the clamour of the market and lumber yards around Waterlooplein, where most Jews settled. There was hardly a more crowded or busier place in town. The Nazi occupation put an end to that. Of the 130,000 Jews living in Amsterdam in 1938 (10 per cent of the total population), 100,000 did not survive the war. For a long time the old Jewish quarter lay empty and derelict, as if the buildings themselves were in a state of shock. Recovery took decades, but the market is now back in place and the area is as lively as ever, though the Jewish community itself is all but invisible.

The walk begins on the edge of the original Jewish quarter, in the elegant, wide streets of the **Plantage** district. The 'Plantation' was a bushy parkland where Amsterdammers would lounge about on feast days, or go on long evening walks. At the end of the 19th century it was flattened by rows of showy neoclassical houses with outrageous colonial embellishments (pineapple pinnacles, exotic festoons, negro figurines propping up the beam ends). Many of the wealthier Jews moved into the grand new houses and by the 1920s it was the suburb of the Jewish élite. In 1897 the **Hollandse Schouwburg** (Holland Theatre) at Plantage Middenlaan 24, after a false start as an operetta theatre, became the home of the Nederlandsche Toneelvereeniging (Dutch Drama Society)—the company that propelled Dutch theatre into the 20th century. Because of the large number of Jews in both the audience and the theatre group itself, the occupying forces during the Second World War renamed it the Joodsche Schouwburg (Jewish Theatre). In 1942 it was designated an assembly point for Jews waiting to be deported. People were kept in the darkened building for days and then (apart from a few children who had managed to escape through the crèche across the road) were herded on to trains bound for Westerbork, a transit camp in the Dutch province of Drenthe. In Amsterdam, Jews spoke of Westerbork as 'the first circle of Hell'. From there trains left weekly for the death camps at Auschwitz and Sobibor. Understandably, after the war no one much wanted to use the Hollandse Schouwburg as a theatre again. In the 1960s it was declared a memorial to the deported Jews who never returned. Today only a secluded memorial garden lies behind the façade. Every year on 4 May (Remembrance Day) the city keeps a two-minute silence to commemorate those who died in the war. Just before 8pm people from the neighbourhood start to arrive at the Hollandse Schouwburg (as they do at similar monuments all over the city). Trendy young things, children, people old enough to have lived through the war all quietly join the swelling groups converging on the theatre. Most carry small posies of flowers. At 8 o'clock the trains stop, cars switch off their engines, people still in cafés put down their drinks and the whole city goes quiet.

> Walk down Plantage Middenlaan past the **Desmet Cinema**. During the war, German Jewish refugees staged theatre and cabaret here. The shows were so good that even the Nazi officer in charge of deportation came to watch. At the end of Plantage Middenlaan you come, on the right-hand side, to **Wertheimpark**, and, left, to the **Hortus Botanicus**.

The tiny Wertheimpark is the last remaining patch of the old Plantage gardens. At the entrance, two sphinxes with lanterns on their heads glower from the top of disproportionately large gateposts. Most of the park seems taken up by a fountain in memory of A. C. Wertheim (1832–97), a philanthropic banker who lived out his motto: 'Be a Jew in the synagogue and a human being in society', by being available in his office for an hour every morning to anyone, Jew or gentile, who needed to appeal to his charity. In one corner of the park, built over an urn of ashes brought back from Auschwitz, is a monument to Jews who perished in the concentration camps. Smashed mirrors lie flat on the ground: a symbol that the Earth can no longer reflect Heaven without distortion.

The **Hortus Botanicus** (Botanical Gardens; *open 1 April–1 Oct, 9–5 on weekdays and 11–5 other days; from 1 Oct to 1 April it closes at 4pm; adm f7.50*), was originally an apothecaries' herb garden in a marshy corner of the Plantage. It was later inundated by tropical plants pillaged by the Dutch East India Company, and has ended up with one of the biggest botanical collections in the world. A coffee shrub cultivated at the Hortus was presented to Louis XIV in 1714. Its seeds were used to initiate the cultivation of coffee in South America. A century later the gardens narrowly survived Louis Bonaparte's attempt to turn them into a zoo. The animals arrived before any cages had been built and the orangery became a volatile dormitory for wolves, lions, monkeys and porcupines. Tranquillity was restored when, after the king's untimely departure from the Netherlands, a relieved directorate put the animals up for auction. During the first half of this century, the gardens' biggest attraction was the massive *Victoria Amazonica* water lily. People would queue for hours on the one night of the year when it flowered, and—so the stories go—could stand, three at a time, on the broad lily pads. The sturdy plant survived this abuse, but not the demolition of its greenhouse in the 1960s. For decades there was no *Victoria Amazonica* at the Hortus, but in the 1990s a new greenhouse was built, and the giant lily once more has pride of place. The Hortus is a tranquil spot, a pocket-sized patch of green that's not really part of the tourist circuit. It won't take you long to nip in and see the ancient varieties of tulip, visit the world's oldest pot plant, warily observe the cabinet of flesh-eating plants, enjoy the tropical climes of the glass-domed palm house or the balmy air in the new three-climate hothouse. Then you can cool off with a fruit juice in the Orangery.

*The National **Vakbondsmuseum** (Trade Unions Museum) at Henri Polaklaan 9, just around the corner from the entrance to the Wertheimpark, is worth a diversion for the building alone (open Tues–Fri 11am–5pm, Sat and Sun 1–5; adm f5).*

The father of modern Dutch architecture, H. P. Berlage, designed the building in 1900 for Holland's first trade union, the mainly Jewish General Netherlands Diamond Workers' Union (ANDB). Wedding-cake layers of brick arches create a light and airy entrance hall. An ornate *Jugendstil* lamp hangs through the depth of two storeys in the centre of the room. Upstairs there is a cosy panelled board-room with more metal lanterns, and murals by the Dutch Impressionist Roland Holst. However, you'll have to be severely interested in the Dutch labour move-ment to appreciate the small exhibitions of photographs, clippings and documents (all in Dutch) in the other room.

*At the end of Plantage Middenlaan you cross the canal to **Muiderstraat**, part of the original Jewish quarter.*

Collectors, on the corner of Muiderstraat, looks more like a museum of 20th-century design classics than a shop. One wall is lined with pinball machines, another with Coca-Cola dispensers. If you have the ready cash, you can pick up a gleaming Maserati or a comfy little Morris Minor Traveller. The **Apotheek De Castro** (De Castro Pharmacy) at Nos.14–16 was established in 1832 during a cholera epidemic. It had a succession of art-loving owners, one of whom, E. M. Vita Israel, exhibited his collection in the rooms above the shop and became the first curator of the Jewish Historical Museum. De Castro's is still a pharmacy, though all that remains of the original shop is the façade.

*Keep to the left side of Muiderstraat. At the end of the street you come to the **Portuguese-Israelite Synagogue** (open April–Oct, Sun–Fri 10–4; Nov–March Mon–Thurs 10–4, Fri 10–3, Sun 10–12; adm f5).*

There was little love lost between the Sephardim and Ashkenazim. Even today old Sephardic Jews can remember being warned off '*vrotte Tedesco*' (filthy Germans) with: '*Je kan nog beter met een Goya trouwen dan met een Tedesco.*' (Rather marry a gentile than an Ashkenazi.) The Sephardim were a smaller but more powerful community with a class of wealthy professionals, and were happily welcomed into Dutch society. Their Portuguese-Israelite Synagogue (or 'Snoge' after the Spanish *esnoga*) was built between 1671 and 1675 as a showpiece. It was more than twice the size of the Ashkenazi temple completed the year before on the site next door. Only in Amsterdam could Jews make such an open display of their place of worship. There was no established building style for synagogues, and the architect, Elias Bouman (who had also designed the Ashkenazi building), claimed he was creating an imitation of Solomon's temple following descriptions in the Old Testament. However, the building he produced, with its mahogany pews and brass chandeliers, bears a remarkable resemblance to the larger Christian churches of the period. It's an imposing brick block that dwarfs the buildings around it. The Hebrew letters of the name 'Aboab' are worked into the text above the door (which translates as 'And I—in Thy great love—shall enter Thy House') in acknowledgement of Rabbi Isaac Aboab de Fonseca's efforts to get the synagogue built.

> *Turn left, along the front of the synagogue, into* **Mr L. E. Visserplein** *('Meester' is the Dutch title for a lawyer), named after the Jewish Dutch President of the Supreme Court dismissed in 1940 for refusing to co-operate with the occupying forces. He later refused to wear a Star of David and worked for* Het Parool, *the illegal Resistance newspaper that developed into a popular Amsterdam daily. The square is a turmoil of traffic hurling in and out of the IJ Tunnel. Hurry down the other side of the synagogue to the relative peace of* **Jonas Daniël Meijerplein**.

Jonas Daniël Meijer (1780–1834) whizzed through his school years and was a Doctor of Law by the time he was sixteen. He was the first Jew admitted to the Bar and one of the first to fight for and get full Dutch citizenship. As a favourite of the potty but enlightened Louis Bonaparte and under William I, Meijer did a lot to improve the legal position of the Jews.

In the middle of the square, standing stalwartly, his sleeves rolled up and chin cocked defiantly—ready for a fight—is Mari Andriessen's bronze statue *De Dokwerker* (The Dockworker, 1952). Every year on 25 February people lay flowers at its feet to commemorate the resistance to Nazi occupation. This is the anniversary of the general strike which swept through a shocked Amsterdam in a matter of hours as an expression of solidarity with the Jews after the first Nazi round-ups. During his brief spell as a theology student in Amsterdam, Van Gogh could be seen 'with his books clamped under his arm, holding snowdrops in his left hand in front of his chest, his head stooped forward slightly', crossing this square to the third floor of the house at No.13, where he studied classics with Mendes da Costa for ƒ1.50 a lesson. (The original house has been demolished.)

> *During one of the brief moments when traffic lights halt the flow on Weesperstraat, you can shoot across to Nieuwe Amstelstraat, once called Shulgas (Synagogue Alley). A complex of four old Ashkenazi synagogues now houses the **Jewish Historical Museum** (open daily 11–5 except Yom Kippur; adm ƒ7).*

The Ashkenazim, fleeing pogroms in Poland and massacres in Germany, arrived in Amsterdam in the mid-17th century. They soon outnumbered the Sephardim (who had begun arriving half a century earlier) by ten to one, but were pitifully poorer. They really had to struggle to build themselves a synagogue. Just as they were about to begin, their attention was diverted by Sabbatai Zvi, a false Messiah who claimed he would lead them back to the Holy Land. They waited for four years before giving up on him and building the Grote Sjoel (Grand Synagogue) in 1671. As the congregation expanded, more temples were built on adjacent plots. The Obbene Sjoel (Upstairs Synagogue, 1686) was followed by the Dritt Sjoel (Third Synagogue, 1700). The Neie Sjoel (New Synagogue, 1752) opened with great ceremony. Tickets were sold at an outrageous ƒ10 (though crowds of poor were let in for free). Ashkenazi Congregation records revel in the pomp of the occasion and bristle with anti-Sephardic rivalry: 'An orchestra pit has been placed next to the *bima* (raised central platform), where the musicians took their places with their music. Below that there was an *uncircumcised* musician playing a contrabass and for the rest only Jews who played for free and *even one Portuguese Jew.*' The complex was gutted during the Second World War and remained empty until the 1980s, when the temples were restored and reopened as the historical museum.

The Museum's displays do not dwell on gruesome images of the Holocaust and tales of woe, but are a combination of works of art, memorabilia and artefacts aimed at explaining Jewish life. Naturally it is moving to see one of the yellow stars Jews had to wear during the war, but the museum also diffuses a positive energy from the delicately embroidered prayershawls, photographs of barmitzvahs and overwhelmingly extravagant silverware also on show. The 'Jewish identity' displays in the New Synagogue explain aspects of tradition, Zionism and the reaction to persecution. Most of the Great Synagogue is given over to expositions of the religion itself—the rituals, festivals and rites of passage. You can see the original Mikveh (ritual bath) unearthed during the renovations, a cute circumcision set and some stylish modern temple silverware. In the galleries of the Great Synagogue paintings and old documents illustrate the history of Jews in Amsterdam. The connecting walkways house temporary exhibitions and work by

Jewish artists (look for Jaap Kaas's fierce, funny bronze monkeys). The museum also has a library and media centre, a kosher café and a good bookshop.

Across the alley from the museum is the Oudezijds Huiszittenhuis (the rather Dickensian-sounding 'Old Side Home for the Domiciled Poor', built in 1654). The Alms Board Wardens would enter through a rather grand public staircase on the other side of the building. Paupers could come in through a gate opposite the Dritt Sjoel and huddle for hours in the courtyard waiting for handouts of bread, cheese and peat. The peat was stored next door in the Arsenaal (built 1610). The road down the side of this warehouse is still called Turfsteeg (Peat Alley).

> *Walk down the narrow Turfsteeg. At the end you pop out into the cheerful din and architectural hotchpotch of Waterlooplein. On your left is the giant pink Stopera, the City Hall/Opera House complex that has caused the biggest public row in recent years (see pp.69–71. Bang up against its back wall, and creeping round the edges, reclaiming the space it has occupied for over a century, is the famous Waterlooplein Fleamarket (open Mon–Sat approx. 10–4).*

Waterlooplein was originally the manmade island of Vlooyenburg, so named because the Amstel flooded it with monotonous regularity. (*Vlooyen* means 'flow', and also 'fleas', which seems rather more appropriate these days.) Vlooyenburg was built on a sandbank in the Amstel in 1593, and soon became a popular neighbourhood for Jews arriving from Portugal. In the mid-17th century they were joined by the Ashkenazim, and Vlooyenburg became the heart of the Jewish quarter. Despite its sogginess, it was at first quite well-to-do. Prosperous Sephardim lived along the water's edge but, with the great influx of Ashkenazim, buildings were constantly subdivided and more and more people were crammed into less and less space. The economic decline of the 18th and 19th centuries made conditions even worse. A contemporary traveller complained that everywhere there were 'horrible piles of excrement and offal, the walls around drenched with urine'. Later in the 19th century, however, the economy boomed and conditions improved. In 1882 the council reclaimed more land, and filled up two canals to create a large market square to replace the squalid, crowded network of alleys. In 1886 the clusters of market traders who had overrun the side streets were moved to the newly created Waterlooplein. There was much grizzling because it was so open and windy (an objection you're sure to sympathize with if the weather is bad) but soon the market had the reputation of being the busiest and most cheerful in Amsterdam.

The district was devastated during the Nazi occupation. Convoys of trucks would rumble into the market and cart away hundreds of people at a time. The empty houses they left behind were stripped of anything burnable during the freezing winters. For decades after the war the square was silent and deserted. A few squatters in the 1960s began to revive the old spirit, but they were evicted to make way for the Stopera, and Waterlooplein ceased to be a residential square.

The Stopera builders' rubble has long since been cleared away, and the market has regained something of its old liveliness. There's a wonderful lack of logic in its layout and a pervasive air of bargain-hunting and money-making. Antiquarian booksellers rub shoulders with purveyors of used porn. Lines of Peruvians, Balinese and Indonesians sell bright national clothing and jewellery. There are heaps of mildewy second-hand overcoats and racks of precision-selected designer classics, tables of used kitchenware and haphazard conglomerations of expensive antiques. The rows of oddities and exotica are punctuated by more down-to-earth stalls selling bicycle parts, underwear or cleaning equipment. A fringe of derelicts gathers around the edge of the market, returning day after day with little spreads of unwanted (and sometimes unidentifiable) bric-a-brac. In one corner a muttering clump of old men surreptitiously flash watches and bits of gold to each other. A relentless stream of collectors, tourists, Amsterdammers looking for bargains and the openly curious flows up and down between the stalls.

The near end of the market is dominated by the **Mozes en Aäron Kerk**. In 1649 it was a clandestine Roman Catholic church, named after the gable stones (one depicting Moses and the other Aaron) on the two house-fronts that hid it. The present heavy-looking neoclassical church (with wooden towers painted to look like sandstone) was built in the 19th century, but you can still see the original gable stones round the back. The church was famous for its choir and even the local Jews would come in for the music on Christmas night. The Jewish philosopher Spinoza lived in the house next door to the original church. The Sephardic community excommunicated him for his secular beliefs, but regretted their haste when he went on to become one of the most lauded intellectuals of his time.

> *Make your way to the far end of the market, where you'll find the **Holland Experience**, a multimedia show that offers 'scent and sound effects' as well as 80,000 litres of water crashing towards you in a simulated dyke collapse (duration 25mins, open daily 9am–10pm; adm adults ƒ17.50, under-12s ƒ15). Turn right and walk up to Jodenbreestraat. Turn right again. The second house on your right is the **Rembrandthuis** (open Mon–Sat 10–5, Sun and hols 1–5; adm ƒ7.50).*

Rembrandt lived at Jodenbreestraat 4–6 for nearly twenty years (*see* p.103) and his old house is now a museum. It has been carefully restored to its original state, using old plans and descriptions to ensure authenticity. In the adjoining modern wing, you can see the pick of Rembrandt's etchings, including a series of tiny self-portraits of the painter pulling funny faces. Rembrandt used himself as a model more than any other 17th-century painter. He even slips into crowd scenes on some of his larger canvases. There's a slide-show on Rembrandt's life, in English, in the basement (hourly on the hour until 3pm).

> Turn left out of the Rembrandthuis and cross the canal at St Antoniessluis (St Antony's Lock). Before the move to Waterlooplein, this was the site of a busy second-hand clothes market. The common Dutch surname 'Sluis' or 'Sluys' can often be traced back to Ashkenazi families who worked here. On the other side of the bridge you come to **St Antoniesbreestraat**.

The great slab of a house at No.69 belonged to the wealthy 17th-century banker, Isaac de Pinto, and was the envy of the neighbourhood. The poorer inhabitants of the surrounding alleys would mutter that someone was 'As rich as de Pinto'. These days it's a public library, so you can nip in for a look at the odd bits of gilding and the brightly painted birds and cherubs which fly all over the ceiling.

> Opposite the entrance to the De Pinto House is a sculpted gateway embellished with a macabre skull motif, which leads you through to the **Zuiderkerk** (open Mon–Fri 12.30–4.30, Thurs 6–9; tower open June–September Wed–Sat 2pm–4pm, adm f3).

The Zuiderkerk, built between 1603 and 1614, was the first Protestant church to be built after the Reformation, and is a triumph of Amsterdam's great steeple designer, Hendrick de Keyser. The soaring spire with its decorative Ionic columns and its clusters of slightly oriental pinnacles was much admired by Christopher Wren, and inspired the designs of his City of London churches. During the harsh winter of 1944–5 more people died in the neighbourhood than the authorities were able to bury, and the church had to be used as a temporary mortuary. Today it's a deeply uninteresting information centre for urban development.

> Walk back through the gateway and turn right, doubling back towards St Antoniessluis, then right again down the stairs before the bridge at the beginning of St Antoniesbreestraat. Follow the canal back along the Zwanenburgwal. Turn right into Staalstraat, a quiet lane of second-hand book dealers and art shops that is a favourite location with film makers for period street scenes. As you cross Groenburgwal, you get a clear view of the elegant Zuiderkerk spire at the end of the canal. Walk on across Kloveniersburgwal and left into Nieuwe Doelenstraat, the address of some of Amsterdam's grander hotels. As the end of Nieuwe Doelenstraat you come to Muntplein and the **Munttoren** (Mint Tower).

The Munttoren, a solitary clock tower with a polygonal base, is yet another steeple by Hendrick de Keyser—a verticomaniac responsible for nearly every spike on Amsterdam's skyline. The base dates from 1490 and was part of Reguliersspoort, one of the gates in the old city wall. The structure gets its name because the guard house was briefly used as a mint in 1672–3, when the French were occupying much of the rest of the Netherlands and the Amsterdam merchants couldn't get at their usual source of Rijksdollars and ductatoons.

*Pass the Munttoren and turn right into the **flower market***.

After all the fuss that's made about it in the brochures, Amsterdam's floating flower market can be a bit of a disappointment. It's not very long, not all that cheap, you can't tell from the street that it's floating, and it's full of confused tourists clutching maps and asking each other: 'Is this it?' But the buckets of cut flowers and rows of potted plants are pretty to look at, and on hot days the mingling scents of the flowers fill the whole passage. If you're a keen gardener there's a tempting variety of seeds and bulbs that can be posted home (but *see* **Travel**, 'Customs', p.4).

> *At the other end of the flower market, cross Koningsplein on to the left-hand side of the Singel. In the 15th century the Singel was the city's line of defence ('singel' means 'moat'). These days it's a sober business and residential canal. Amsterdam's smallest house is at No.312.*

> *If you're interested in Judaica you may want to visit the **Bibliotheca Rosenthaliana**, housed in the University Library, the modern building on the other side of the canal (open Mon–Thurs 9.30–5, Fri 9.30–1, closed public and Jewish holidays).*

This priceless collection of over 100,000 volumes, dating from the 15th century, disappeared during the Second World War, but was later tracked down to a village near Frankfurt. As well as old Hebrew manuscripts, there's a large collection of Spinoza, old broadsheets, engravings and photographs.

> *Walk on up to Raadhuisstraat and turn left.*

Just off Raadhuisstraat, at Herengracht 168, you'll find the **Nederlands Theater Instituut** (*open Tues–Fri 11–5, Sat and Sun 1–5; adm f7.50*) which always has good exhibitions, usually of the sort where you push buttons or pull levers and make things happen. If there are three of you, you can raise a storm with the wind, thunder and lightning machines on the ground floor.

> *Carry on along Raadhuisstraat. An elaborate Art-Nouveau shopping arcade takes up much of the left-hand side. It was built for a life insurance company, which might explain the frightening crocodiles and other dangerous creatures which adorn the canopy. At the end of Raadhuisstraat you come to Westermarkt and the towering spire of the **Westerkerk**.*

The Westerkerk was consecrated in 1631. Its sober Protestant interior is brightened by large painted organ shutters showing a dancing King David and a voluptuous Queen of Sheba laden with gifts for Solomon. Rembrandt was buried here, but no one knows where the body is. There's a flutter of academic excitement every time old bones are found, but it's most likely that he was crunched up during the digging of an underground car park. A memorial plaque has been put up near his son Titus's grave. The church tower, known as the **Westertoren**, built by (you guessed it) Hendrick de Keyser, is Amsterdam's highest (85m) and contains its heaviest bell (7,500kg). In the 1940s a fervent engineer climbed out on to the top of the tower during a violent storm and, with the help of a theodolite, worked out that it swayed all of 3cm. During the summer months you can climb up rather more sedately for a rare view of Amsterdam from high up (*open April–Sept, Mon–Sat 10–4; adm f3*). At the top is the gaudily painted imperial crown of Maximilian of Austria. Amsterdam's merchants gained considerable international clout when, out of gratitude for support given to the Austro-Burgundian princes, he granted them the right to use the crown in the city coat of arms.

If you walk around the outside of the church you can see the house where Descartes lived when he was in Amsterdam (Westermarkt 6); the pink marble triangles of the **Homomonument** which commemorates gays killed in the concentration camps; and a sad little statue of Anne Frank, who wrote her diary just around the corner.

> *At the far end of Westermarkt, turn right and walk down the right-hand side of Prinsengracht.* **Anne Frank Huis** *is at No.263 (open Sept–May Mon–Sat 9–5, Sun 10–5; June–Aug Mon–Sat 9–7, Sun 10–7; adm f10).*

Well over half a million people visit the Anne Frank Huis annually. The house has been restored to its pre-war condition, giving a moving impression of what life was like for the families who hid there. In new premises next door you'll find an exhibition on Jews in Amsterdam and racial oppression.

> *Turn right out of the Anne Frank Huis, walk up the Prinsengracht and cross it at the first bridge you come to. You are now in the* **Jordaan**.

The inviting side streets, alleys and intimate canals of the Jordaan are lined with cosy cafés, curious shops and good restaurants, all luring you to ferret about in your own way. The last part of this walk leads you quickly through the quarter and gives you just enough of an idea of what you might like to come back and explore later. Jordaan comes from the French '*jardin*', but during the housing crisis in the 19th century this 'garden' on the outskirts of the city disappeared under rows of working-class housing. The houses were small, dark and close together and all the smellier industries (such as tanning) were banished to the

Anne Frank

Anne Frank, the second daughter of German-Jewish immigrants living in Amsterdam, got her diary for her thirteenth birthday on 12 June 1942. Three weeks later her family were '*onderduikers*' ('divers')—in hiding from the Nazi occupying forces. They lived for two years in a small suite of rooms at the back of Anne's father's herb and spice business on the Prinsengracht. The windows had always been painted over to protect the herbs previously stored there, the entrance was hidden behind a hinged bookcase and, apart from four trusted office workers who supplied them with food, nobody knew they were there. Later they were joined by a dentist Fritz Pfeffer (whom Anne calls 'Dussel') and the Van Pelses ('Van Daans') and their son Peter. For two years they were cooped up in what became known as the Annexe, and Anne wrote in her diaries about life with the petulant and demanding Mrs Van Daan and her hen-pecked spouse, of the tiresomely childish Dussel, and of moments of joy and desperation within her own family. No one knows who betrayed them, but in August 1944 German police barged into the offices, walked straight up to the bookcase and demanded entry. All the hideaways, except Anne's father, died in concentration camps in Germany. The office cleaner found the diary in which Anne had written with astonishing lucidity about life in the 'Annexe' and about growing up. When it was given to her father, he found that she'd already began to edit it for publication. It appeared in 1947 with the title *The Annexe*, the one Anne herself had chosen. Now it's printed in over fifty languages and an estimated thirteen million copies have been sold.

Jordaan from the posher areas of town. Naming the streets after flowers didn't cheer things up much. Conditions were appalling, but the Jordaaners developed a pride and a culture akin to London's cockneys. The true Jordaaner is born in the small patch bound by Prinsengracht, Brouwersgracht, Lijnbaansgracht and Looiersgracht, in the shadow of the Westertoren. The church tower is the symbol of the Jordaan. Jordaaners have their own accent and are renowned for a wry sense of humour and for being adept pigeon-fanciers. Everyone over the age of forty is known as '*ome*' or '*tante*'—uncle or aunt. (Until a decade or so ago, you could still be woken by Ome Hein, a professional 'waker-up', as he made his early morning rounds with a pet goat.) They're a rebellious lot. There have been a number of historical riots, including one in 1886 when police tried to put a stop to the gory-sounding pastime of 'eel-jerking'; and another when the council threatened to reduce the dole in 1934. Recently, traditional Jordaan life has been given a new edge by an influx of artists and music students. You're quite likely to be accompanied on your walk by strains of Mozart and will probably encounter odd art objects suspended over the street.

> *Turn right up Prinsengracht, and almost immediately left down Egelantiersgracht. Keep to the left side of the canal. At Nos.107–145 you'll find one of several **hofjes** in the district, St Andrieshofje.*

Hofjes, the courts of almshouses, are magically quiet garden courts, often completely hidden from the street. You reach this one (built 1616) through a door that looks like any other front door along the canal and down a passage lined with Delft tiles. Most *hofjes* are private residences, but as long as you're sensitive to that, residents don't mind you popping in for a few calming moments.

> *Outside St Andrieshofje, double back a little and cross over to the other side of the canal. Walk back up towards Prinsengracht and turn left into Tweede Egelantiersdwarsstraat, a narrow road of shops and cafés typical of the Jordaan's quirky charm. It changes its name to Tweede Tuindwarsstraat and then Tweede Anjeliersdwarsstraat before spilling out into **Westerstraat**, where you turn right.*

Westerstraat (once a canal) is too wide to be really attractive, but at No.67 there's a tiny shop full of good, old-fashioned, low-tech toys. Skipping ropes, bright-coloured balls, red wooden buses, pretty paper cut-outs are stacked on shelves and hanging from the walls and ceiling. There are boxes and boxes of all sorts of little things that will keep parents and kids digging about for ages.

> *Westerstraat, and the walk, end at **Noordermarkt**.*

The square is quiet, and usually empty, but if you come back early on a Monday morning you'll find a crush of trendies, students and down-and-outs at Amsterdam's cheapest clothes market. The **Noorderkerk** was Hendrick de Keyser's last church and, as befits an old man, is solemn and austere with only the teeniest of spires. You could end the walk with a quiet coffee in one of the cafés around the square, plunge back into the Jordaan (Bloemgracht and Lindengracht are both very much worth a look) or cross the canal to two more *hofjes*: 'De Ster' at Prinsengracht 89–133 (one of the best, though now closed to the public) and 'Zons Hofje' at Nos.159–171.

> *When you've had enough, wander back up Prinsengracht towards the omnipresent Westertoren. One of the trams from here (13, 14, 17 or 21) will probably be able to take you home.*

Walk IV: The Port of Amsterdam

Start: *Take Tram 1, 2, 5, 13, 17, 21 to the stop marked 'Nieuwezijds Kolk' on Nieuwezijds Voorburgwal.*

Walking time: *3½ hours not counting museums and café stops. You won't need more than an hour in the Maritime Museum (unless you're a sailboat fanatic). The suggested short-cuts will knock off over half an hour.*

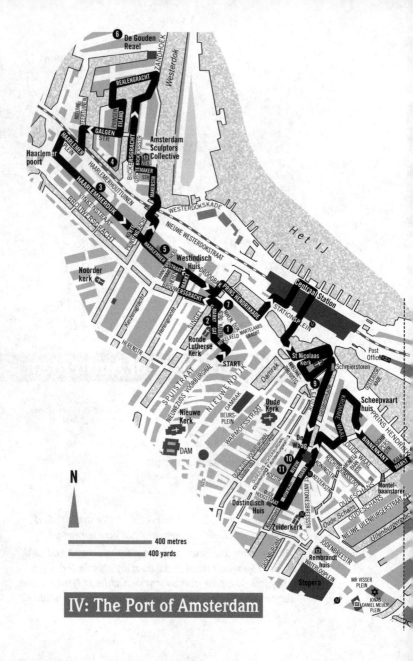

6 De Gouden Reael

ZANDHOEK

Westerdok

REALENGRACHT

NIEUWE TEERTUINEN

PRINSEN EILAND

GALGEN STR

Amsterdam Sculptors Collective

Haarlemer poort

HAARLEMER PLEIN

4

BICKERSGRACHT

PRINS BICKERSSTR

BICKERS EILAND

ZEILMAKER STR

MAKERSTR

HAARLEMMERDIJK

3

HAARLEMERHOUTTUINEN

KORTE PRINSENGRACHT

WESTERDOKSKADE

VINKENSTRAAT

NIEUWE WESTERDOKSTRAAT

BROUWERSGRACHT

HAARLEMMER

Het IJ

Noorder kerk

BINNEN WIERINGERSTR

BINNEN DOMMERSSTR

Westindisch Huis

5

DROOGBAK

BROUWERSGRACHT

Keizersgracht

Hekelveld

PRINS HENDRIKKADE

Centraal Station

STATIONSPLEIN

Herengracht

HERENSTR

SINGEL

MARTS GAT

OUDE BRUG NIEUWE BRUG

KORTE KOLK

1

2

1

MARTELAARS GRACHT

Ronde Lutherse Kerk

St Nicolaas Kerk

Schreierstoren

Post Office

OOSTER DOKS KADE

SPUISTRAAT

NIEUWEZIJDS VOORBURGWAL

START

NIEUWENDIJK

Damrak

WARMOESSTRAAT

ZEEDIJK

KROMME WAAL

9

Scheepvaart huis

PRINS HENDRIKKADE

Nieuwe Kerk

Oude Kerk

DAMRAK BEURS-PLEIN

De Waag

OUDE WAAL

SCHIP PERSTR

BINNENKANT

'S GRAVEN HEKJE

NES

OUDEZIJDS VOORBURGWAL

OUDEZIJDS ACHTERBURGWAL

10

11

MONNIKENSTR

KONINGSTR

RECHTBOOMSSLOOT

KEIZERSTR

Montel-baanstoren

DAM

OUDE HOOGSTRAAT

Oostindisch Huis

KLOVENIERSBURGWAL

GELDERSEKADE

ST ANTONIESBREESTR

OUDESCHANS

Oude Schans

OUDESCHANS

NIEUWE UILENBURGERGRACHT

Uilenburgergracht

Zuiderkerk

N

Rembrandt huis

JODENBREESTR

GROENBURGWAL

Stopera

WATERLOOPLEIN

MR VISSER PLEIN

JONAS DANIEL MEIJER PLEIN

400 metres

400 yards

IV: The Port of Amsterdam

Amsterdam's harbour hides behind the massive Centraal Station. Few visitors even know it's there. This walk takes you around the old port and through island neighbourhoods redolent of the days when wooden ships bulging with corn, spices, silks and gold came from all over the world to fill the city's warehouses.

It starts in the shadow of the imposing copper dome of an old Lutheran church, touches briefly on Amsterdam's prettiest canal, then ducks under the tracks to a secluded area of crumbling warehouses, startling new apartment blocks and colourful houseboats. You cross town to fortify yourself in the city's oldest bar. Then you skirt the red-light district and follow the course of the old city wall, passing the tower where weeping sailors' wives waved their farewells and the market square where 'poor sinners' were branded, flogged, hanged and/or cut into bits. Then it's through the old shipyards, past the centre's one remaining windmill and into the bowels of a 17th-century sailing ship at the Maritime Museum.

It's a good walk for a Sunday, taxing the legs rather than the mind. Start quietly in the peaceful Koepelkwartier, then blow out Saturday night's cobwebs with a vigorous walk around the islands (though if you're a diesel engine enthusiast you'll have to do the walk on a weekday to visit the Kromhout Museum). The Maritime Museum is closed on a Monday.

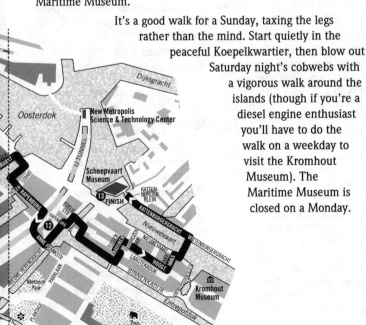

Lunch and Cafés

1 Koepelcafé, Kattengat 1, in the Koepelkwartier. Part of the Renaissance Hotel. A rather bland café, but open on a Sunday morning.

2 't Monumentje, Stromarkt 2, alongside the Koepel (*open 9am–10pm; closed Tuesdays*). Cheap and cheerful. Serves filling breakfasts.

3 Jordino, Haarlemmerdijk 25. When the heart begins to flutter and the knees begin to fail, ice cream and mega-chocolates from heaven will set you on your way again. Homemade and way over the top.

4 Rosereijn, Haarlemmerdijk 52, near Haarlemmerplein. Brown café with a neighbourhood atmosphere, huge plates of wholesome Dutch home cooking and an 'English Lunch' that involves fried eggs and baked beans.

5 Dulac, Haarlemmerstraat 118, in the Scheepvaartbuurt (*open daily 4pm–1am, to 2am at weekends*). Peter Barent, the owner, is inspired by Gaudí and the French illustrator Edmund Dulac. He's transformed a 1920s bank into a grown-up's fairy grotto. Gothic spires stick out horizontally from pillars; it's lit by huge brass chandeliers (salvaged from a nearby church); stuffed fish hang from the ceiling, wooden figures, strange paintings and more brass adorn the green-blue walls.

6 De Gouden Reael, Zandhoek 14, Realeneiland, ☎ 623 3883 (*open Mon–Fri noon–1am; Sat and Sun 5pm–1am*). Situated in a 17th-century house in the heart of the Western Islands. Pop in for just a drink or sample excellent French provincial cuisine (from a different region every three months).

7 Café Karpershoek, Martelaarsgracht 2, opposite Centraal Station. Claims to be Amsterdam's oldest bar (dating from 1629—but *see* Café Chris, **Walk III**, p.116). Once right on the waterfront, it was a popular seamen's tavern. It still has sand on the floor, as in the 17th century.

8 Café Ot en Sien, Buiksloterweg 27, across the water from Centraal Station (*open 12–9pm; closed Saturdays*). A friendly, family-run café in a lane of country gardens and old wooden houses. Pancakes from ƒ8.

9 In 't Aepjen, Zeedijk 1 (*open daily from noon*) fills the tiny ground floor of a 15th-century seamen's lodging house. It's a '*rariteitencafé*' crammed with antiques, leather armchairs and barrels. The painted wall-panels were rescued from a 1920s travelling dance hall.

10 De Waag Café, Nieuwmarkt. The medieval city gate and weigh-house is now a café with long communal tables, plenty of reading material, a high-tech Internet table, and a terrace on the Nieuwmarkt.

11 Tofani, Kloveniersburgwal 16. Genuine Italian ice-cream parlour that also has great espresso and warm rolls stuffed with tomato, fresh basil and meltingly soft mozzarella cheese.

12 De Druif, Rapenburgstraat 83, at the gate to the Entrepotdok. Opened in 1631. A brown café with barrels to the ceiling and a rare antique *jenever* pump on the counter. Locals maintain that naval hero Piet Heyn was a regular visitor. His entrance would have caused a stir, as Heyn died in 1629.

13 Maritime Museum Café is a good place to sip coffee and look out over the harbour.

*The walk begins in the Koepelkwartier, but nearest tram stop is on the busy Nieuwezijds Voorburgwal. To get to the Koepelkwartier you can walk up Nieuwezijds Voorburgwal and duck down Klimopstraat, a rather dull alley. A more intriguing route is through **De Klompenboer**, Nieuwezijds Voorburgwal 20 (open daily 10–6).*

From the outside, De Klompenboer looks like an ordinary souvenir shop. Inside, however, live chickens and guinea fowl peck their way between rocking-horses, wood carvings and piles of pewter. The shop assistant sits burning patterns into freshly carved clogs. Through a door at the back you can see craftsmen working hard to keep up the supply.

*Leave though the small workshop at the back of the shop. You emerge into the quiet and leafy **Koepelkwartier** (Dome Quarter), aptly nick-named the Montmartre of Amsterdam.*

It's easy to see where the Koepelkwartier gets its name. The enormous copper dome of the old **Lutherse Kerk** (Lutheran Chuch) towers over the narrow lanes and pavement cafés. The church (also known as the Ronde Lutherse Kerk— Round Lutheran Church) was built in 1668 by Adriaan Dortsman, a leading light of the appropriately named Restrained Dutch Classicists. A careless plumber caused a fire which burnt it down in 1822; it was rebuilt the following year and was used as a church until the early 1930s, when dwindling congregations resulted in its closure. After some years of disuse, the church was converted into a conference hall for the hotel across the road, but in 1993 it burned down again. The gutted building cost ƒ4 million to restore and opened for business again in 1995. The round brick walls look impenetrable (conference delegates reach it through an underground tunnel).

In 1614 Laurens Spiegel, a wealthy soap-manufacturer, built the dainty twin step-gable houses next door to the Koepel as an investment. He seemed to rather enjoy punning on his surname (which means mirror). He called his own house (in a classier part of town) 'De Drie Spiegels' (The Three Mirrors), and the two houses on the Kattengat (possibly in view of the profits he hoped to make by let-ting them out) were called 'De Goude Spiegel' (Golden Mirror) and 'De Silveren Spiegel' (Silver Mirror).

*Walk past the Koepel, up Kattengat ('Cat-hole'—it was once a narrow ditch), along Stromarkt and left over the bridge. A brass propeller and black anchor on the street corners mark the beginning of the **Scheepvaartbuurt** (Shipping Neighbourhood).*

For centuries, most travellers arrived in Amsterdam by boat. Their first view of the spikes and spires of the city was through a forest of wooden masts. From the shore you looked out at a floating extension of the town. Large seagoing ships made up the horizon. Small boats scuttled between the larger craft. Flat barges plied to and fro carrying fresh water and other supplies. Offices, warehouses and inns were built on timber platforms far out in the water. Amsterdam was the nexus between extensive inland waterways and the open seas, and its port provided welcome protection from the elements for the tiny, rather clumsy sea-going trade ships on their journey 'within the dunes' across the Wadden Sea, the Zuider Zee and the River IJ.

Under the auspices of the famous Dutch East India Company (founded in 1602, *see* p.37) and the smaller West India Company (founded 1624), shipbuilding and navigational skills quickly improved, and Dutch ships were soon travelling all over the world. But the Napoleonic wars completely disrupted the Netherlands' trade and the newer, larger ships built in the 19th century had trouble reaching Amsterdam. By 1882 sea trade had declined to such an extent that P. J. H. Cuypers was happy to curtain off the harbour with his palatial Centraal Station. The docks have all but disappeared from view, but there are still corners of Amsterdam where you can find vivid reminders of the bustling, prosperous old port.

> *To begin an exploration of the Scheepvaartbuurt, turn left and double back along Singel. Cat-lovers might like to nip down to **De Poezenboot** ('The Cat Boat', a houseboat full of stray cats, opposite Singel 40; open 1pm–2pm daily, closed at present for rebuilding). Fat moggies pad non-chalantly around their own terrace, or stare complacently from baskets and wait for you to go away. Lean days of alley fights and tough living seem a dim memory. An enormous platter of very dead day-old chicks lies untouched in the corner. A leaflet assures you that all strays are neutered so that the 'problem is dealt with by its roots'. If the idea of 101 floating felines doesn't take your fancy, then turn right into **Brouwersgracht**, keeping on the right-hand side of the canal.*

The Brouwersgracht (Brewers' Canal) is quintessential Amsterdam. Its neat, gabled houses, humped bridges and shady towpaths feature in almost every brochure intended to lure you to the city. Yet the crowds that tramp up and down the grand canals seem to pass it by. There are no neon lights or noisy cafés. It's a quiet, residential canal for the hopelessly romantic. Most of the houses are converted warehouses. In the 17th century the Brouwersgracht, right at the harbour's edge, seethed with traders and reeked of fish and beer. Stockfish warehouses and no fewer than twenty-four breweries crowded its banks. Amsterdam had to import fresh water from the surrounding countryside to feed its industries and populace. Most of the long flat boats carrying this water entered the city along the Brouwersgracht, so breweries sprang up along the canal that afforded them the pick of the incoming supplies.

> *Walk up Brouwersgracht and turn right into Herenmarkt, a small square dominated by* **Westindisch Huis** *(West India House).*

The dumpy red-brick exterior of Westindisch Huis (West India House) dates from the 19th century, when it was rebuilt as a Lutheran orphanage. Nowadays it's an adult education college, but you can usually nip in for a glimpse of the 17th-century courtyard—the only remnant of the building's romantic past as headquarters of the West India Company. In the courtyard there's a memorial to Peter Stuyvesant, the notoriously grouchy peg-legged Governor of Nieuw Amsterdam—the Company's chief American trading post. In 1664 he surrendered the settlement to the British, who renamed it New York.

> *Turn left, in front of Westindisch Huis, along Haarlemmerstraat. Cross the bridge and turn right into Korte Prinsengracht. Follow the pedestrian walkway under the railway bridge to Bickerseiland, the first of the* **Western Islands**.

The Western Islands are man-made. They're close together, criss-crossed by canals and connected by little wooden bridges. There's an eerie sense of isolation, even though they are nowadays very much part of the mainland. In the 17th century Amsterdam burst beyond the boundaries that had contained it for generations. More and more land was created by draining off water into new canals. The area of the city increased by nearly 40 per cent. The poet Vondel wrote some histrionic verse in praise of the achievement (as was very much his wont), using the sort of hyperbole usually reserved for military victories. Travellers marvelled at the size and number of the warehouses. Buildings shot up all over the new islands, and were immediately filled with tobacco, salt, tin, wine, draperies, spices, copper, furs, gold—almost any commodity that could realize a profit.

On **Bickerseiland** (Bicker's Island, named after the original developer), modern concrete apartment blocks with bright red and blue window frames line one side of the narrow walkway. The other side is a jumble of houseboats. Rafts, tugs, canal boats, barges—anything that floats (and some things that almost don't) have been commandeered to solve Amsterdam's chronic housing problem. In the 1950s, when the canal transport industry went into an almost terminal decline, skippers were only too pleased to offload their craft on the oddballs who wanted to live on the water. By the 1970s there were around 800 legally licensed moorings and countless illegal ones. The council outlawed all newcomers and granted an amnesty to over a thousand of the unlicensed boats that were already occupied. Recently, moves have begun again to get rid of them.

Their occupants were allowed (like those on the legal boats) to connect up to the water and electricity supplies. Arrangements for the latter are alarmingly Heath Robinson. Wonky home-made poles hold up yards of black flex as it snakes along the canalside and between the boats. Wet washing flutters from these improvised clothes lines. The electricity supply is temperamental. Anyone who wants to use a washing machine has to check that the neighbours aren't watching TV, or everyone could be plunged into darkness. There are other drawbacks to boat life—like having to get up in the middle of the night to check your moorings in a storm, or chase off drunk men who pee over the edge of the canal on to your bedroom roof. Despite the hazards, houseboats are popular. Originally they were the domain of the weird and rebellious, but now lawyers and stockbrokers sun themselves on deck and talk for hours about waterproofing techniques. One boat even houses a community of nuns. But the old eccentrics are still there. From Bickerseiland, if the city council hasn't had its way by the time you visit, you can see the boat of a 'collector', piled high with scrap metal, rusting machines and bits of wood.

> *Carry on along the pedestrian walkway, then make a left turn into Zeilmakerstraat.*

Streetnames like 'Sailmaker's Street' and 'Blockmaker's Street' are all that's left of the shipbuilding yards for which Bickerseiland was renowned. (It was also famous for its dogs. There were so many that the local church had to employ two dog-chasers to keep the aisles free during services.) Most of the island is taken up by soulless 1970s housing estates. At Zeilmakerstraat 15, in one of the few buildings to escape post-war redevelopment, you'll find the **Amsterdams Beeldhouwers Kollektief** (Amsterdam Sculptors' Collective; *open Thurs–Sun 1–5*). The sixty members (some of the city's best young sculptors among them) keep the gallery well supplied. Exhibitions change frequently. Most work is on sale, and not all of it is of a size to preclude taking it home in your overnight bag.

> *At the end of Zeilmakerstraat turn right, then immediately left into Minnemoerstraat. Turn right again into Bickersgracht where there's a tiny urban farmyard. Fat rabbits lie stretched out in the sun next to curly-horned goats. Various fowl peck about the edge of the concrete. If you find the pong a bit much, hurry on around the corner and over the white wooden bridge to **Realeneiland**.*

Realeneiland is named after Jacob Real, the original owner. Ahead of you as you cross the bridge is a neat little row of 17th-century houses. Jacob Real's own, rather modest house (now a restaurant) is at the end. He was a fervent Catholic. The gold-painted coin on the gable stone commemorates the treasures he saved from the iconoclasts by smuggling them out of a monastery in the nick of time.

Real's surname (also the name of a coin) afforded an appropriate pun, and the house became known as 'De Gouden Reael'. There's a tang of tar and varnish in the air. The diligent occupants of the rather stately row of boats on the dockside seem perpetually involved in maintenance.

> *After you've nosed about a bit, make your way left from the bridge along Realengracht, past the floating police station. Across the bridge at the end of Realengracht is* **Prinseneiland**.

Hidden in the middle of the Western Islands, Prinseneiland is the best of all. Its little lanes are a mish-mash of architectural styles. Tumbledown warehouses crumble quietly next to smart, sharp-edged new apartments. Tall, carefully restored façades grace the canal. The island is perfumed by freshly sawn timber from the working boatyard. There's seldom any traffic. All you hear is the sound of sawing, workmen calling to each other and (to jolt you back down to earth) pop music from their ghettoblasters.

> *Turn left, past the Walvis shipyard, and follow the road as far as* **Galgenstraat**.

'*Galg*' means 'gallows'. The bridge at the eastern end of Galgenstraat used to afford a fine prospect of the city's Golgotha. The curious were not always afforded a view of the whole process. Offenders were often executed in the city centre. The heads, sometimes with the heart stuffed into the mouth, were posted on the city wall and only the discarded bits ended up on the grassy mound near the Galgenbrug.

> *Turn right into Galgenstraat and leave the island over the small white bridge leading to Nieuwe Teertuinen. Just to the left of the bridge, behind a matching pair of white doors, George Breitner (1857–1923) had his studio. Breitner's paintings of Amsterdam have made him a local favourite. He loved the low life and, when he went to The Hague, he used to prowl the seedy areas with his good friend Van Gogh, looking for inspiration.*

> *Turn left into Nieuwe Teertuinen. Walk back under the railway tracks to* **Haarlemmer Houttuinen** *on the mainland.*

The gaudy daubings in the arches under the tracks are part of Amsterdam's longest painting. Five hundred metres of bright colour were commissioned of Fabrice Hünd, who seems to have ended up covering up ugly concrete surfaces all over the city. (He's also responsible for the walls of the Stopera car park.) Fabrice's murals are so ubiquitous that one local outdoor artist has taken to signing his work '*not* Fabrice'.

*Haarlemmer Houttuinen opens out into **Haarlemmerplein**. Bewildered old men, looking for all the world like retired sailors, sit in rows on the benches, puffing pipes and staring at the traffic as it whizzes round them.*

Willemspoort (a.k.a. Haarlemmerpoort), a neoclassical gatehouse built for the entrance of King William II in 1840, takes up all of one end of the square. The masons botched the rather special *trompe-l'œil* effect that has to be achieved to keep the perspectives right: the central columns appear to taper rather suddenly at the top. It's never been a popular structure. At a town council meeting at the turn of the century it was saved from demolition by only four votes. If you walk through the gate you'll see four small rectangles set into the second pillar on the left. They mark the position of the old *stokmaat*, the measure by which horses were judged large enough for military service. It was used right up to the First World War.

*From Haarlemmerplein you can catch Tram 18 or 22 to Centraal Station for the second part of the walk. This will save about half an hour. If you have the time and energy you can walk it. Coffee and chocolate cake in the bizarre Café Dulac (see 'Lunch and Café' listings, p.132) will reward you for the extra effort. Leave Haarlemmerplein by **Haarlemmerdijk**, which becomes Haarlemmerstraat.*

Over the past few years Haarlemmerdijk and Haarlemmerstraat have developed into one of the quirkiest and most varied shopping quarters in town. New Age stores, junk shops, galleries, zany boutiques and ethnic gift shops all contribute to the appeal. Among the more curious attractions is Beune's confectioners at No.156. If you take them your photograph, they'll reproduce it in icing on the cake of your choice. The result is a white slab with a sombre sepia image, rather like a Portuguese tombstone. There's a chess and *go* shop (No.147) and a shop selling wildly coloured hand-woven Tibetan tiger rugs. A church by the 19th-century grandfather of modern Dutch architecture, P. J. H. Cuypers, has (like so many of his others) been converted into offices. Towards the end of the street you'll have to concentrate hard not to miss De Groene Lanteerne which, at 128cm wide, claims to be the world's narrowest restaurant.

*At the end of Haarlemmerstraat, turn left into Prins Hendrikkade. Trains, trams, buses, lorries, cars and phalanxes of cyclists hurtle by. A little Dutch courage may be needed to cross this manic fray. Luckily, Café Karpershoek, which claims to be Amsterdam's oldest bar, is close at hand (see 'Lunch and Café' listings p.132). Suitably fortified, you can cross to **Centraal Station**. Walk in the main entrance, right through the concourse, and out the back for a **free ferry trip across the IJ**.*

P. J. H. Cuypers' grand, gilded red-brick Centraal Station (*see* p.84) so effectively blocks out the city's view of the water that the harbour on its back doorstep comes as a complete surprise. The IJ is quite narrow at this point, so the modern docks have moved far out to the west. Most of the *steigers* (piers) now provide mooring for tour boats and the water police. Two (free) ferries that look like floating air traffic control buildings work in tandem, making the journey to the opposite bank (the crossing takes only a few minutes). There, in the shadow of the towering Shell laboratory, you'll find a neat country lane of dapper wooden cottages, cheerful houseboats, gardens and trees. The wide wooden houses in **Buiksloterweg** date back to the 16th century and are examples of a style that has now entirely disappeared from the city centre.

> *Retrace your steps through the station. Diagonally across the intersection in front of the main entrance you'll see the rose window and spires of **Sint Nicolaaskerk** (St Nicholas's Church; open April–Oct, Mon–Fri 11–4, Sat 2–4).*

Sint Nicolaaskerk is a sprucely restored 19th-century neo-Renaissance building with a murky interior. A small ship set above the door at the back is the only remainder that it was a seamen's church. Every March during the *Stille Omgang* (Silent Procession), Roman Catholics walk silently through the streets to the Sint Nicolaaskerk to commemorate Amsterdam's miracle (*see* p.33). Paintings in the left-hand transept depict the story.

> *Turn left out of the church, past the Barbizon Hotel and left again into **Zeedijk**.*

In the 14th century Zeedijk marked the city limits. Modern Amsterdammers associate it with the *rode knipoog en witte kick* (the 'red wink' of prostitution and 'white kick' of heroin). A massive clean-up campaign by the council and police has got rid of the drug dealers and is turning Zeedijk into a respectable street of restaurants and galleries. The red wink is still just around the corner.

The timber house at No.1 is one of the oldest buildings in the city and one of the two remaining wooden buildings in central Amsterdam. It was built in 1550 as a seamen's hostel. The innkeeper allowed sailors who'd drunk or gambled away their wages to leave pet monkeys in payment. The hostel became infested with apes and fleas and became known as **'In 't Aepjen'**: you could always spot the scratching seamen who'd slept 'in the monkeys'. The Dutch still say of someone who is in difficulty that they have *in de aap gelogeerd* (literally, 'stayed in the monkey'). You can still visit In 't Aepjen—*see* 'Lunch and Café' listings, p.132.

> *Turn left down Oudezijds Kolk, a canal with doors opening, Venetian style, directly on to the water. Walk down to the **Schreierstoren** (the 'Weepers' Tower').*

The Schreierstoren (built 1480) is a dwarfish brick tower with a pixie-hat roof. It's one of the few remnants of Amsterdam's first city wall. Romantics maintain the tower gets its name because sailors' wives would gather on the battlements to see the men off the sea. Well might they weep and wave. Voyages could take up to four years and, on average, two thirds of the men who set off never returned. More pedantic linguists point out that '*schreier*' comes from the old Dutch word for 'astride' or 'angle' and that the tower straddles two canals. The romantics win: a stone tablet on the wall depicts the wailing wives. Henry Hudson also has a plaque, as it was from here, in 1609, that he went off to discover a new route to the East Indies and found Manhattan instead, giving his name to the Hudson River. The Schreierstoren was orginally a solid defence tower. The top storey, windows and doors were all added later. Nowadays it houses a café.

> *Double back and walk south along the right-hand side of the* **Geldersekade**.

The old city wall ran along the far side of the canal. Along this stretch it was covered in a tangle of herbs and camomile. Centuries later Van Gogh's Uncle Stricker lived on the site of No.77. When Vincent was in Amsterdam studying for the priesthood, Uncle Stricker had the fairly hopeless task of supervising his lessons. The drinking houses on the right-hand side of Geldersekade were notorious. A 17th-century British ambassador to the Netherlands was horrified: 'There are tolerated in the city of Amsterdam, amongst other abuses, at least 50 musick-houses where lewd persons of both sexes meet to practise their villainies.' His moral outrage didn't preclude him from having a detailed knowledge of the prices and opening times of the 'Long Seller', a public meeting house where 'rogues and whores make their filthy bargains'. The red-light district has moved fractionally eastward. Geldersekade is now a grimy collection of downmarket Chinese shops and restaurants.

> *At the end of Geldersekade you come to* **Nieuwmarkt** *(New Market).*

Nieuwmarkt is an open, brick-paved square that connects some of the more sinister alleys of the red-light district. Furtive men pop out of side streets, blink uncertainly in the bright light, then slip away. The police have cleared out the junkies and dealers who used to hang about the square, and it's been given a facelift. Now that the underworld is banished, Nieuwmarkt has moved into limbo. Cafés are opening in the area, and the once barren square is beginning to fill up with terraces and regain some of its old liveliness, but it retains an edge of seediness. On Sundays in the summer months there's a bustling antiques market and on feast days you can sometimes find a fairground or one of the old Dutch travelling dance halls.

A ring of modern street lamps, like giant mauve praying mantises, seem about to devour the solid medieval **St Antoniespoort** which huddles, flanked by dumpy towers, in the middle of the square. St Antoniespoort began life in 1488 as one of the main gates in the city wall. It was a popular spot for public executions. If you have a look on the south side you can see the rectangular holes (now bricked up) where the support beams of the scaffold slipped in. In one of the octagonal towers was a *galgekamertje* (little gallows room). From here the hapless prisoner got a foretaste of what was to happen to him. A small window looked out on the hangings, brandings and chopping off of bits going on a few feet below. In 1617 the gate was converted into a public weighing house. As all wholesale goods had to be weighed for taxes, '*De Waag*' was the centre of trading activity. Liveried porters carried produce to and fro. Fierce armed guards were posted everywhere to keep an eye on the filling coffers and to arrest defaulters. (The sewer below the square was a highway for smugglers and bandits.) In 1691 St Antoniespoort housed the dissecting room of the Guild of Surgeons (cadavers being so conveniently at hand). You can just make out their inscription above the door in the south tower. On the other side bricklayers decorated the door to their guild room with elaborate wreaths of trowels. Today *De Waag* houses a trendy café.

Before you leave the square, treat your nostrils to the herbalists Jacob Hooy & Co at No.12. In one half of the shop barrels and boxes of herbs are piled to the ceiling; in the other half it comes right up to date with a range of ecologically sound products.

> *Cross Nieuwmarkt and walk as far as the police station down the right-hand side of* **Kloveniersburgwal.**

Kloveniersburgwal was a fashionable address in the Golden Age. The grand classicist house at No.29 (across from the police station) belonged to the Trip brothers. The brothers were powerful arms dealers: together with their rival, De Geer, they controlled almost all of Europe's munitions supply in the 17th century. In an ostentatious display of wealth, they clubbed together and built two separate houses behind a vast single façade. The chimney pots were made to look like cannons. When they were moving in, the coachman grumbled that he would be happy with a house the size of their front door. He got what he wanted, across the canal at No.26.

> *Walk on up to Oude Hoogstraat. The monumental red brick building on the corner was* **Oostindisch Huis** *(East India House), the headquarters of the Dutch East India Company.*

It used to fill the whole neighbourhood with the scent of spices. Nowadays it's part of the university. At first glance it seems rather austere—though if you take a peek into the courtyard (off Oude Hoogstraat) you'll be surprised by the richly decorated entrance. A rather small door is surrounded by wedding-cake embellishments of volutes and scrolls.

The company treated sailors well, but found recruiting seamen to be a problem—the odds on ever returning from a voyage were pretty low. 'Soul merchants', employed by the company, would ensnare Amsterdam's (often foreign) poor by paying their board and lodging. When the drums and trumpets announced enlistment day, the soul merchants stopped paying the rent. For many the only alternative was to sign up as indentured seamen to work off their debt (the soul merchant earning a commission on the deal). Once at sea sailors were well paid. They were given danger money and supplements for sighting land. Most did a bit of trading on their own account—smuggled goods weighed down some ships so much that they sank. Sailors who got back home found themselves wealthy men—and in relief at having returned safely would often go on a frenzy of spending. A favourite prank was to hire three coaches, in an ostentatious display of their new wealth. The first would contain the sailor's hat and would have to drive fast enough to keep a flag constantly flying. Careering behind would be a coach with the sailor's pipe and tobacco box, and the third contained the sailor himself. These 'six-week masters' were as poor after a few weeks as they had been before the voyage.

> Cross over the bridge and walk back to Nieuwmarkt along the other side of the canal. Cross Nieuwmarkt and walk down the east side of Geldersekade. Turn right into Recht Boomsloot, a quiet residential canal. Keep to the left-hand side of the canal. Turn left into Lastageweg. Cut through the children's playground and turn left into Kromme Waal. Turn right over the bridge on Prins Hendrikkade.

> From Kromme Waal you begin to see the monumental ship-shaped **Scheepvaarthuis** (Shipping House). By the time you're on the bridge, it's bearing down on you at full steam.

The house was built in 1916 (on the site of the place where the first Dutch fleet set sail for the East Indies) as the offices for six big shipping companies. After serving as the headquarters of the municipal transport authority during the 1980s and most of the 1990s it was closed for renovation, and will probably reopen as an hotel. It was the first building designed by the team of architects (Van der Meij, Kramer and De Klerk) who became known as the Amsterdam School, a sort of fantastical Dutch Art Nouveau movement (*see* pp.155–6). Nothing escapes decoration. The building comes to a prow-like point crowned by a statue of Neptune. He waves his trident while his wife Salicia takes the wheel. Four female figures represent the points of the compass. The walls are encrusted with unflattering reliefs of sea heroes. Doors, stairs, window frames and any wall space left are patterned with appropriate images—wave forms, sea horses, dolphins, anchors, seals and ship's wheels. The roof line is a cheval-de-frise of moulded lead. It's as if you're viewing the building in a distorting mirror: there's hardly a smooth surface in sight. Inside, the maritime motifs continue inside with filigreed metalwork ornamentation, beautiful stained-glass skylights and windows and much of the original furniture (also designed by the architects). Door-knobs, lamps, wall-panels, floor patterns all reflect the theme. No detail is missed.

*Pop across the road for a look at the magnificent moustachios of Prince Hendrik, 'the seaman' (1820–79). (He did a lot to promote sea trade, and the bust was erected in gratitude.) Walk down **Binnenkant**, to the right of the Scheepvaarthuis.*

Binnenkant was created in 1644 to provide more mooring. Its sedate charm is a relief after the traffic on Prins Hendrikkade. It was always a quiet spot in the harbour and a popular place to live. You can still see some fine old merchant houses. At the end of Binnenkant is the **Montelbaanstoren**, a defence tower built in 1512 when the wharves were still outside the city walls. In 1606 (when the tower was no longer used for defence) the builder Hendrick de Keyser added a wonderfully gratuitous spire. This was an activity he apparently enjoyed: he's responsible for much of Amsterdam's spiky skyline. Five years after it was built, the Montelbaanstoren began to tilt over. The good burghers of Amsterdam, unlike their more flamboyant counterparts in Pisa, would have none of it. They attached ropes to the top and pulled it straight again. Rembrandt loved to draw it, and it's still a favourite subject for visiting artists. VOC sailors left from the Montelbaanstoren to join the large seafaring East Indiamen which were too bulky to navigate as far as Amsterdam and were moored far to the north. These days it houses the city water authority. There's a delightful grotto of antiquarian and second-hand books in a shop opposite the tower.

*Turn left into Kalkmarkt, right over the bridge, then right again down **tsGravenhekje**.*

On the corner of 'sGravenhekje you can see the old warehouses of the West India Company. Their monogram is on the pediment. In its later years the ailing company gave up its head office in the western docks and moved the administrative sections in here too. The impoverished owner of No.5, further up the street, had to sell off part of his property to the neighbours, and as they expanded they cut his house in half.

Follow 's Gravenhekje round, across Peperstraat into Rapenburgstraat. Pepper was the most prized commodity of the VOC—enough for a street to be named after it. The Dutch still use the expression 'peper-duur'— 'pepper-expensive'. Piet Heyn—the admiral who captured the Silver Fleet—lived at Rapenburgstraat 13.

At the end of Rapenburgstraat, cross the main road at the lights to your right and walk up Anne Frankstraat. Turn left along the Nieuwe Herengracht canal and across the middle of three bridges, Scharrenbiersbrug, which gets its name from the cheap beer that used to be sold to smugglers and stowaways.

Whenever boats pass, the low bridges here have to be raised in succession. The operator bicycles swiftly from one to the other, just beating the boat. Across the bridge is the solid neoclassical entrance to the **Entrepotdok**, a customs-free area where goods in transit could be stored. It was once the largest warehouse complex in Europe and recently it was converted into apartments. The architects created an indoor street at first-floor level to combat the gloom.

The weary can cut straight across Prins Hendrikkade to the Maritime Museum. Others can go through the Entrepotdok gates and nose about this district a little more. The stairs marked Binnenkadijk take you up to the internal street. The long row of simple step-gabled warehouses is named in alphabetical order. There's no motor traffic: all you hear is the lap of water and the odd squawk from the zoo on the other side of the dock.

*At the end of the line of warehouses, turn left into Laagtekadijk. Cross the playground and walk up the steps to Hoogtekadijk. Across the bridge to the right is the **Kromhout Museum** (open Mon–Fri 10–4; adm f3.50).*

The Kromhout Shipyard, one of Amsterdam's oldest, was one of the few to survive the 19th-century decline in shipbuilding. It had a new lease of life in the 20th century when it produced the diesel engine used by most Dutch inland craft. In the 1960s it moved to larger premises and the old yard became a museum. Some boat building and restoration still goes on, but rows of diesel engines form the bulk of the exhibits. It's very much a place for the enthusiast.

*If the smell of oil and tar doesn't excite you, cross Hoogtekadijk, walk down Overhaalsgang and over the brightly painted modern bridge to the **Eastern Islands**.*

To your right as you cross the canal, central Amsterdam's last windmill pokes up out of squat 1960s architecture. The Eastern Islands (Wittenburg, Kattenburg and Oostenburg) are now joined together by a wide boulevard, but were once not only separate, but fiercely isolationist. There are islanders still living who remember neighbours who never once went to central Amsterdam. In 1928 the council built a public bath-house on Wittenburg and a bridge across to Kattenburg. It was a long time before anyone could be persuaded to cross the bridge and bath on 'foreign territory'.

> *Walk left up the boulevard to the sturdy* **Nederlands Scheepvaart Museum** *(Maritime Museum), built as an admiralty warehouse in 1655 (open Tues–Sun 10–5; adm f14.50).*

It's a wonder the building's still upright: workers were bribed with '*drinkgelt*' (drinking money) and finished it in an amazing nine months and fourteen days. The new warehouse had a system of cisterns and sprinklers to put out fires and an army of rat-catching cats with their own office and keeper. The museum's main attraction—a full size replica of the *Amsterdam*, one of the VOC's ships— is moored outside (though occasionally it pays visits to other ports). You can swan about the captain's cabin, have a look at his tiny loo then descend into the ship's murky maw where up to 200 sailors would live for months at a stretch.

From the upper deck you can look across to the VOC warehouses on the end of Prins Hendrikkade, or back over the water to the **New Metropolis Science & Technology Center** (*see* **Museums and Galleries**, p.180), designed by Renzo Piano, architect of the Pompidou Centre in Paris, to resemble the prow of a gigantic ship. Beyond that the harbour cranes poke up into the skyline. Don't be alarmed if you see a small figure hurtling off the top of one of them. It's the Amsterdam Bungee-jumping Club at play.

Back in the museum you can see a cutaway of an 1840s outrigger and the osten-tatiously gilded (and rather uncomfortable) Royal Barge used for state occasions and for paddling visiting dignitaries around the canals. You can also climb up to the Second World War room to peer out at Amsterdam through a periscope. The rest of the museum comprises room after room of maps, navigational equipment from previous eras, and models and pictures of ships. Everything is informatively labelled in Dutch and English, giving you a good introduction to the history of Dutch seafaring. The 'Time Voyage' multimedia show takes you a step further, portraying—with smoke machines, movies, slide shows and special effects— how unjolly it was to be a tar in the 17th century.

The museum shop is well-provisioned with books on ships, and is a treasure chest of maritime flotsam and jetsam. In an unmarked room in the cellar a man sells model kits of awesome complexity (*Thurs–Sat only*).

Bus 22 takes you from outside the museum back to Centraal Station, or you can end the walk more appropriately by making the journey in the Museum Boat (day ticket f25; departure details from Lovers on Prins Hendrikkade, ☏ 622 2181).

Start: *Take Tram 2, 3, 5, 12, 16 to Paulus Potterstraat/Museumplein.*

Walking time: *2 hours—but allow at least another two for museums, markets and relaxing in a café.*

Walk V: Modern Amsterdam

This is a walk to do once you've explored the canals, seen the main sights and want to escape from the 17th century. It begins at the city's trendiest museum and skirts round the hallowed Concertgebouw to the secluded Nieuw Zuid (New South)—a nook of eccentric modern architecture that few visitors know about. Then it's back to the crush of Holland's longest street market. Just when you need it, the Heineken Brewery Museum gives you enough free beer to propel you happily through the crowds in Rembrandtplein, and on to a coffee in the modern city hall.

It's a good weekday walk, though not one for too early a start as the Stedelijk Museum doesn't open until 11am. A mid-morning start on a Wednesday will mean that you're in time for a lunch-hour recital at the Concertgebouw. The fancy brickwork of Amsterdam School architecture looks its best in the afternoon sunlight—and if you really want that beer you'll have to make the brewery by 2.30 (earlier in the winter). If you're only in town for the weekend, you'll find the brewery closed, and a deserted market-place on Sunday. And if you're a fan of modern art, you might like to do the walk in reverse, so that you don't exhaust yourself at the outset in the Stedelijk Museum.

Lunch and Cafés

❶ Stedelijk Museum Café is the best café on the museum circuit. You can lounge about in basket chairs reading art magazines, or sit in the sun and look out at the sculptures.

❷ Café Welling, J. W. Brouwersstraat 32, behind the Concertgebouw (*open daily from 3pm*). A traditional brown café. The main door is always locked—the entrance is around the side.

❸ Meidi-Ya, Beethovenstraat 19–20, just into the Nieuw Zuid. Japanese delicatessen. Sushi to take down to the canal, or more elaborate dishes to eat there.

❹ Delcavi, Beethovenstraat 40. Haunt of the well-heeled locals. Sandwiches and home-cooked meals.

❺ Café/Restaurant Kort, Amstelveld 2, tucked behind the Amstelkerk. Sleek and modern with one of the few terraces in central Amsterdam where the traffic doesn't hurtle between you and the canal.

❻ Café Schiller, Rembrandtplein 26. A perfectly preserved Art Deco interior and a haven from the tourist throngs.

❼ De Kroon Royal Café, Rembrandtplein 17, (upstairs). All air and light with Louis XV chairs, modern paintings and chandeliers hanging from distant ceilings.

❽ Coffeeshop Le Monde, Rembrandtplein 6. The friendliest of the otherwise indistinguishable pavement cafés.

❾ Café L'Opera, Rembrandtplein 19. Catches the last patch of afternoon sun.

❿ Café Dantzig, Zwanenburgwal 15, part of the Stopera complex. Deeply trendy, post-modern café.

V: Modern Amsterdam

N

500 yards

SPUI
ROKIN
KALVERSTR.
NWE DOELENSTR.
HEISTEEG
KEIZERSGRACHT
KEIZERSGRACHT
PRINSENGRACHT
PRINSENGRACHT
HERENGRACHT
MUNTPLEIN
Tuschinski
ROKIN
VIJZELSTRAAT
REG. BREESTR.
BAKKERSTR.
AMSTELSTR.
9
8 7
10 FINISH
Stopera
WATERLOO PLEIN
M
BLAUW- BRUG
REMBRANDT- PLEIN
6
Amstel-
Binnen- amstel
NWE SPIEGELSTRAAT
Reguliersgracht
5
Amstelkerk
KERKSTRAAT
Amstel-
veld
WETERINGSCHANS
VIJZELGRACHT
WETERINGSCHANS
UTRECHTSESTR.
Nederlandse
Bank
Vondel-
park
Rijksmuseum
VAN
VELDE
POTTERSTR.
M
WETERING PLEIN
Singelgracht
STADHOUDERSKADE
MUSEUM
START PAULUS
STR.
PLEIN
Stedelijk
Museum
1
MUSEUMPLEIN
Heineken Brewery
Museum
FERDINAND
TEL.V.D.
Post
Office
2
BAERLESSTR.
HOBBEMAKADE
CUYPSTRAAT
Concertgebouw
J.W. BROUWERSTR.
CONCERTGEBOUW-
PLEIN
ALBERT STR.
CUYPSTRAAT
Albert
Cuypmarkt
J. VERHULSTSTR.
OBRECHTSTR.
BOSBOULEVARD
SARPHATI-
PARK
Sarphati-
park
JACOB
OBRECHTPLEIN
HARTPLEIN
R.HARTSTR.
CEINTUURBAAN
2E V.D. HELSTSTR.
Jacob
J. M.COENENSTR.
BURGERSTRAAT
JACOB
HEINZE-STR.
BARTH.
Synagogue
OBRECHTSTR.
RUSTEN-
VAN DER
BOERENWETERING
HELSTPLEIN
COÖPER-
ATIEHOF
De
Dageraad
APOLLOLAAN
MOZART KDE
Apollolaan
LUTMA-
STRAAT
J.
PASSTOOR-
STR.
W.
2E V.D. HELST STRA.
SCHWARTZE
STR.
BURG.
P.L.TAKSTR.
GEN.
Coöperatiehof
BEETHOVEN STRAAT
GERRIT V.D.VEENSTR.
3
4
Sociale
Vezekeringsbank
HENRIETTE
Amstelkanaal
MUZEN-
PLEIN
CHURCHILLAAN
JOSEF
ISRAELS
THÉRÈSE
SCHWARTZEPLEIN
SCHELDESTRAAT
MAASSTRAAT

149

The Stedelijk Museum is a solid 19th-century red brick building with fussy plaster decorations and spiky gables. A row of rather haughty architects stares down at you from niches on the first floor. The widened entrance and glass box extension at the back were part of a drive in the 1950s to make art more accessible: the guiding principle was that a museum loses its sense of mystery when works can also be viewed from the street. A good idea—if the blinds didn't have to be drawn every afternoon against the damaging sunlight.

Don't be deceived by appearances. It's a bright, lively museum of modern art. You'll find not only conventional paintings, but all sorts of applied art (designer chairs, feather hats and gaudy teapots) and work by less established artists.

The museum owes its existence to two benefactors. Sophia Augusta de Bruyn, the eccentric dowager of Jonkheer (Lord) Lopez Suasso, spent as little as she could on clothes (scandalizing Amsterdam society by wearing the same dress more than once). Instead she amassed as many jewels, trinkets, curios (and especially clocks) as she could. When she died, she left everything to the City of Amsterdam. There was so much that the council felt obliged to build a museum to display it all. At the same time the wealthy Vereeniging tot het Vormen van eene Openbare Verzameling van Heedendaagsche Kunst (Society for the Formation of a Public Collection of Contemporary Art) or VvHK, was looking for a home.

The city council and the 'society with the long name' (as it was understandably nicknamed) got together and the museum opened in 1895. It wasn't until the early 1970s that the last of Sophia Augusta's bric-a-brac was dispersed to specialist museums and the Stedelijk became devoted exclusively to modern art.

Successive directors have left their imprint on the collection, but it was the imagination, energy and skill of Willem Sandberg—'part poet, part artist, part designer, part administrator, part magician'—that between 1945 and 1963 established the Stedelijk as one of the world's leading modern art museums. He built up an important collection and held a series of notable, usually controversial, exhibitions. In 1949 there were fisticuffs in the foyer at the opening of the first COBRA exhibition. (COBRA was a group of artists from **Co**penhagen, **Br**ussels and **A**msterdam whose colourful, childlike painting was the first to provoke the response that 'a three-year-old could do better'.) Though that's not happened again, daring new acquisitions still spark off public uproars.

Space is limited, so only a small portion of the collection is shown at any one time. Outside the summer months (May–September) you may even find that much of the museum is taken over by a special exhibition, though present museum policy is to show the core of the permanent collection on a more stable, long-term basis. A plan of what is currently on view is available from the information desk (to the left of the entrance). The catalogue (a survey of the entire collection, in English) is a bargain at *f*35.

> *You'll find whatever is being exhibited of the **permanent collection** up the wide marble staircase, on the top floor.*

In 1972 the large Van Gogh collection, which had been kept at the Stedelijk, moved next door to its own museum (*see* **Walk VI**, pp.164–9). Because Van Gogh is considered so important to modern art, a few paintings were left behind. *La Berceuse* (The Cradle) was inspired by a story Gauguin told Van Gogh about fishermen who pinned prints of their patron saint—Stella Maris (Maria, Star of the Sea)—to the cabin wall. Van Gogh felt that a portrait of Madame Roulin (a postman's wife), holding a cord for a rocking cradle, would be ideal for such a print. He imagined the seamen 'would feel the old sense of being rocked come over them and remember their own lullabies'. It's a pity that the painting isn't hung the way Van Gogh suggested—as a triptych with sunflower paintings on either side. Don't miss the paintings by George Breitner, Van Gogh's contemporary and drinking partner. In *De Dam*, a view of Dam square, he captures that special Amsterdam light in a way that makes the exact time of year, even the time of day, immediately recognizable. Keep an eye open also for his highly patterned, exotic *Woman in a Red Kimono* (in reality a hat shop assistant).

The museum has a good collection of modern art classics. You'll probably find Manet's picture of a barmaid (staring out at you saucily), a study for his famous *Bar at the Folies-Bergère*. There are some gentle Cézanne landscapes and a range of Picassos—from bright early collages to nudes from his Blue Period. One wall is sure to be filled by Matisse's vast paper cut-out *The Parakeet and the Mermaid*, done towards the end of his life when his eyesight was too poor for painting, and painstakingly restored in 1996. You'll find at least one of Kandinsky's vivid *Improvisations*—paintings where he used colour to represent the sounds of various musical instruments—and some rather good Chagalls. The 1960s are well represented by Warhol screen-prints, Roy Lichtenstein's comic strip blow-ups and Bruce Nauman's neon light installations, and the museum comes right up to date with works by some of the best living European and American arists.

The high point is the museum's collection of the Russian artist, Kazimir Malevich and the Dutch movement, *De Stijl*. Side by side, these two collections show how abstract art began and we see the gradual disappearance of any reference to outside reality. The visionary director of the museum, Willem Sandberg, was responsible for tracking down the Malevich collection, unearthing a treasury of works that had been forgotten in a cellar in Germany. Malevich had left the entire contents of an exhibition for safe-keeping with a friend in Beieren, but was subsequently never allowed to leave Russia. He died in 1935, so there the cache remained (under a pile of rubble after the war) until Sandberg swooped down and bought it in the late 1950s. The museum has a complete range of his work, from early Impressionist pieces, through a Cubist period to the completely abstract—solid shapes of colour on a white background. Malevich composes these shapes at such angles that the paintings seem full of movement.

At around the same time (1917) *De Stijl* artists were coming up with very similar work. The best known is that of Piet Mondriaan (he dropped the last 'a' to appear French, but the Dutch prefer the original). His *Compositions* of vertical and horizontal black lines with blocks of primary colours, so shocking at the time, now appear on everything. When Theo van Doesburg (co-founder of *De Stijl*) after ten years of rectilinear painting produced a *Contra-composition*, in which he daringly tilted his lines through 45°, Piet left the movement in a huff. They were never reconciled, though Mondriaan later took up the challenge by tilting his *canvas* through 45° and keeping the lines vertical.

*Halfway down the staircase you'll find the **Print Room**.*

Here you could find anything from a Toulouse-Lautrec poster to Mapplethorpe's startling close-up photographs of male nudes. Keep an eye open for the innovative work of Dutch photographer Cas Oorthuys, and Roland Topor's blackly comic cartoons. Work not on display can be viewed by appointment in the study-room.

*Carry on down to the ground floor, most of which is given over to **travelling exhibitions** and **applied art**.*

The small door to the left of the ticket office leads to rooms of odd-shaped furniture, gaudy ceramics and lumpy mats. There's a video art room under the stairs, and the glass box extension at the back of the building occasionally displays work (often dire) by contemporary Amsterdam artists. Two installations on the ground floor shouldn't be missed. The *Appelbar* (through a door to the right of the information desk), adorned with murals of colourful birds, fish and children, is the work of the COBRA artist Karel Appel. It was used as a café until the opening of the present restaurant in 1956. The commission was offered to Appel as a palliative after a débâcle at the Town Hall in 1951: a mural in the canteen, commissioned by the Building Department, had to be boarded over when the Catering Department insisted that it would put people off their food. Edward Kienholz's *Beanery* is a near-life-sized version of a poky Los Angeles bar. You can wander about in the dim light, examining the bric-a-brac. Rusty music scratches away in the juke-box. There's a murmur of conversation. A couple sit at the bar.

Someone has passed out in the corner. A waitress clears the remnants of a disgusting meal. But all the faces of the figures are clock-faces, and as you're the only thing that moves it is a surreal and rather disorientating experience. Luckily, the real bar (bright and airy) is just across the corridor. (Unlike the *Appelbar*, the *Beanery* is not a permanent installation, so sometimes disappears on tour.)

> *Leaving the museum, turn right at the main entrance and then right again down the side of the museum. A gate leads into the small* **Sculpture Garden**. *You can't help noticing the American Richard Serra's 12m-high Sight Point. The best place to view these three precariously balanced sheets of steel is from inside the sculpture itself.*
>
> *There's not much else to detain you in the Sculpture Garden. Walk back out of the gate and turn right into* **Museumplein**. *Turn right again and walk up the side of the square to the* **Concertgebouw**.

The city's greatest cultural institutions border Museumplein—the Rijksmuseum (*see* **Walk II**) and Concertgebouw at either end, the Van Gogh and Stedelijk Museums up one side. Until recently Museumplein was bisected by a busy road nicknamed 'Europe's's shortest motorway', and was windswept, deserted and nasty. But dramatic relandscaping in the late 1990s created a green and stylish spot with a long pool, a café and underground garages that suck up all the cars.

As you wander through the square, stop briefly to look at the *Vrouwen van Ravensbrück* memorial, a series of vertical steel slabs erected to commemorate the 92,000 women who died in concentration camps during the Second World War. The text translates as 'For those women who until the bitter end refused to accept fascism'. The flickering light and thumping sound emanating from the sculpture are intended to call people to the monument and to continue the fight.

The **Concertgebouw** at the southern end of the square was designed by A. L. van Gendt (one of the collaborators on the Centraal Station design) and completed in 1888. It is solid Dutch neo-Renaissance; no French frivolity here—indeed, the few urns and obelisks he included in the design either never went up for lack of funds, or have fallen off through lack of funds. The twin staircase towers are intended to harmonize with Cuypers' Rijksmuseum across the way (more out of toadyism than artistic integrity—Cuypers headed the committee that chose the design). Busts of Beethoven, Bach and Sweelinck (Holland's one claim to musical fame) grace the façade. The gilded lyre on top is a 1960s replacement of the original (which fell off). The entrance is no longer through the front, but through a shiny glass extension built in 1988 as part of a complete renovation of the building, which had been subsiding dangerously. It certainly meets the general manager's stipulation that if there was to be a new front door, he didn't want to have to hang an 'Entrance around the Corner' notice on the old one.

In the 1870s Amsterdam, a city with metropolitan aspirations, found itself without a concert hall and with Brahms's admonition ringing in its ears: '*Ihr seid liebe Leute aber schlechte Musikanten*' (You are lovely people but awful musicians). The government maintained that art was not its business, so it was a committee of private citizens that raised the money, bought some cheap land outside the city limits next to an evil-smelling candle factory and commissioned Van Gendt (more for his figures than his design). Van Gendt prided himself on being a salesman rather than an artist and was completely unmusical. It is ironic that he should have produced a concert hall with possibly the best acoustics in the world.

Under the baton of conductors like Mengelberg (who was sacked for his Nazi sympathies in 1945 after 50 years of service) and Haitink, the resident Royal Concertgebouw Orchestra has become world-famous. If you're passing on a Wednesday, pop in for a free 'lunch concert' (*12.30pm, though it's a good idea to be there by 12*). These are usually recitals given in the Kleine Zaal (Small Hall—a chamber music room upstairs), but if you're lucky you might catch the RCO itself in open rehearsal in the Grote Zaal (Big Hall—the main auditorium).

> *Walk down the left-hand side of the building following Jan Willem Brouwersstraat and turning left into Johannes Verhulststraat.*

At the turn of the century there was a garden, since sold to developers, behind the Concertgebouw. On summer afternoons it would rustle with silk as Amsterdam's élite gathered for outdoor concerts. Those (literally) outside the charmed circle would have to crush around the railings. If you walk a short way up J. Verhulststraat and look back you'll get the only view now available of the little gilded mermaid blowing her trumpet on top of the *Kleine Zaal*.

> *Turn left into Jacob Obrechtstraat and carry on down to Jacob Obrechtplein. The block-like **synagogue** (1930) on the square isn't usually open to the public, but if you spot an open door, nip in for a look at the vibrant expressionist stained glass windows by W. Bogtman, whose Haarlem studio is responsible for much of Amsterdam's best modern stained glass. Leave the square by Bartholomeus Ruloffsstraat, turn right into Johannes M. Coenenstraat and cross the bridge. On the other side of the Amstel Canal lies the **Nieuw Zuid** (New South).*

The Nieuw Zuid was created by the architect H. P. Berlage (1856–1934), the father of modern Dutch architecture (*see* p.63–4), after a new law had revolutionized Amsterdam housing conditions. In 1915–17 he drew up a plan of wide avenues and narrow side streets that reflected the 17th-century canals. He died before he could implement it, and his work was taken on with even greater enthusiasm by Michel de Klerk and Pieter Kramer, architects of what became known as the Amsterdam School. De Klerk was a working-class *wunderkind*

Features of the Amsterdam School

Shape: Their whimsical brick buildings are instantly recognizable by the curves and bulges of their façades. Entire blocks were seen as one building—waves of roofs and balconies give a delightful sense of horizontal movement. Soaring chimneys and stairways accentuate the vertical lines.

Bricks: Decorative, polychromatic, almost sculptural brickwork is used lavishly. Like Berlage, the new builders used 'honest' Dutch materials of wood and brick, but the buildings are constructed around a reinforced concrete frame, so the bricks can do what they like. The pleats and folds earned the movement's work the nickname *schortjesarchitectuur* (apron architecture). Straight edges are often softened by a frill of vertically placed roofing tiles.

Windows and Doors: Odd parabolic and trapeziform windows and angulated carved doors contrast startlingly with the general symmetry of the buildings.

Sculptures: Stone and brick sculptures are integrated into the building's design, especially at corners and on bridges. In the Nieuw Zuid these are usually the gnome-like mythical figures by Hildo Krop (1884–1970). Krop was the municipal sculptor for many years and his chunky work is all over Amsterdam. Recently it was revealed that for much of that time he was working for the Soviet KGB, and it's even been suggested that he was involved in the recruitment of Anthony Blunt and other famous British spies.

Details: House numbers, letterboxes and hoists are all designed to fit into the larger scheme. Egyptian and oriental influences are evident in the metalwork.

headhunted from primary school to begin work with the city's leading architectural firm at the age of 14. He and Kramer set out to design buildings that were, in his words, 'sensationally shocking'. They were successful. When the Nieuw Zuid was finished nobody wanted to live there. The area eventually became a ghetto for Jews fleeing persecution in Germany. (The Frank family lived on Merwedeplein before going into hiding.) In the past few years there's been a revival of interest in the Amsterdam School. Houses, bridges and even public lavatories are being declared national monuments.

In reacting against their sober, rational Dutch predecessors, the Amsterdam School produced an idiosyncratic cross between Old Dutch and Art Nouveau, which has led to some quirky and amusing, but also rather beautiful building. You can see why they're sometimes called the 'Gaudís of the North'. As you walk through the New South, a checklist (*see* above) of some of their innovations might help you to recognize and enjoy the style.

> Having crossed the bridge (by Kramer, sculptures by Krop), cross Apollolaan. In 1969 there was great commotion at the **Amsterdam Hilton** (to the right, up Apollolaan) when John Lennon and Yoko Ono staged a week-long 'Bed-in', the starting point of their world campaign

*for peace. For f1750 a night you can stay in the some room as the late
Beatle, surrounded by John and Yoko memorabilia.*

*The desultory trio on the central island of Apollolaan commemorates
the shooting on the spot of 29 people by the Germans in reprisal for
Resistance action in 1944. Walk across to Beethovenstraat, a chic but
unimaginative shopping street mainly frequented by children of diplomats and bored expatriate housewives. Before turning left into **Gerrit
van der Veenstraat**, look west and you will see the clocktower
marking the school building used as the Gestapo headquarters during
the war. The Frank family were brought here after their capture.*

Gerrit van der Veen—sculptor and Resistance hero—led the raid on the
Amsterdam Registry in 1943 in an attempt to burn the records. The mission was
only partially successful, but the firemen who were called to the blaze obligingly
drenched what was left. Van der Veen was later shot in the back while
attempting to free some Resistance prisoners, arrested and executed in the dunes
near Bloemendaal. The building that rises out of the surrounding domestic architecture at the end of the street like a huge ocean liner is the **Sociale
Verzekeringsbank** (Social Insurance Bank, built 1937–9). It has an almost
magical monumentality, but doesn't seem at all out of place. Its shape is even
echoed in the curved windows of the houses towards the end of the terrace.

*Walk down the right-hand side of the Sociale Verzekeringsbank and
turn right over the bridge (another by Kramer). The **Apollohal** (a sports
hall) on the corner before the bridge is an early example of Nieuwe
Zakelijkheid (the functional concrete-and-glass style that began in the
1920s, begetter of many 1960s monstrosities). Neglected and rather
sad, it's hard to judge whether it was ever pleasing to look at. Across the
water the **Amstel Boat Club** reverberates with the hearty shouts of
boaties. They brave the vilest weather and seem to resent the occasional
winter freezes when the rest of the world comes out to skate. Walk on
down Churchillaan—a leafy avenue where even the trams appear to run
over grass. Look out for little sculptures by Krop set into the walls,
expressionist lettering and some bizarre front doors. Turn left at
Maasstraat, then turn right on the canal and over the white footbridge.
Turn right and immediately left into **Pieter Lodewijk Takstraat**.*

On the side of the building opposite the footbridge are powerful sculptures of
rearing horses and straining figures—*De Geboorte van de Daad* (The Birth of
the Deed), some of Krop's best work. Once you turn the corner you're in a patch
of streets and squares designed entirely by Kramer and De Klerk. In 1918 the
housing association *De Dageraad* (Daybreak) gave the young men free rein to
design the neighbourhood. Strikingly curved staircase towers, wavy rooftops,

jutting sharp-edged windows and fancy coloured brickwork are the results of this freedom from restriction. The buildings are wonderful to look at, but residents complain their furniture doesn't fit in the odd-shaped rooms.

*Walk anti-clockwise around **Burgemeester Tellegenstraat** and cut left through Coöperatiehof.*

The two crescents of Burgemeester Tellegenstraat are completely symmetrical. Look at the lettering in the doorways. You'll occasionally even find corresponding lettering on one side reflected in mirror image on the other.

*Walk on to Thérèse Schwartzestraat, turn up and walk to **Thérèse Schwartzeplein**.*

De Klerk died in his 30s. The barn-like houses on Thérèse Schwartzeplein are among the last he built. Tiny butterfly-wing windows interrupt vast sheets of yellow brick (it must be dark in there). The houses are linked by bulbous little balconies and tall arrow-shaped chimneys.

*Leave the square along Paletstraat, turn right along the canal and walk along as far as Tweede Van der Helststraat where you turn right (behind the towering Hotel Okura). Wander up past (or through) the tiny, but rather pretty Sarphatipark (named after a 19th-century philanthropist who gave Amsterdam an efficient rubbish disposal service, an hygienic bread factory and its own Crystal Palace; see pp.40–1). Carry on up what is now Eerste Van der Helststraat as far as Albert Cuypstraat. The area between the Amstel Kanaal and the Singelgracht is known as **De Pijp** (The Pipe) for the long thin passages between the 19th-century tenement houses.*

Once a slum, it's now a lively neighbourhood populated by artists and immigrant communities. The streets seem to get brighter, busier and nosier as you get closer to the **Albert Cuyp Market**, where it all explodes into a cacophony of national musics, a kaleidoscope of colour and a press of eager shoppers. Between the piles of silk, gaudy modern clothes and cheap shoes, boxes of dried herbs and teas, people slip raw herrings down their throats, guzzle home-made chocolates, queue for freshly cooked waffles, taste farm cheese and stock up on fish, fruit and vegetables. Behind the stalls there's yet another layer of life—tacky clothing shops, ethnic stores and cheap Indian and Surinamese restaurants.

After whatever market shopping you might do, leave by Eerste Van der Helstraat (straight across from where you arrived). Walk on up to the canal. The building on the left is the **Heineken Brewery Museum** (✆ 523 9666; *guided tours only: Mon–Fri 9.30 and 11am, 1pm and 2.30pm, also at noon and 2pm on Saturdays in July and Aug ; allow 2 hours; adm f3, which goes to charity*).

This is the birthplace of Heineken beer. The brewery, established here in 1867, stopped production on this site only a few years ago when Amsterdam began to drink more than the brewery could produce. Now smart guides lead you through the stables (old dray horses *in situ*) and past huge copper vats; but the real purpose of the visit, however, seems to be the free beer at the end of the tour.

> *If two hours of hops and dray horses doesn't appeal to you, turn left along the front of the brewery and cross the canal to Weteringplein—a rather hectic traffic intersection. On the left,* **De Gevallen Hoornblazer** *(The Fallen Trumpeter) is a poignant tribute to a number of people shot by the Germans and left on this spot on 24 March 1945 in a last-minute display of Nazi power as liberation was becoming inevitable. There's also a Krop sculpture (Mother Earth) and a monument erected in appreciation for aid given during the disastrous 1953 Zeeland flood. Leave the square by the corner diagonally opposite the bridge towards the right and walk to the right along* **Weteringschans**.

The concrete and glass monstrosity that looms at the end of Weteringschans is the **Nederlandse Bank** built in 1968 by M. F. Duintjer (he has a string of unpopular buildings to his name, including the 'coal scuttle church' in Amsterdam West). A cylindrical mirror tower, from the 1980s, has made it even worse.

> *Escape left to the quiet gables and bridges of the* **Reguliersgracht**.

A little way up Reguliersgracht you pass along the side of **Amstelveld**, a secluded square with a white wooden church and small Monday flower market, tucked away from the surrounding bustle. The recently restored 17th-century **Amstelkerk** has a popular left-wing preacher and is the one of the few churches in central Amsterdam that packs in a congregation. It isn't continuously open to the public, but sometimes stages chamber recitals. Further up Reguliersgracht, at Nos.57–9 and 63, you come across two elaborately carved façades designed by I. Gosschalk in the late 19th century—rather like two extravagant sisters flanking a maiden aunt. One is a wild combination of Old Dutch and German, the other a modest mingling of Old Dutch with Old English and Queen Anne.

> *Turn left to follow* **Keizersgracht**, *one of the grand 17th-century canals, then turn right into* **Vijzelstraat**.

In the 1920s Vijzelstraat was a tiny shopping street, in places only a few metres wide. Over fifty 16th and 17th-century houses were demolished down the west side to turn it into a traffic thoroughfare. The council promised a mixture of housing, businesses and shops in the rebuilding programme. To the Amsterdammers' horror, the first building to go up, on land leased from the council, was the huge brick Nederlandse Handelsmaatschappij (Netherlands Trading Company). Ten days before the opening, the company's president donated his Herengracht mansion to the city as an official home for the mayor. A whole wall of heavyweight commercial buildings has since gone up—all the way down to Muntplein. Each has caused a storm of protest.

> *Walk down the right hand side of Vijzelstraat towards Muntplein. Before turning right into Reguliersbreestraat pop into the **apothecary** on the corner. A remnant of the old Vijzelstraat, it's stuffed to the ceiling with scents, spices and cough drops that can cure at twenty paces. At Reguliersbreestraat 26 you'll find the **Tuschinski Cinema**.*

Abraham Tuschinski, a Jewish refugee from Poland, saw his first film in 1910 and immediately wanted to own a cinema. His first 'bioscope' opened in 1911 in a disused seamen's church with a converted outside lavatory as the box office. But Tuschinski wanted a cinema where his 'guests' could lose themselves in another world. In 1921 he was wealthy enough to achieve his dream. You walk through a soaring Art Deco façade with flagpoles, camp statuary and curly iron lamps into an interior that lurches between heady luxury and high kitsch. It's a stylistic cocktail of five different colours of marble, Persian carpets, and thousands of electric lights. You can go on a guided tour (*Sun and Mon during July and Aug, 10.30am, f10*), or come back later and see a film. Ask for a balcony ticket in the main cinema. On the first Sunday of each month during the winter, there's a special morning screening of a silent movie, with musical accompaniment and sound effects from the original Wurlitzer organ.

The concrete and glass **Cineac** (opposite the Tuschinski) seems from another century. It's hard to believe it was built only 13 years later. The architect, J. Duiker, was a movie fanatic. The auditorium opened directly on to the street and the projectionist could be seen from outside through the glass wall on the first floor. Rebuilding in the 1960s and 1980s all but destroyed the original concept. In the late 1990s Cineac got yet another facelift, this time emerging as a restaurant in the Planet Hollywood chain.

> *Reguliersbreestraat opens on to **Rembrandtplein**.*

Rembrandtplein was a butter market until the mid 19th-century when a group of worthy burghers plonked a statue (Amsterdam's first) in the middle and grew some grass around it. Cafés sprang up. Variety artists from the halls along the Amstel would meet their agents at the posh Café Kroon, then retreat across the square to the darker recesses of the Hotel Schiller where they felt more at home among the artists, writers and other friends of proprietor Frits Schiller (whose paintings still decorate the walls). Nowadays the square is a favourite after-work stopover and a magnet to tourists, who come for the relaxed Amsterdam conviviality. Traffic is banished from most of the square but buskers keep the noise level high. When the sun sets, things get even livelier. The cafés change gear as the night staff come on duty. Music systems are turned on full, jazz from one corner, Dutch sing-along from another. Congas of drunken Dutchmen snake out of pubs and around bemused policemen. At one bar the three barmen break out at intervals into a well rehearsed dance routine. Whether you're carousing with the revellers, or just sitting and watching it all, it's a cheerful place to stop for a drink.

> *Leave the square at Bakkerstraat, turn right and cross the Amstel via the Blauwbrug (and its maritime-inspired decorations) to reach* **Waterlooplein***.*

Waterlooplein was once the heart of the Jewish neighbourhood. For decades after the war it lay desolate. When the city council announced plans (in 1979) to build a combined city hall and opera house on the site, there was public outrage (*see* pp.69–71). The city hall was ugly, the opera house seemed unnecessary, and the few people still living in the neighbourhood would have to be evicted. The building was nicknamed the Stopera—from *stadhuis* (city hall) and opera. 'Stop the Stopera' campaigns were held all over Amsterdam but, as always, the council won. The new **Muziektheater** (the opera house) opened in 1986, followed two years later by the Stadhuis. The city hall is indeed bland, but most Amsterdammers grudgingly admit to the beauty of the Muziektheater. Its glass walls, sweeping stairways, soft pink colour scheme and marble coliseum-like shell look their best in the early evening. As the light fades, the whole building seems to glow. The artists themselves are delighted with the state-of-the-art equipment and huge dressing rooms. But acoustics experts from around the world haven't been able to solve the (severe) problems in the auditorium and there have been some massive architectural blunders backstage—the ballet rehearsal rooms have ceilings so low that dancers can't practise lifts, the orchestra doesn't have a rehearsal room at all and the scenery lifts are at the opposite end of the building from the loading entrances. Both the Netherlands Ballet and Opera are resident, and the programme is varied, with many international visitors (*see* p.210).

In a passageway connecting the Stadhuis and Muziektheater three water columns show the tides at IJmuiden and Vlissingen (below knee-level) and the sobering sight of the level reached during the 1953 Zeeland flood (way above your head). You can walk down a flight of stairs, below sea level, and touch the bronze knob (its position was calculated in the 17th century) which represents the **zero point** from which heights in much of Europe are calculated.

> *Behind the Stopera, and creeping slowly around it, is the Waterlooplein fleamarket—but that's best saved for* **Walk III***; see p.122. Pop into the post-modern Café Dantzig which overlooks the river on the Amstel/ Zwanenburgwal corner of the Stadhuis, or wander back across the bridge and end the walk café-crawling on Rembrandtplein.*

Walk VI: Van Gogh, Diamonds and Shops

Start: *Take Tram 2, 3, 5, 12 to the corner of Van Baerlestraat and Paulus Potterstraat, or take Tram 6, 7 or 10 to the Rijksmuseum and cut through to Museumplein.*

Walking time: *About 3 hours, though that depends on how long you linger in the shops. Allow at least another hour for the Van Gogh Museum.*

Few artists have a national museum all to themselves, but there's a sad irony in the long queue that snakes back under the simple silver lettering 'Vincent van Gogh' to one side of Amsterdam's top tourist attraction. The lonely artist, who sold just two paintings and got only one good review in his lifetime, is now the still point in a money-spinning world of multi-million dollar picture sales, bizarre art theft, pop songs, novels, films and tacky souvenirs.

This walk gives you a close insight into Van Gogh, then whisks you out to a more frivolous Amsterdam. You can relax in the park, become party to the city's best kept secret, and have hashish with your coffee on the Leidseplein. The walk then takes you to classy antiques shops in the Spiegelkwartier and to the Keizersgracht's modern galleries. After exploring a network of fanciful shopping alleys, you saunter down a dapper little canal and end the day looking for bargains in an indoor antiques market. It's a good walk for a Saturday: the museum is open all day, Vondelpark is festive and the markets are well-stocked and buzzing.

You'll find most shops closed on a Monday, and on Friday the De Looier Antiques Market is shuttered and grim.

Lunch and Cafés

1 't Ronde Blauwe Theehuis, Vondelpark. 'The Round Blue Teahouse' is an odd piece of 1930s New Functionalist architecture in the middle of the Vondelpark. After years of mediocrity as a café, it has taken on a new life as a trendy watering hole.

2 Café Vertigo is in the cellar of the Film Museum and spills out into the park in good weather. The cuisine surpasses that of any museum restaurant in town; even has appropriate theme menus during film festivals.

3 Hollandse Manege Café, Vondelstraat 140, overlooks the arena of the elegant 19th-century riding school. It's a quiet place to sip coffee and watch the horses, though there are occasional invasions of groups of 11-year-olds in jodhpurs.

4 Café Américain, American Hotel, Leidseplein. Art Nouveau grand Café.

Once the hangout of Amsterdam's literati, it's now visited mainly by tourists, but is just the right environment for a pot of fresh coffee and an extravagantly gooey cake. It also serves snacks and fuller meals.

5 Café Cox, beneath the Stadsschouwburg. Named after the theatre's erstwhile director Cox Habbema. It serves scrumptious salads and light meals.

6 The Bulldog, Leidseplein. A 1970s institution. One of the first places allowed to sell marijuana on the premises. It's now a slick commercial enterprise with alcohol upstairs, dope downstairs and even a souvenir shop.

7 Le Soleil, Nieuwe Spiegelstraat 50. Traditional Dutch pancakes (sweet and savoury) served at communal tables. The chairs are painted in the pastel pink and green enamels you usually find in seaside

VI: Van Gogh, Diamonds and Shops

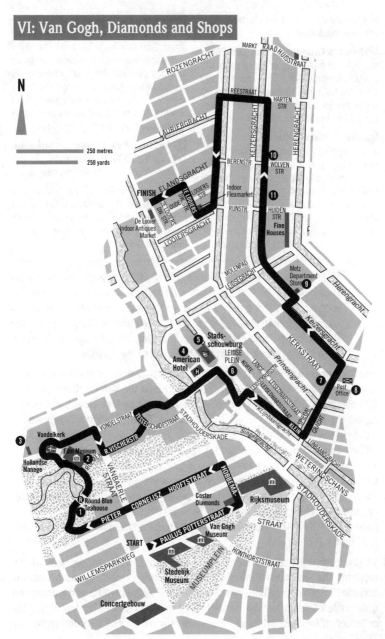

tearooms and the walls are cluttered with Art Deco knick-knacks.

8 Sarah's Grannies, Kerkstraat 176, in the Spiegelkwartier. Run and frequented mainly by women. It's calm and friendly, with classical music, a speciality tea menu (from mango to Earl Grey), hot home-cooked lunches and a good salad menu.

9 The Metz Café, corner of Leidsestraat and Keizersgracht. Amsterdam from high up is a rare sight. The glass cupola on top of one of its poshest department stores is a good place to sip a coffee and change your perspective of the city—but not for a meal. It dishes up dull railway-station fare. Service is rather indifferent until you try to take a photograph.

10 Pompadour, Huidenstraat 5. A chocolaterie and pâtisserie. The interior—hardly bigger than an average kitchen—somehow incorporates carved oak panels, a staircase and a balustrade from an 18th-century town hall near Liège. Sit in this matchbox splendour and choose from a selection of nearly 50 different hand-made choccies, or (and?) have a pastry with your coffee.

11 Café Aas van Bokalen, Keizersgracht 335. Good brown Café with an arty crowd and a restaurant-sized menu.

The alleys criss-crossing the canals, from **Huidenstraat** to **Reestraat**, are a rich hunting-ground for good restaurants, should you wish to return for an evening meal (see **Food and Drink**, p.183).

If you've arrived on Tram 2, 3, 5 or 12, walk down Paulus Potterstraat—the Van Gogh Museum is halfway down, on the right. If you've taken Tram 6, 7 or 10, then you'll need to cross the Singelgracht and Stadhouderskade and walk through the walkway under the Rijksmuseum. This brings you to Museumplein. A walk up the right-hand side of Museumplein will bring you to the museum.

The **Rijksmuseum Vincent Van Gogh** (National Vincent Van Gogh Museum, *open daily 10–6; adm f12.50*) has really cornered the Van Gogh market with 200 paintings, 500 drawings, a collection of works by Van Gogh's contemporaries, the letters from Vincent to his brother Theo, Vincent's collections of Japanese woodcuts and 19th-century engravings, a press archive dating from 1899—and publishing copyright for the lot. The museum was completed in 1973 and is based on an initial drawing by the influential Dutch architect, Gerrit Rietveld (see p.64), who died before working the plan through. Brave efforts by later architects to realize his rather sketchy ideas produced a hard-edged and unsympathetic building. But in 1999, a new wing by renowned Japanese architect Kisho Kurokawa gave the museum the sort of proud architectural profile it deserves.

Works from the permanent collection are displayed in the old part of the museum, the Kurokawa wing is used for temporary exhibitions and houses the darkened Print Room, where you can find Van Gogh's drawings and studies, and trace some of his influences—sketches by friends, pictures he copied and his collection of Japanese prints and magazine engravings. The selection on display

Vincent Van Gogh

Vincent van Gogh was born in 1853 in the tiny village of Zundert, near the Belgian border. We have an image of him as a wild, schizophrenic bohemian; a simpleton, out of touch with the world and reliant on his younger brother's handouts. This isn't the full truth. He came from an old Dutch family of clerics, naval officers and gallery owners. Though he was constantly at odds with his relations, and offended almost everyone he met, he was in many ways part of the Establishment. He spoke three languages fluently, had a wide knowledge of European art and had the connections needed to organize two exhibitions of friends' work in Paris. He signed himself 'Vincent' because he thought his surname, difficult for foreigners to pronouce, would be bad salesmanship. (You say it with two guttural 'gs'—'fun HGoHG'). Yet all his life he was desperately lonely, dogged by a sense of failure and frustrated by how few people appreciated his art. Towards the end he was beset by bouts of madness which left him exhausted and depressed. He was acutely sensitive to his surroundings. The colours, people, light or weather in one environment would become loathsome to him and the need to move would become consuming. Suddenly he'd up sticks and go—to the sun, to the city, to the country. These moves were often reflected in a change in his work.

Vincent's first job, at the age of 16, was as an assistant with the art dealer Goupil & Cie in The Hague. In 1873 he went to work at the London branch and was impressed by Constable, Turner and especially the Pre-Raphaelite John Everett Millais. An unhappy love affair made him grumpy at work. He began to be rude to customers about their taste, was shuttled between London and Paris and, finally, dismissed. Still obsessed by his English rose, he returned to Britain as a teacher, but was soundly rebuffed. He went back to Holland to work in a bookshop, but still didn't know what he wanted to do with his life.

But in May 1877 it all suddenly seemed clear: following in his father's footsteps, he set off for Amsterdam to study theology. Greek, Latin and algebra proved an uphill struggle, and after less than a year he went to a crammer for evangelists in Brussels. But he couldn't preach either. Yet again the family pulled strings. The Brussels Evangelist Committee sent him to work among the coalminers of the Borinage in south Belgium, but he was soon dismissed for over-zealous involvement with the poor.

He stayed on in a hovel for another year, almost starving to death, and began to draw. He was 26 and had found his direction. His younger brother, Theo, rescued him and started to pay him the monthly allowance that was to be Vincent's only income for the rest of his life.

Van Gogh was largely self-taught, though he spent a brief period studying perspective and anatomy in Brussels in 1880. The following year he fell in love with his widowed cousin, Kee Vos. He stormed into her father's house on the Keizersgracht and held his hand over a candle yelling, 'Let me see her for as long as I can hold my hand in the flame.' But Kee had fled. He was thrown out of home and went to The Hague, where he met members of the Hague School of painting, a movement characterized by muddy colours and gloomy skies. He was given lessons by one of its leading members, Anton Mauve (a cousin by marriage), and was also much influenced by Jozef Isradls' earthy studies of peasants. He was especially friendly with George Breitner, who later became known as one of the best Amsterdam Impressionists. They discovered a mutual interest in Zola and together drew the street life in the seedier parts of town. An uncle who had commissioned twelve views of the city was horrified by Vincent's unconventional approach and refused to pay up. The relationship with Mauve grew tense when Van Gogh began to reject the older painter's advice, and family relations soured on a wider scale when it became known that he was living with the prostitute Sien Hoornik 'in order to reform her'.

In September 1883 Van Gogh suddenly left The Hague for the countryside of Drenthe in the north of Holland. He had begun to paint in oils, but still with a muddy Dutch palette. The good people of Drenthe thought him a dangerous lunatic and a tramp, and refused to pose for him—so this became a period of landscapes with small figures in the distance. After a few months, loneliness drove him to a reconciliation with his parents and he went back south to live with them in Nuenen. Weavers and peasants in the surrounding Brabant farmland were his dominant motif. The period culminated in the dim glow and gravy browns of *The Potato Eaters* (1885). Van Gogh loved this 'real peasant picture'—he felt you could smell the bacon, smoke and potato steam.

In *The Old Church Tower at Nuenen*, the tower stands crooked and solitary in a flat, empty churchyard, crows flutter against the overcast sky. Van Gogh painted it in May 1885, a few months after his father, an unpopular preacher in a declining sect had been buried there, and just before it was demolished and all the wood—including the graveyard crosses—sold to peasants. *Open Bible, Extinguished Candle and Book* (1885) has been seen as Vincent's homage to their difficult relationship.

Margot Begemann, a neighbour, took poison after her family had refused permission for her to marry Vincent. She survived, but Vincent got the blame and the village turned against him. He went to Antwerp, studied Rubens, covered his walls with Japanese prints and enrolled in the academy—which he left a few months later without ever learning of the academy's decision to demote him to the beginners' class. He then went to Paris, and moved inwith his brother, Theo. The first few canvases in Paris (such as *View over Paris*, 1886) still use the Dutch browns and greys. But when Theo introduced him to a few Impressionist friends, the shock of their fresh, bright canvases changed Vincent for life. At first the colour creeps in gradually (*Woman Sitting in the Café du Tambourin*, 1887) but soon he is copying the flat colours of the Japanese prints and painting some of the familiar bright self-portraits. He began to long for harder light and a less hectic milieu than Paris could offer. Writing to his sister Wil about *Self-portrait at the Easel* (1888), he draws her attention to his sad expression. He's had enough of Paris and wants the sun.

On 20 February 1888 Vincent escaped to the Mediterranean warmth of Arles in the south of France. Here in the famous 'Yellow House', which he shared for a while with Gauguin, his best known works were painted. It is hard to believe that the raucous yellows and bright reds and blues of *Harvest at La Crau* were painted only three years after *The Potato Eaters*. Look closely at one of the versions of *Sunflowers*. Between the greens and yellows are bright streaks of ice blues, mauves and reds—colours you never notice in the reproductions. Portraits of the postman, Roulin, and his wife are drenched in sun and colour. Even the *Night Café* has a bright, steamy heat. The solitary *Sower at Arles* works under an enormous yellow orb in a green and pink sky. The most ordinary things around him evoke intense response. Vincent's *Bedroom at Arles* is filled with a brilliant light but the smooth paintwork, the mauves and blues of the walls have a calming effect.

Van Gogh was very excited by Gauguin's arrival on 20 October 1888 and went to great pains to furnish his room comfortably. The money to do this, of course, came from Theo. *Gauguin's Chair* shows a piece Vincent bought for his friend (elaborate in comparison with his own). On the seat are novels intended to indicate Gauguin's spirituality and modernism. A candle burns as well as the gas light, to suggest Gauguin's fiery nature. Together they visited nearby towns such as Les Saintes-Maries-de-la-Mer, where Vincent painted *Boats on the Beach*. The small red, green and blue boats had reminded him of flowers.

Gauguin's stay was not a happy one. The two artists had tempestuous arguments. After a particularly violent dispute on Christmas Eve, Vincent threatened Gauguin with a razor, then slashed off his own right ear and presented it to a prostitute who had complimented it. Gauguin left for Paris. Another nervous crisis followed Van Gogh's recuperation, and he was voluntarily admitted to the asylum of St-Paul-de-Mausole at Saint-Rémy. Paintings from this period—usually of fields around the asylum, the hospital garden or of individual trees and flowers—are in softer hues. In February 1890 Vincent painted *Branches of an Almond Tree in Blossom* for Theo's newly born son— blossom-laden branches stand out against an eggshell blue background.

By May he felt well enough to leave the asylum, though he could only bear Paris for three days. He travelled to Auvers-sur-Oise where an eccentric art-lover, Dr Gachet, promised to keep an eye on him. But Vincent became more and more overwrought: his colours became harder, brush strokes more violent. In *Crows in the Wheatfields* (July 1890) it seems difficult for the birds to fly into the thick, dark sky. A path curves and goes nowhere. One of his last paintings, *Roots and Tree Trunks*, has even more disorientating perspectives and thick layers of paint in unexpected colours. The painter seems completely self-engrossed, and the viewer is quite alienated.

On 27 July Vincent went into the fields and shot himself, but he bungled even this. He staggered back to the inn where he was staying and died on 29 July, in Theo's arms. After a short illness, Theo himself died six months later, at the age of 32. The brothers are buried side by side in the churchyard at Auvers-sur-Oise.

Dedication, or desperation, drove Theo's widow—Johanna van Gogh-Bonger—to promote the works stacked all over her apartment. The art world began to take notice. In 1891 there was an exhibition in Brussels, followed by numerous others all over the Netherlands and in Paris. After Johanna's death in 1925 her son, Vincent's namesake, took over the collection and in 1931 put it on permanent exhibition in the Stedelijk Museum in Amsterdam. To prevent the break-up of the collection after his death, the Van Gogh Foundation was formed in 1960 and set about building the present museum. With three members of the Van Gogh family on the board of the foundation, there's a feeling that it's still very much a family concern—and Vincent, once the black sheep, is again part of the Establishment.

changes frequently, but you can usually follow his development through some rather conventional Dutch landscapes, with all the expected perspectives, and studies of gnarled hands and heavily jowled peasant faces to the wild movement of *Women Dancing* (1885). Millet's *Labours of the Field* and woodcuts by Hiroshige and Kesai Yeisen clearly had an influence on some of Van Gogh's better known oils. The museum has an exceptionally good library, where you can view photographs of Vincent's letters to Theo. Training courses, and all sorts of activities to help working artists, are held regularly. (*Details from the museum.*)

> *Turn right out of the museum past the quirky little statue of Van Gogh (by André Schaller, 1962) towards* **Coster Diamonds**, *on the corner of Hobbemastraat (open daily 9–5; adm free).*

Jews fleeing persecution in Antwerp set up the diamond-polishing industry in Amsterdam in the 16th century. Roaring trade with South Africa established it in the 19th century. (Diamond-cutters would light their cigars with a $f10$ note, more than the average weekly wage.) The city is still a focus for diamond-dealing and processing. This means you can buy the gems for half the price you'd pay in London or New York. All over the city factories invite you in to see the craftsmen at work in order to lure you into their salerooms.

Coster Diamonds is one of the biggest. The 'Koh-I-Noor' (Mountain of Light), one of the prize gems in the British crown jewels, was cut here, and there's a glassy replica in the exhibition hall. Smart, uniformed hostesses conduct you on a short tour through the cutting and polishing works (done with whizzing discs coated with diamond dust and olive oil) and then propel you past a room temptingly labelled 'Self-Service' (it turns out to be a café) into the jewellery shop. It's an interesting ten minutes, though if you want to buy it might be worth shopping around (*see* p.219).

> *Turn left down the side of the Coster building into Hobbemastraat, and left again into* **Pieter Cornelisz. Hooftstraat**.

Amsterdam's most chic shopping street is named after a 17th-century poet. It's one of the few streets in the city where you can confidently window-shop without fear of stepping in dog turds. There are a few exotic delis, certificated Delft porcelain at Focke & Meltzer (No.65) and some elegant, but dull, cafés. Mostly it's clothes: shops for the hip toddler or the fashion-anxious adolescent. If you're past voting age then things range from well-cut classics to the *outré* (well, almost). All the favourite names (Armani, Gucci, Hamnett) can be found. Some (like MaxMara and Stephane Kelian) have their own shops. P. C. Hooftstraat and Van Baerlestraat, which crosses it further up, are also home to some of the better Dutch designers—Edgar Vos, Rob Kroner and Sissy Boy.

> *P. C. Hooftstraat leads right into the* **Vondelpark**.

Joost van Vondel (1582–1674; pronounced in the way an old English army officer might say 'fondle') is proclaimed the Dutch answer to Shakespeare. He excelled in ornate poems in celebration of public events, clocking up over a thousand lines for the opening of the Town Hall alone. The lack of action in his dramas is notorious: he went in for static pictorial representations accompanied by long flowery descriptions of anything exciting. His play *Gijsbrecht van Amstel* is a Dutch literary classic. It's said that one of the scenes inspired Rembrandt's *Night Watch*. By all accounts the Master would have had quite enough time to paint it during the performance. From humble beginnings in his father's busy hosiery shop on the edge of the red-light district, Vondel built up a considerable reputation and small fortune. The former counted for little in mercantile Amsterdam when his son squandered the latter. At the age of 70 he had to go back to work in the city pawnbrokers. He was sacked after 10 years' service for writing poetry in office hours and finally, in his eighties, was granted a state pension. He died at 92 of hypothermia, and suggested his own epitaph:

> *Hier ligt Vondel zonder Rouw,*
> *Hij is gestorven van de kou.*
>
> Here lies Vondel, without regret [or unmourned],
> He was killed by the cold.

During the so-called 'Second Golden Age' at the end of the 19th century, when the butter market was turned into Rembrandtplein and the neighbourhood around the museums was being developed as an upmarket residental area, some local burghers got together to commemorate the poet by creating the Vondelpark. It's a large park by Amsterdam standards and J. D. Kocher's informal English landscaping gives it calm, graceful lines and wide perspectives. Curved tree-lined avenues, irregularly shaped lakes and ponds, little furrow-like paths through shrubberies, hidden gardens and wide stretches of lawn attract Amsterdammers from all over the city—especially at weekends. A lone accordionist sits on a bench and plays for the ducks. Refugee guitarists from South America play heartrending tunes, homesick for a stronger sunlight. Jugglers meet to learn, practise and show off. There's a party atmosphere whenever the sun shines, and in the summer the festivities go on well into the night with concerts, theatre performances and an open-air cinema. On holidays (especially Queen's Day) enjoyment reaches carnival pitch.

There are dainty bridges, a few sculptural surprises and some odd architecture to catch your eye. Entering the park, you can see, across the pond, one of the more attractive examples of Nieuwe Zakelijkheid (Functionalist) architecture: H. J. Baanders' **'t Ronde Blauwe Theehuis** (Round Blue Teahouse), a cross between a pagoda and a flying saucer that seems to hover over the water. Across the way Vondel himself, in badly fitting laurels, looks gouty, prosperous and entirely oblivious of the Muses playing at his ankles. His ornate pedestal was made in 1867 by P. J. H. Cuypers (architect of the Centraal Station and Rijksmuseum).

The pavilion (to your right as you enter the park) was designed in 1881 by P. J. and W. Hamer, and is now the **Netherlands Film Museum** *(no exhibition—cinema shows from the archive only, details published in listings magazines).*

The first director, Jan de Vaal, was a voracious but secretive collector. He hoarded his treasures and seemed wary of the outside world. The result was that no one bothered about the film museum until the dynamic duo—director Hoos Blotkamp and film buff Eric de Kuyper—took over in the late 1980s and discovered an archive of world significance. Funding was secured, the building was revamped, the long process of cataloguing begun (unearthing such gems as hand-coloured silent movies) and the occasional screenings were boosted to three times a day. There are all sorts of special events and films are shown in the original language. On summer Saturdays there are free screenings on the terrace (*around 10pm*), when you can buy a beer and giggle at Charlie Chaplin or Abbott and Costello. The main hall is worth a peek. Its interior is from Amsterdam's first cinema, the Cinema Parisien built in 1910. The Parisien had declined ungracefully into a porn pit when the daughter of the orginal owner heard, in 1987, that it was about to be gutted by the hotel next door. Armed with coffee flask and screwdriver she went to rescue the interior (still intact after a 1930s redecoration) and, aided by the Monuments Trust, the old atmosphere was bottled and transferred to the Film Museum. The library, with a good selection of magazines and reference works and a stash of posters and publicity material, is in the building alongside the pavilion (*open Tues–Fri 10–5, Sat 11–5, adm free*).

Leave the park by the gate next to the Film Museum. The grand 19th-century Gothic of the **Vondelkerk** *(Heilige Hartkerk) fills a tiny oval in Vondelstraat. The architect P. J. H. Cuypers was highly respected for his churches, and this is acknowledged as one of his best. Unfortunately it's been converted to offices, so the interior is lost. Turn left down Vondelstraat. The houses at Nos.73–9 were also designed by Cuypers. The tiled tableaux on the wall show the architect, the mason and the jealous critic. The motto translates as: 'Jan conceives it, Piet realizes it, Claes tears it apart. Oh, who cares?'*

Further up Vondelstraat, at No.140, through the arch and up a long passage lies one of Amsterdam's best kept secrets. As you walk up towards the black door at the end of the passage, you'll notice a clue—the earth and cumin-musty smell of horses. Open the door and *immediately you are in the vast, light and eerily silent **Hollandse Manege** (open daily, usually from 10am–midnight).*

The architect, A. L. van Gendt (who also designed the Concertgebouw), was influenced by the Spanish Riding School in Vienna. The beautifully plastered interior, with horses' heads worked into the classical design and elegant open iron roofing, comes as a complete surprise.

Walk up the wide staircase (to the left) past marble vases and gilded mirrors, and you come to two more doors.

The one marked 'Tribune' leads to a balcony overlooking the arena. Sawdust muffles all sound and the occasional sharp command from the instructor is all that breaks the thick silence. The door marked 'Foyer' takes you to a café that runs the width of the building. It has the relaxed grandeur of a palace stables. The wooden floor is dusty; there's even an odd wisp of straw. The tall smoke-yellowed walls are encrusted with plaster flowers and graces. An eighteen-stick brass candelabra hangs from the ceiling. A brass stallion shies at the clock on the mantelpiece. More gilded mirrors. You can see the horses in the arena through glass doors all up one side of the café—and the drinks are the cheapest in town.

Double back along Vondelstraat and on to the busy Stadhouderskade. On the way you might like to duck down Roemer Vischerstraat (turn right at Eerste Constantijn Huygensstraat, then first left) to see a row of quaint 19th-century houses (Nos.20–30a) designed to illustrate seven national architectural styles: German, French, Spanish, Italian, Russian, Dutch and English.

*Across Stadhouderskade, in the lower branches of a tree opposite the Barbizon Centre Hotel, is another of Amsterdam's secrets. Once you've spotted it, cross the bridge over the Singelgracht to **Leidseplein**. As you do so you come to the **American Hotel**.*

The jutting balconies and odd protruding windows are a Dutch interpretation of an original Art Nouveau design. The architect, W. Kromhout, is considered a forerunner of the fanciful Amsterdam School (*see p.154–5*). The writers and artists who used the **Café Américain** (*open daily 10am–midnight*) for most of this century have fled the tourist armies of the Leidseplein, but it's still worth a visit for the glass Japanese parasol lampshades and patterned windows that filter the hard Amsterdam light into a soft and playful kaleidoscope.

*Next door is the **Stadsschouwburg (Municipal Theatre)**, open nightly; backstage tours (1 hour) in summer daily at noon; adm f5.*

State theatres in Amsterdam were usually out in the sticks, and kept burning down. The first one on this site was built in 1774 (when Leidseplein was on the edge of town) and, after suffering the usual fate, was replaced by the present building in the late 19th century. The new building was designed by Jan Springer, the bohemian kingpin of Architectura et Amicitia, a wickedly unrestrained artists' society. Budget cuts put a stop to his more florid decorations, yet still the public disapproved. Springer sulked and virtually abandoned his career. The building has a small stage and the new Muziektheater on Waterlooplein has rather stolen its thunder, but it continues to host local and international productions.

Leidseplein is Amsterdam's tourist vortex with more than the usual complement of British boys in Union Jack shorts learning the strength of Dutch lager. Fire-eaters and itinerant musicians busk while your pockets are picked, though at night the atmosphere improves a little as the square becomes the festive hub of late-night transport. As a 17th-century traveller cautioned, 'Here be sure to furnish yourself with money.' The neon alleys leading off the square are lined with expensive and nasty restaurants and nightclubs with names like 'Cash'. Leidsestraat, the northern exit, is clogged wtih pedestrians and bicycles travelling on no particular side until, bells clanging, a yellow tram hurtles down the central rails scattering all. Mainly airline offices, 24-hour bureaux de change and shops selling clogs and Taiwan Delft, Leidsestraat is happily avoided.

Escape Leidseplein down Kleine Lijnbaansgracht. This you do by taking the main road opposite the Stadsschouwburg, but keeping to the smaller left-hand fork following the canal. Just before the fork you pass Amsterdam's new casino and night-life complex. It's a colourful heap of post-modernist design—an architectural style ideally suited to the wry, up-front Amsterdam temperament. What other city would allow, in its centre, a massive colonnade topped with a frieze bearing the inscription Homo Sapiens non Urinat in Ventum (Wise Men Do Not Pee In The Wind)?

*Kleine Lijnbaansgracht takes you to the **antiques shops and galleries** of the **Spiegelkwartier**, one of the two quarters in Amsterdam dedicated to one particular business (the other one being the red-light district). Turn left into Spiegelgracht and walk on to the Prinsengracht.*

The Spiegelkwartier has gone upmarket in recent years—these days even museums buy here for their collections—but it hasn't lost its charm, and the prices are still lower than in most other major cities. (There are even cheaper antiques markets at the end of the walk, and it's not too far to double back to the Spiegelkwartier should you want to look those over before buying anything.) Here you'll find shops crammed with elaborate clocks, solemn rows of carved wooden dressers and ornate gilded furniture. Enormous chandeliers hang at eye-level, and gold, silver and colourful gems shine at you from all sides. Tucked amongst all this grandeur, you can still find idiosyncratic little shops, obviously the domain of a single collector. Aalderink (No.15) has a sparse but expertly selected range of oriental pieces and Africana. Anneke Schat (No.20a) makes delicate, sculpted jewellery inspired by spiders' webs and butterflies and much favoured by Dutch glitterati and the royal family.

*Continue over the bridge to **Nieuwe Spiegelstraat**, where the price tags begin to get serious.*

If your souvenir budget runs to multiple noughts you could pop into Elisabeth den Bieman de Haas for a little Chagall litho or bright modern oil from COBRA, the post-war expressionist movement (see p.59). Roel Houwink (No.57) has one of those shops you could potter about in for ages—everything from musical boxes to escutcheons nicked from under the nose of a Prince of Orange. Kramers (No.64) has tangles of old jewellery and trinkets, barrels of clay pipe bowls and a roomful of Delft tiles ranging from the 15th to 20th centuries.

*Turn left up the left-hand side of **Keizersgracht**, one of the three grand 17th-century canals, where there are a number of galleries showing 20th-century Dutch art.*

Even if you show no signs of buying, gallery-owners are usually friendly and informative and it's a pleasant way to learn. At No.546 nothing of the façade, except the windows, has changed since it was built in 1760. The bell-gable is a good example of the playful cake-icing Louis XV decoration. Walk on as far as Leidsestraat. The ornately decorated building that cuts the corner with Leidsestraat is German inspired—the Dutch were more into solid right angles at corners. A frieze of fat naked babies, lurking in shrubberies and grumpily pushing carts and canoes, runs around the wall. The bust commemorates the 17th-century poet Pieter Cornelisz. Hooft.

*Cross to the other side of the canal. The pompous building on this corner was built on the site of Van Gogh's uncle's art shop for an insurance company in the late 19th century, but is now the refined **Metz** department store.*

Inside, you can mount stairs, passing racks of tasteful kitchenware and mounds of Liberty prints. As you climb, the atmosphere becomes increasingly rarefied and the floors emptier and emptier. By the time you're nearing the top, there's hardly anything for sale at all. The few pieces of designer furniture scattered about look more like museum pieces than anything you could put in the dining-room. At the top is a café designed by Gerrit Rietveld. Gazing through its glass cupola, you have a rare opportunity to view Amsterdam's spider's web from on high.

Carry on up the right-hand side of the Keizersgracht and across the Leidsegracht.

The startlingly large windows of the public library at No.440 (built 1897) originally lit a clothing design studio and factory. It must have been the world's most gracious sweatshop. The bank at No.452 was once a private residence. Designed by Outshoorn in 1860 it is one of the last of a series of grand canal houses, influenced by French and Italian architecture, that were built by the three great domestic architects—Vingboons, van Campen and Outshoorn—over a period of 200 years. One of Vingboons's early houses can be seen further up the canal at No.319 (built 1639), the façade virtually untouched. It's the first one in which he combined classic elements (the Doric pilasters) with the traditional Dutch style.

> *Short streets lead off from both sides of the three bridges beyond the Leidsegracht. These alleys offer the most **intriguing shopping** in Amsterdam. Keep a steady progress up the Keizersgracht, ducking down each in turn, only as far as the next canal.*

The first on the right, Huidenstraat, has trendy **second-hand** clothes stores and shops crammed with lamps and light fittings—from original Art Nouveau to bright and bulbous 1960s products. In the Third World Charity shop you can buy all sorts of cheerfully coloured clothes and Zulu weaponry, and Pompadour at No.5 sells impossibly tempting **hand-made chocolates**. Across the bridge in Runstraat is the Witte Tanden Winkel (White Teeth Shop) for nothing but the tooth—psychedelic and electric toothbrushes, pastes galore, curious aids and sound clinical advice. Just the place to expiate your sins after Pompadour.

Furniture from **antiques shops** tumbles out into the streets, though they're not always as cheap as the image suggests.

> *On the way up to the second bridge, you pass the imposing **Felix Meritis** building (No.324 on the left-hand side; open daily 5pm–12am).*

It was built in 1778 to house an arts and scientific society founded in the spirit of Voltaire and Rousseau. With an observatory, library, laboratories and a small concert hall, the Felix Meritis Foundation became the cultural centre of the Dutch Enlightenment. When Napoleon made his triumphal entry to Amsterdam, he was punted up the canal and ushered with pride into the building. He got no further than the foyer, spat on the floor, said the place stank of tobacco smoke, and strutted back to the boat. Towards the end of the 19th century the society went into terminal decline.The building was later used as the Communist Party headquarters, but won back its cultural prominence in the 1970s when it housed the Shaffy Theatre, in the forefront of the European avant-garde. The theatre lost some of its significance and impact during the 1980s, but the Felix Meritis Society has been revived. As an arts complex and the home of Amsterdam's Summer University, the building is once again playing host artists and intellectuals from around the world.

Continue up the Keizersgracht.

Wolvenstraat, to the right of the second bridge, has more second-hand clothes shops (one with Queen Mother hats) and a **button shop** (some in such shapes and sizes that their function is barely recognizable). Berenstraat, across the bridge, is home to some of the younger, trendier **art galleries**. One, Animation Art: 'Name that Toon' (see p.182), sells storyboards and cels (the acetate originals from which cartoons are made) of everyone from Betty Boop to Winnie the Pooh. Hartenstraat (at the third bridge) has more **fashion shops** and another eccentric collector's outlet—this time **vintage electronic equipment**. The jolly naked illustrations of Eddie Varekamp that have found their way on to T-shirts and coffee mugs are on sale from his studio shop (No.30). Reestraat has a *poppendokter* (**doll's doctor**). Puppets hang from the ceiling, dolls of all sorts crowd the window and a disconcerting catalogue of dolls' faces hangs on the wall. Next door is a **candle shop**. Coloured, scented, sculpted, altar candles and erotic candles hang from the ceiling, are stacked on shelves or poked into odd candlesticks and elaborate candelabra—and they're not at silly prices.

At the end of Reestraat cross the Prinsengracht and turn left down the far side. Walk along to Looiersgracht. On the way down have a look at the house at No.300, nicknamed 't Vosje (the fox) after a 17th-century furrier's on the site. Above the doors a red fox holds a bird in its mouth. There's another below the hoist beam. Turn right into Looiersgracht. At No.38 is the **Rommelmarkt** *(literally 'rubbish market'), an indoor flea-market that seems almost subterranean.*

Entering through a small street door, you seem to walk forever down a long, dim corridor lined with piles of old toys, tea caddies, zippo lighters, 1960s records and magazines. The further you penetrate, the more precious things become. You might even pick up some antique Japanese lacquerware or an Art Deco vase. Up the stairs you're assaulted by the bright light that streams in through skylights. Here the real 'rommel' lies spread out on tables. It all seems a bit unwanted: there's an air of dead people's things. Perhaps it's the light. Perhaps it's time to leave.

If you double back down one of alleys and turn left down Elandsgracht you come to the De Looier Indoor Antiques Market, a collectors' and dealers' market pitched halfway between Rommelmarket junk and Spiegelkwartier splendour. Stallholders have a lively commercial spirit—they even have their own newspaper and weekly bridge drives. There are regular specialist fairs. In this honeycomb of little stands selling furniture, glass, old lace and even older Delftware, Walk VI fades to FINIS.

Museums and Galleries

Amsterdam has over 40 museums. You can admire world art treasures, or poke about in back rooms crammed with one hoarder's booty. Most museums (except the Rijksmuseum, Van Gogh and Stedelijk Museum) are closed Mondays, and swarm with schoolchildren on Wednesday afternoons. Many keep Sunday hours on public holidays, but some close entirely.

All but seven of the museums are privately owned and nearly all charge an entrance fee. Most offer discounts to children, but not all offer reductions to students. If you intend visiting more than one or two, the **Annual Museum Card** or **CJP** (youth pass) is a must (*see* **Practical A–Z**, 'Discounts').

A **Museum Boat** will chug you pleasantly along the canals between 16 of Amsterdam's museums. Tickets valid for a day (*f*25) also entitle you to discounts on some admissions. Boats leave every 45 minutes, 10–3.15 daily, from one of six stops: Centraal Station (main boarding point and office, © 622 2181); Prinsengracht/ Egelantiersgracht (Anne Frank Huis); Singelgracht (Van Gogh, Stedelijk, Rijksmuseum); Herengracht/Leidsegracht (Bijbels, Fodor, Amsterdams Historisch, Allard Pierson); Amstel/ Zwanenburgwal (Rembrandthuis, Jewish Historical); Oosterdok/ Kattenburgergracht (Tropenmuseum, Werf 't Kromhout).

Public Museums and Galleries

Agnietenkapel, Oudezijds Voorburgwal 231, © 525 3339 (*open Mon–Fri 9–5, though phone first to check; adm f3.50*). Prints and trivia relating to Amsterdam university life. The 15th-century chapel is infinitely more interesting than the collection it houses (*see* **Walk I**).

Ajax Museum, Arena Boulevard 3, © 311 1333 (*open daily 9–6; adm f12.50, under 13s f10*). Ephemera relating to Amsterdam's most famous sports team.

Allard Pierson Museum, Oude Turfmarkt 127, © 525 2556 (*open Tues–Fri 10–5, Sat, Sun 1–5; adm f9.50, children f3*). Superb archaeological collection, poorly presented. Few English texts, but children like the Roman chariot.

Amsterdams Historisch Museum, Kalverstraat 92, © 523 1822 (*open Mon–Fri 10–5, Sat and Sun 11–5; adm f11, under 16s f5.50*). DIY carillons, paintings that play music, and bits and pieces dug up around town making an accessible introduction to the city's history (*see* **Walk I**).

Anne Frank Huis, Prinsengracht 263, © 556 7100 (*open Sept–May Mon–Sat 9–5, Sun 10–5; June–Aug Mon–Sat 9–7, Sun 10–7; adm f10, under 18s f5, under 10s free*). The building which housed the Frank family's hide-out has been restored to its Second World War condition, and an exhibition on racial repression occupies the building next door (*see* **Walk III**).

Artis Museum (Zoo Museum), Plantage Kerklaan 38–40, ✆ 523 3400 (*open daily 9–5; adm included in zoo ticket: ƒ23.50, children ƒ15.50*). Slides and stuffed animals in a corner of the zoo.

Aviodome, Schiphol Centre, Schiphol Airport, ✆ 406 8000 (*open Oct–March Tues–Fri 10–5, Sat and Sun noon–5; April–Sept daily 10–5; adm ƒ12.50, under 13s ƒ10*). Aeronautics and space travel. Models from a flimsy 1903 Wright Flyer to American Mercury capsules—some open to clamber in.

Beurs van Berlage Museum, Damrak 277, ✆ 530 4141 (*museum open Tues–Sun 10–4; adm varies*). Berlage's epoch-marking Stock Exchange houses a small display on the history of the building and larger travelling exhibitions.

Bijbels Museum (Bible Museum), Herengracht 366, ✆ 624 2436 (*open Mon–Sat 10–5, Sun 1–5; adm ƒ5, under 16s ƒ3.50*). Another museum that is worth visiting more for the building than the collection. The 17th-century Vingboons house, complete with original kitchen and 18th-century ceiling paintings by Jacob de Wit, far outshines old Dutch Bibles (*see* **Walk III**).

COBRA Museum, Sandbergplein 1–3 Amstelveen, Tram 5, 51; ✆ 547 5050 (*open Tues–Sun 11–5; adm ƒ7.50, under 16s ƒ3.50*). Permanent displays and temporary exhibitions focusing on one of the most important modern Dutch art movements (*see* **Art and Architecture**).

Elektrische Museumtramlijn (Electric Tramline Museum), Amstelveenseweg 264, ✆ 673 7538 (*open April–Oct, Sun 10–6; July–Aug,Tues–Sat 1–4; adm ƒ5 (return), ƒ3 (single), under 12s half-price*). A museum on the move. Antique trams rattle along a 20-minute ride to the Amsterdam Forest.

Hash & Marijuana Museum, Oudezijds Achterburgwal 148, ✆ 623 5961 (*open daily 11am–10pm; adm ƒ6*). History of dope—exhibits are occasionally confiscated by the authorities (*see* **Walk I**).

Heineken Brewery Museum, Stadhouderskade 78, ✆ 523 9666 (*guided tours only: Mon–Fri 9.30 and 11am; June 1–Sept 15 also at 1 and 2.30pm, Saturdays in July and August also noon and 2pm; adm ƒ2. Tours may be booked out in advance in high season—phone to check*). Copper vats, dray horses and a glass or two of free beer (*see* **Walk V**).

Holland Experience, Jodenbreestraat 6, ✆ 422 2233 (*open daily 9am–10pm; adm ƒ17.50 adults, ƒ15 under-12s*). Multimedia show and exhibition on Holland's top sites, including an 80,000-litre dyke-burst (*see* **Walk III**).

Joods Historisch Museum (Jewish Historical Museum), Jonas Danidl Meyerplein 2–4, ✆ 625 4229 (*open daily 11–5, closed Yom Kippur; adm ƒ8, under 18s ƒ3.50, under 10s free*). Converted synagogue complex (*see* **Walk III**).

Kattenkabinet (Cat Museum), Herengracht 497, ✆ 626 5378 (*open Mon–Fri 10–2, Sat, Sun 1–5; adm ƒ10*). Art with a feline theme in a restored canal house.

Madame Tussauds, Peek & Cloppenburg Building, Dam 20, ✆ 622 9949 (*open daily 10–5.30, July and Aug 10–7.30; adm ƒ17.50, under 15s ƒ15, under 5s free, family ticket ƒ57.50*). Waxworks; some good re-creations of 17th-century life (*see* **Walk I**).

Max Euwe Centrum, Max Euweplein 30, ✆ 625 7017 (*open Tues–Fri and first Sat of the month 10.30–4; adm free*). Chess memorabilia and the chance to play the game with live people or clever computers.

Museum Amstelkring ('Our Lord in the Attic'), Oudezijds Voorburgwal 40, ✆ 624 6604 (*open Mon–Sat 10–5, Sun 1–5; adm f7.50*). Magical 17th-century clandestine church and restored canal house (*see* **Walk I**).

Museum van Loon, Keizersgracht 672, ✆ 624 5255 (*open Fri–Mon 11–5; adm f7.50*). The most charming of the canal house museums, with a cosy, lived-in atmosphere.

Museum Willet-Holthuysen, Herengracht 605, ✆ 523 1870 (*open Mon–Fri 10–5, Sat and Sun 11–5; adm f7.50, children f3.75*). Grand, if over-embellished, canal-house museum (*see* **Walk II**).

Nationaal Vakbondsmuseum (Trade Unions Museum), Henri Polaklaan 9, ✆ 624 1166 (*open Tues–Fri 11–5, Sat and Sun 1–5; adm f5*). One of the best examples of Berlage's architecture after the Beurs (*see* **Walk I**) houses a collection of interest only for those in quest of knowledge about the Dutch labour movement (*see* **Walk III**).

Nederlands Filmmuseum, Vondelpark 3, ✆ 589 1400 (*Library open Tues–Fri 10–5, Sat 11–5; adm free; see* **Walk VI**.). Screenings from the archives daily.

Nederlands Scheepvaart Museum, Kattenburgerplein 1, ✆ 523 2222 (*open Tues–Sun 10–5; adm f14.50, under 18s f8*). The Royal Barge, a reproduction 17th-century sailing ship, and rooms and rooms of maritime models (*see* **Walk IV**).

Nederlands Theater Instituut, Herengracht 168, ✆ 551 3300 (*open Tues–Fri 11–5, Sat and Sun 1–5; adm f7.50, under 17s f4, under 7s free*). A beautiful canal house (18th-century ceiling paintings by Jacob de Wit) with enticingly presented costumes, scenery and backstage equipment (*see* **Walk III**).

New Metropolis Science & Technology Center, Oosterdok 2, ✆ (0900) 919 1100 (*open Tues–Sun 10–6, Sat open until 9pm; adm f24, after 4pm f14, under 17s f16*). All sorts of interactive equipment in a giant ship-shaped museum designed by Renzo Piano (*see* **Walk IV**).

Open Haven Museum, KNSMlaan 311, ✆ 418 5522; bus 32 (*open Wed–Fri 1–5; adm f5*). Journals, uniforms and seafaring paraphernalia celebrating the age of steamship travel.

Pianola Museum, Westerstraat 106, ✆ 627 9624 (*open Sun 1–5 only; adm f7.50*). Pianolas and player-pianos demonstrated using part of a massive hoard of music rolls.

Rembrandthuis, Jodenbreestraat 4–6, ✆ 520 0400 (*open Mon–Sat 10–5, Sun 1–5; adm f7.50, under 17s f5, under 10s free*). Rembrandt's house faithfully restored to its 17th-century glory. Good selection of Rembrandt's etchings in the modern wing next door (*see* **Walk III**).

Rijksmuseum, Stadhouderskade 42, ✆ 674 4700 (*open daily 10–5; adm f15, under 18s f7.50*). Dutch art from its earliest moments to the 19th century, as well as a warren of rooms stacked with Delft, furniture and ecclesiastical knick-knacks (*see* **Walk II**).

Sex Museum, Damrak 18, ✆ 622 8376 (*open daily 10am–11.30pm; adm f3.95*). Lurid evidence that the pornographer's imagination has changed remarkably little over the centuries.

Stedelijk Museum, Paulus Potterstraat 13, ✆ 573 2911 (*open daily 11–5; adm f9, under 17s f4.50*). Lively municipal museum with an up-to-the-minute collection of modern art (*see* **Walk V**).

Tattoo Museum, Oudezijds Achterburgwal 130, © 625 1565 (*open Tues–Sun noon–6; adm f6*). Not as tacky and sensationalist as one might expect, but a genuinely well-researched survey of the history of tattooing and body art in a variety of cultures (*see* **Walk I**).

Tropenmuseum (Tropical Museum), Linnaesusstraat 2, © 568 8200 (*open Mon–Fri 10–5, Sat and Sun noon–5; adm f12.50, under 18s f7.50*). Tapes, models and life-sized installations evoke the atmosphere of life in the Third World. The splendid 1920s building also houses exhibits of ethnic musical instruments and reminders of Holland's colonial past.

Van Gogh Museum, Paulus Potterstraat 7, © 570 5200 (*open daily 10–6; adm f12.50, under 18s f5*). Over 200 of Vincent's paintings and 500 drawings as well as work by his contemporaries (*see* **Walk VI**).

Verzetsmuseum (Museum of the Resistance), Plantage Kerklaan 61a, © 620 2535 (*open Tues–Fri 10–5, Sat and Sun 1–5; adm f8, under 18s f4*). Newspaper clippings, photographs, tape-recordings and makeshift secret equipment give intimate insight into the 1940s Resistance movement.

Werf 't Kromhout (shipyard museum), Hoogte Kadijk 147, © 627 6777 (*open Mon–Fri 10–4; adm f3.50, under 12s f1.50*). The working shipyard restores antique vessels—but most of the exhibits are rather esoteric bits of patent diesel engines (*see* **Walk IV**).

Woonbootmuseum (Houseboat Museum), Prinsengracht opp. 296, © 427 0750 (*open Tues–Sun 10–5; adm f3.75, children under 152 cm f2.50*). A glimpse of the nitty-gritty of life in a houseboat.

Commercial Galleries

There are over 140 commercial art galleries in Amsterdam. They're scattered all over town, though you'll find a number of the more established ones along the Keizersgracht and in the Spiegelkwartier.

The listings magazine *What's On in Amsterdam* (f3.50 from the Amsterdam Tourist Board, newsagents and hotels) will guide you to mainstream exhibitions.

For a fuller picture, pick up a copy of *Alert* (f4 from most galleries), the monthly Amsterdam gallery diary. Although this is in Dutch, the pages of photographs, clear symbolic coding and detailed maps give you a good idea of what's showing around town and where to find it.

Look out also for 'Open Atelier' posters—artists working in one neighbourhood will open their studios for a day, and you can wander in for a chat, a look and possibly (they hope) a happy purchase.

'Open Ateliers' are also listed on the Gallery pages ('Beeldende Kunst') of the *Uitkrant* (a 'what's-on' freebie available at cafés and from the Uit Buro).

Ten Contemporary Art Galleries

Carla Koch, Prinsengracht 510 (*open Wed–Sat noon–6*) Top of the list for arty glass and ceramics.

De Appel, Nieuwe Spiegelstraat 10 (*open Tues–Sun noon–5*). Innovative gallery that shows anything from artsy chairs to videos, from a spectrum that runs from lesser-known artists to famous names.

Galerie Atelier Amsterdam, Weteringschans 221 (*open Mon–Sat 10–5*). Bright and imaginative art from a group of people with mental disabilities, who also have their studio on the premises.

Mokum, Oudezijds Voorburgwal 334 (*open Wed–Sat 11–6*). Dutch realistic art—a good place to find work by Magic Realists (*see* p.59).

Rob Jurka, Singel 28 (*open Wed–Sat 1–6*). One-time establishment-rattler Rob Jurka has linked up with go-getting digger-out of new talent Barbara Farber to make one of the most respected galleries on the Amsterdam scene.

SBK Kunstuitleen, Nieuwe Herengracht 23 (*open Tues, Thurs 1–8, Fri 1–5, Sat 9–5*). Art library that hires out original work by Amsterdam artists from *f*25 per month—and you get the option to buy.

Stedelijk Museum Bureau Amsterdam, Rozenstraat 59 (*open Tues–Sun 11–5*). An offshoot of the museum that exhibits and sells work by challenging up-and-coming artists on the international scene.

Swart, Van Breestraat 23 (*open Wed–Sat 3–6*). Run by the queen of the city's art scene. She rules with a rod of iron and her exhibitions seldom fail to excite.

Torch, Lauriergracht 94 (*open Thurs–Sat 2–6*). Specializes in video and photography, but is currently a leading light in other media too.

W 139, Warmoesstraat 139 (*open Wed–Sun 1–6*). Cavernous space used by fledgling artists. Sometimes the work is dire, sometimes plain curious—but occasionally you'll find a gem, and will seldom be bored (see **Walk I**). (*Undergoing extensive rebuilding, so not all of the gallery will be open.*)

Some Specialists

ABK (Amsterdam Sculptors' Collective) (*open Thurs–Sun 12–5*). Sculpture of all sizes (*see* **Walk IV**).

Animation Art, Berenstraat 19 (*open Tues–Fri 11–6, Sat 10–5*). Original drawings of everyone from Popeye to Betty Boop (*see* **Walk VI**).

The Frozen Fountain, Prinsengracht 629 (*open Mon 1–6, Tues–Fri 10–6, Sat 11–5, Thurs open until 9pm*). Household items from wastepaper baskets to sofas elevated to high art.

Food and Drink

Erasmus, the great 16th-century Dutch humanist and man of letters, was pleased to note that his fellow countrymen were not given to much wild or ferocious behaviour, treachery or deceit, indeed were 'not prone to any serious vices except, that is, a little given to pleasure, especially to feasting'. Two centuries later the national ability to tuck in and drink up was still impressive enough to shock the British—themselves no mean feasters. In 1703 the seven or so deacons of the Arnhem guild of surgeons dispatched, at one sitting, 14lb of beef, 8lb of veal, six fowl, stuffed cabbages, apples, pears, bread, pretzels, assorted nuts, 20 bottles of red wine, 12 bottles of white wine and some jugs of coffee. Today, eating is still a supreme Dutch enthusiasm, and one in which any visitor can happily join.

Paradoxically, native Dutch cuisine is not all that inspiring. The Dutch culinary clichés are *hutspot* ('hotchpotch'), a well-boiled stew that was much appreciated by starving citizens after the siege of Leiden and to be enjoyed still requires a similar state of ravenousness; and *erwtensoep*, a porridgy pea soup which comes (vegetarians beware) with bits of sausage floating in it and a side-dish of bread and raw bacon. The quality of *erwtensoep* is judged by testing whether or not your spoon will stand up on its own in the middle of the bowl. These are the staples of many a 'tourist menu', but (like the English) the Dutch have recently begun to explore more exciting avenues in their local cuisine—with game and fish especially. Other palatable traditional foods include *pannekoeken* (pancakes) with sweet or savoury fillings, and *haring* (herring) eaten raw by tossing your head back and dropping a whole fillet down your throat. If you can stomach it, this is a marvellous cure for a hangover. *Belegde broodjes* are crusty rolls filled with a delicious variety of fillings—travellers' tales of sliced beef layered on buttered bread predated anecdotes about Lord Sandwich's invention by about a century. Waffles, dripping with syrup or smothered with fruit and cream, are sold on the streets and are treacherously gooey and unmanageable, but quite irresistible. Cones of *frites* (potato chips), usually with a large dollop of mayonnaise, are ubiquitous. They're normally cooked with good-quality potatoes in clean oil.

In the absence of a stimulating local tradition, Dutch chefs have looked further afield. French cuisine first came into fashion during the Napoleonic occupation, and remains the cornerstone of many of the best kitchens. Nowadays most menus are tantalizingly eclectic, showing influences from Japan, Indonesia, Surinam and Turkey. This makes for some curious—but usually delicious—combinations. Don't be surprised to find peanut sauce, saffron pasta and oysters on the same menu. The Dutch were enjoying 'fusion cuisine' years before trendy London and New York chefs could distinguish lemon grass from lime leaves.

Ingredients are usually market-fresh and microwave cookers are pleasingly thin on the ground. Food is cooked to order in most restaurants, so expect an unhurried meal. The Dutch eat early in the evening—between 7 and 9pm—and many kitchens are closed by 10 or 11pm.

Specialist ethnic restaurants abound. Reasonable Indian and Italian food is to be had all over town, with Thai and Japanese restaurants an increasingly popular alternative. It's the culinary heritage of Holland's imperial past, however, that makes for the best ethnic binge. Treat yourself to an Indonesian *rijsttafel*—a personal banquet of rice or noodles with myriad spicy side dishes. (*See* **Language**, p.238–9, for a selection of Dutch and Indonesian food terms.)

Vegetarians will have a difficult time. The Dutch are great carnivores, and if you enquire about vegetarian dishes you're often offered *kabeljauw* (cod). However, in the 1970s the tastes of the hippies spawned a few vegetarian restaurants and more have opened recently. Chefs in better kitchens are beginning to be more imaginative with their vegetarian options, and most restaurants will have at least one vegetarian meal on the menu.

Budget eating is easy, and needn't be boring. Many restaurants offer a three-course 'Tourist Menu' for under *f*30, but you're generally better off looking out for signs advertising a *dagschotel* (dish of the day). You usually end up with an oversized white plate with some well-prepared meat and a constellation of pickles and salads. Many cafés serve food—menus change daily and often offer the best value of all (see 'Cafés', below). Best bet budget restaurants: **Axum** (Central), **Keuken van** 1870 (Central), **La Place** (Central), **Moeders Pot** (Central).

Take-away foodstalls punctuate markets and shopping streets all over town. As well as *frites*, *haring* and waffles you can sample all sorts of foreign delights: Turkish kebabs, Israeli falafel, Japanese sushi and spicy nibbles from Surinam and Indonesia. Under signs flashing *Automatiek* you can select a deep-fried croquette from a row of tiny windows displaying this and similar wares: drop in your *f*1.50, pull a lever and collect your reward. 'Snack' was originally a Dutch word. Snack Bars are the Amsterdam equivalent of street food. At worst they sell pre-prepared mushy croquettes, but at best they are tiny family-run establishments that hover in the middle ground between restaurant and take-away. Often run by immigrants, they have simple décor, a scattering of tables and some of the best foreign food in town. Try **Bird** (Thai; Zeedijk 77), **Kismet** (Turkish; Albert Cuypstraat 64), **Maoz** (Israeli falafel; Reguliersbreestraat 45), **Riaz** (Surinam; Bilderdijkstraat 193).

Amsterdam is very much a cash city. Many smaller restaurants don't accept credit cards, and there's an air of reluctance about those that do. Even some of the larger establishments don't like plastic—so it's always a good idea to check in advance. Feasting Amsterdammers and hungry tourists fill up most good restaurants pretty quickly, so it's wise to reserve a table by telephone.

The restaurants below are all graded according to the approximate price of a three-course meal, without wine. You'll find eating out cheaper than in most large cities.

∞∞	expensive	over ƒ80 (though seldom more than ƒ175)
∞	moderate	ƒ45–ƒ80
○	cheap	under ƒ45

The bill will include tax and a 15% service charge—though if you feel you've been well looked after you can leave a little extra. It's usual to leave behind any small change (or round up larger bills to the nearest ƒ5). It's worth checking out expensive restaurants, even if they seem above your budget, as many offer special three- or four-course meals for between ƒ45 and ƒ75.

Restaurants

The following list is a very personal selection from the hundreds of good restaurants Amsterdam has to offer. An exploratory wander around the Jordaan, through the alleys that criss-cross the canals (from Reestraat to Huidenstraat), or along Utrechtsestraat will reveal even more. Restaurants are listed in three areas. 'Central' refers to the semi-circle bounded by the three main canals; the Jordaan is the area in the west of the city, just beyond the canals. Restaurants in the north, south and east will be found under 'Further Afield'.

Central

∞∞ **Excelsior**, Hotel l'Europe, Nieuwe Doelenstraat 2–8, ℰ 531 1705. Grand without being pompous. Waiters in tails bring you haute cuisine classics or the very best in new Dutch cooking, and there's a superb view over the Amstel. ƒ110. Dress: jacket and tie.

∞∞ **Breitner**, Amstel 212, ℰ 627 7879 (*open till midnight; closed Sun, Mon*). An even more sublime view than from the Excelsior, with a menu that is perhaps even more imaginative. The relaxedly chic atmosphere and excellent cuisine are a great attraction to artistes from the Opera House. ƒ95.

∞∞ **Sichuan Food**, Reguliersdwarsstraat 35, ℰ 626 9327. Proud possessor of the first Michelin star awarded to a Chinese restaurant in the Netherlands. Aperitifs made from flowers, sautéed oysters with tangy sauces; local western restaurants are beginning to imitate the seafood dishes. ƒ90.

∞∞ **De Silveren Spiegel**, Kattengat 4–6, ℰ 624 6589. The building, all Delft tiles and cosy corners, dates from 1614. The visionary chef comes up with such dishes as guinea fowl with rose petal sauce, and uses prime local ingredients, such as lamb from the North Sea island of Texel (where the creatures frolic freely and eat wild herbs). Service is personal and friendly. ƒ80.

't Swarte Schaep, Korte Leidse-dwarsstraat 24, ✆ 622 3021. Up a steep staircase in a 300-year-old building with oak beams, antiques, superb wines, an eclectic cuisine and passing members of the Dutch royal family. *f*90.

De Utrechtsedwarstafel, Utrecht-sedwarsstraat 107, 625 4189 (*closed Sun, Mon*). Igor, a culinary whizz, works single-handedly in the kitchen, Hans, an expert on wines, is front-of-house. There's no menu, just a grid offering three, four or five courses, at a simple, medium or gourmet level. Wine is included in the price. You pick your level, tell them if there is anything you prefer not to eat, and wait to be surprised. Igor comes out to tell you about the meal; Hans chats about the wine, tailor-making choices as you go along. On a matrix, from *f*60 to *f*180, wines included.

Van Harte, Hartenstraat 24, ✆ 625 8500. Modest, yet excellent kitchen. Berries and wild mushrooms in the sauces, tender meats and charming service. *f*75.

Vasso, Rozenboomsteeg 12–14, ✆ 626 0158. Fresh pasta and fine Italian food in a restaurant that has the lively atmosphere of the kitchens of a faded palazzo. *f*75.

D'Vijff Vlieghen (The Five Flies), Spuistraat 294–302, ✆ 624 8369. An intriguing conglomeration of antique-filled rooms in a wonky 17th-century inn. It gets its unfortunate name from the original owner, Jan Vijff Vlieghen. In the 1950s and 1960s it was frequented by the likes of Orson Welles, Benjamin Britten, Jean Cocteau and Walt Disney. These days the restaurant rests on its laurels, and doesn't give good value for money. *f*90.

le Klas, Platform 2B, Centraal Station, ✆ 625 0131 (*see* **Walk I**). Well-prepared (though not adventurous) Dutch fare in the beautifully restored First Class restaurant. *f*60.

Centra, Lange Niezel 29, ✆ 622 3050. Busy, garish, cafeteria-like atmosphere, and the best Spanish food in town. *f*40.

De Compagnon, Guldehandsteeg 17, ✆ 620 4225. Down an alley in the red-light district, through a green door, a series of tiny rooms, perched on top of each other, filled with antique bric-à-brac, and with views across the little harbour on the Damrak. An unexpected find, romantic and intimate—but sadly the atmosphere outdoes the cuisine, which is run-of-the-mill Franco-Dutch. *f*75.

Hemelse Modder, Oude Waal 9, ✆ 624 3203 (*closed Mon*). Haunt of writers. Before you get to the divine chocolate mousse that gives the restaurant its name ('Heavenly Mud'), try some of the delicious fish or vegetarian dishes. *f*55.

Kort, Amstelveld 2, ✆ 626 1199. Freshly prepared food with simple sauces. Somewhere for the health-conscious gourmet. Quiet terrace on the water's edge, and a coolly rational Wiener Werkstätte interior. *f*60.

Krua Thai, Spuistraat 90a, ✆ 620 0623. After much audible campery in the kitchen, spectacular dishes issue forth. The hot-and-spicy beef salad is unbeatable, and the stuffed chicken wings divine. *f*60.

∞ **Maison Descartes**, Vijzelgracht 2, ℗ 622 4936. Excellent regional French cuisine in the depths of the French cultural institute, surrounded by the Delft tiles of a 17th-century Dutch kitchen. *f*75.

∞ **Memories of India**, Reguliersdwarstraat 88, ℗ 623 5710. Top-class Indian cuisine in curious sub-continental post-modern surrounds: copper palm trees and stubs of marble column. Fried pomfret, chicken with cinnamon and cardamom sauce, or searing curries. *f*65.

∞ **Pier 10**, De Ruyterkade Steiger 10 (behind Centraal Station), ℗ 624 8276. A little wooden hut, once a shipping line office, right on the end of a pier in the IJ. Watch the boats chug past as you devour scrumptious Dutch/French food. *f*70.

∞ **Rose's Cantina**, Reguliersdwarsstraat 38, ℗ 625 9797. Crowds of Bright Young Things, tasty Tex-Mex food and lethal margaritas. *f*50.

∞ **Saturnino**, Reguliersdwarsstraat 5h, ℗ 639 0102. Trendy Italian restaurant on Amsterdam's main gay street. The atmosphere is glitzy, but the food has a wholesome home-made touch.

∞ **Sluizer Visrestaurant**, Utrechtsestraat 45; and **Sluizer**, Utrechtse straat 41–3, ℗ 622 6376. Two adjacent trendy restaurants, evocative of the thirties with marble-topped tables and fringed lamps. Both are usually packed and open till midnight. The fish restaurant especially has a good reputation. *f*65.

∞ **d'Theeboom**, Singel 210, ℗ 623 8420. Georges Thubert scorns rip-off prices and culinary pretension. He runs his restaurant, in a converted canalside warehouse, in classic French style, and offers excellent value and fine cooking. *f*50.

∞ **Tujuh Maret**, Utrechtsestraat 73, ℗ 427 9865 Treat yourself to a flavoursome feast of Indonesian *rijsttafel*. The *soto ayam* (chicken broth) has a fine bouillon base, and the different chicken and meat dishes are just that—different. Beef in a mild sauce of soya and nutmeg, or a zippier version cooked with red peppers and tamarind; chicken as a tangy curry, or with a gentle coconut sauce. *f*60.

∞ **Turquoise**, Wolvenstraat 22–24, ℗ 624 2026. A bizarre combination of wood-panelled Art Nouveau décor and Turkish cuisine. Under Tiffany lamps, beside cherubs rampant, you can tuck into a feast made up of different starters or try such main courses as chicken breast with cheese and garlic. Warm, friendly service. *f*55.

∞ **Le zinc...et les dames**, Prinsengracht 999, ℗ 622 9044 (*closed Mon*). Converted 17th-century warehouse adorned with portraits of women. The clientele may all seem under 25 and on their first date, but the French cuisine is robust and tasty, with dishes from various regions and wines-by-the-glass to match. *f*75.

∞ **Zuid Zeeland**, Herengracht 413, ℗ 624 3154 (*closed Sat and Sun*). Specializes in fish dishes from Belgium and the south of Holland, but also meat dishes with a French and Japanese influence. *f*65.

∞ **Anda Nugraha**, Waterlooplein 339, ℗ 626 6046. Tasty home-cooked Indonesian food. *Rijsttafel f*45 for 2 people.

Axum, Utrechtsedwarsstraat 85–87, ✆ 622 8389. Authentic Ethiopian cuisine—a giant communal pancake and a few sizzling pots of stews and curries. Toss on some salad and yoghurt sauce, add a spoon of stew, and roll up mouth-sized bites with your fingers. Appropriately ethnic décor and utterly charming service. ƒ35.

Balthazar's Keuken, Elandsgracht 108, ✆ 420 2114 (*open Wed–Fri*). The kitchen takes up a third of the room, and diners crowd around a few small wooden tables. Starters are usually *meze*-style: cockles with ginger and parsley or red-pepper salad with anise pepperoni. There's a fish-or-flesh choice for the main course: try buttery pink salmon in a crackly coat of nori, scattered with crisp-fried green asparagus, served with sepia risotto and a perky anchovy sauce. ƒ45.

De Blauwe Hollander, Leidsekruisstraat 28, ✆ 623 3014. Cheap and cheerful, if heavy, Dutch cooking. ƒ30.

Bird, Zeedijk 77, ✆ 420 6289. Tiny Thai snack bar with a kitchen one end, a trendy crowd and tantalizing Thai cuisine. ƒ25.

Casa di David, Singel 426, ✆ 624 5093. Pizzeria with wooden beams and canalside charm. The food is good too—pasta made on the premises, excellent antipasti, and fragrant, crusty pizzas cooked in a wood-burning oven. Pizzas around ƒ20.

Et Alors, Nes 35, ✆ 421 6056. Run by two sisters in the heart of the alternative theatre district. The small restaurant is decorated with a comfortable clutter of old furniture picked up on treks through France, all for sale. The cuisine is unpretentious French fare, with a cared-for, home-cooked touch. Try tasty home-made sausages with rocket salad, or monk fish with an aïoli and vegetable sauce. ƒ40.

Goodies, Huidenstraat 9, ✆ 625 6122. Arty hangout that sells good sandwiches and salads by day, and pasta by night. ƒ30.

Haesje Claes, Spuistraat 273–5, ✆ 624 9998. Touristy, but unhurried. Folksy Old Dutch interior, solid tasty Dutch food, lots of salad and vegetables. Tourist menu ƒ30.

Keuken van 1870, Spuistraat 4, ✆ 624 8965 (*kitchen closes 8pm weekdays, 9pm Sat, Sun*). Began as a soup kitchen in 1870. Punks, pensioners and passing backpackers come in for enormous, tastily cooked meals for under ƒ17.

Pancake Bakery, Prinsengracht 191, ✆ 625 1333 (*see* **Walk III**). The best pancakes in town. Around ƒ10.

La Place, Rokin 162, ✆ 620 2364. Serve yourself at various counters—a great salad bar, fresh pastas and grilled meats cooked while you wait. Most of the ingredients are organic, you sit in one of a honeycomb of rooms in an atmospheric 17th-century building—and it's cheap. ƒ30.

Song Kwae, Kloveniersburgwal 14, ✆ 624 2568. The place to go for Thai food when you've been unable to squeeze into Bird (*see* above). Lots more space, and good food too. ƒ30.

Surinam Express, Halvemaansteeg 18, ✆ 622 7405. Tiny sandwich shop off Rembrandtplein with searingly authentic Surinamese food—spicy vegetable and tangy curry fillings. Eat fuller meals too, at a counter along the wall. ƒ25.

- **Upstairs Pannekoekhuis**, Grimburgwal 2, ✆ 626 5603 (*see* **Walk I**). Teeny pancake parlour suspended above a bustling lane. From *f*10.
- **Woeste Walmen**, Singel 46, ✆ 638 0765 (*open Sat and Sun only*). Decorated with quirky flair and run by squatters who come up with food that they have obviously enjoyed cooking. Usually one meat and one non-meat option for the main course. *f*30.

The Jordaan

- **Christophe**, Leliegracht 46, ✆ 625 0807. A liitle stuffy but Algerian-born Jean-Christophe Royer comes up with superb French cuisine enlivened by zesty north-African flavours. *f*100.
- **Caramba**, Lindengracht 342, ✆ 627 1188. Lively South American restaurant where an arty crowd consumes tortilla and vicious margaritas. *f*45.
- **De Luwte**, Leliegracht 26, ✆ 625 8548. Romantic candlelit restaurant, *trompe-l'œil* on the walls, overlooking a small canal. Delicious meals with fresh (often organic) ingredients. *f*55.
- **Speciaal**, Nieuwe Leliestraat 142, ✆ 624 9706. Reputedly the best Indonesian in town. *Rijsttafel f*50.
- **Stoop**, 1e Anjeliersdwarsstraat 4, ✆ 639 2480. Small, busy restaurant: pastrami salad with ginger and yoghurt dressing, Peking duck with a chutney of aubergines and dried figs. *f*55.
- **Ristorante Toscanini**, Lindengracht 75, ✆ 623 2813 (*closed Tues*). Cavernous, rowdy and very Italian. A gastric and sensual delight, but service is exceeding slow. *f*50.
- **De Eettuin**, 2ᵉ Tuindwarsstraat 10, ✆ 623 7706. Forests of greenery, generous Dutch portions and a modest salad bar. *f*30.
- **Moeders Pot** (Mother's Cooking), Vinkenstraat 119, ✆ 623 7643. A one-person affair run by a huge hairy man. Meat and ten veg for under *f*20.

Further Afield

- **Beddington's**, Roelof Hartstraat 6–8, ✆ 676 5201 (*closed Mon*). Austere décor, but sumptuous meals by a chef with culinary experience from Derbyshire, the Far East and the summits of French *haute cuisine*. *f*95.
- **Ciel Bleu**, Okura Hotel, Ferdinand Bolstraat 333, ✆ 678 7111. On the 23rd floor with wonderful views. The cuisine is appropriately haut. *f*120. Dress: jacket and tie.
- **De Gouden Reael**, Zandhoek 14, ✆ 623 3883. A 17th-century house on a quayside in the Western Islands (*see* **Walk IV**). Renowned for its French provincial cuisine—a different area every three months. *f*75.
- **De Groene Lanteerne**, Haarlemmerstraat 43, ✆ 624 1952. The narrowest restaurant in the world, run by a couple who are renowned for their hearty French fare. *f*75.
- **De Knijp**, Van Baerlestraat 134, ✆ 671 4248 (*open till midnight*). Near to the Concertgebouw. Fresh oysters are a speciality. *f*75.
- **Vis aan de Schelde**, Scheldeplein 4, ✆ 675 1583. Minimalist décor. Fish comes perfectly cooked: marinated salmon with asparagus steeped in vanilla and orange, tuna with just a tinge of pink, meltingly soft monkfish, excellent *bouillabaisse*, tuna in a red-wine and flageolet bean sauce. *f*100.

Yamazato, Hotel Okura, Ferdinand Bolstraat 333, ✆ 678 7111. Superb Japanese cuisine, exquisitely presented. ƒ110.

Yoichi, Weteringschans 128, ✆ 622 6829. Amsterdam's oldest Japanese restaurant, and still one of the best. Traditional food, high prices. ƒ80.

Basak, Frans Halsstraat 89, ✆ 664 9534. Unassuming Turkish restaurant serving tasty casseroles and grills accompanied by heaps of salad. ƒ45.

La Brasa, Haarlemmerdijk 16, ✆ 625 4438. One of the more intimate of the Argentinian grills. Cowhide seats and juicy beef on a wood grill. ƒ55.

Griet Manshande, Keerpunt 10, ✆ 622 8194. Relaxed, neighbourhood restaurant hidden in a corner of a modern housing estate on the Bickerseiland. The daily selection includes anything from *coq au vin* to roast skate with *beurre noir*. Friendly service and skilled cooking. ƒ55.

Bodega Keyzer, Van Baerlestraat 96, ✆ 671 1441 (*closed Sun; open till midnight*). Next to the Concertgebouw. Writers and musicians have been coming here for nearly a century to eat smoked eel and fresh sole. ƒ55.

Kilimanjaro, Rapenburgerplein 6, ✆ 622 3485. Fish soup from Guinea, crocodile from Senegal, Tanzanian red snapper curry and Castle lager from South Africa, home-made ginger beer or hibiscus and baobab cocktail. ƒ50.

The Movies, Haarlemmerdijk 159, ✆ 626 7069. Crowded restaurant attached to an old Art Deco cinema offers challenging concoctions such as red bass with kumquats. ƒ50.

De Ondeugd, Ferdinand Bolstraat 15, ✆ 672 0651. Just minutes from the Albert Cuyp market: the fish and vegetables are alarmingly fresh. Goose liver on apple compôte, Thai soup or grilled swordfish with tomato *beurre blanc*. Main dishes come with delicious *frites* and homemade mayonnaise.

Sparks, Willemsparkweg 87, ✆ 676 0700. Friendly neighbourhood brasserie, with a small garden courtyard, understated décor, and Sander van Ommeren's inspired Mediterranean cooking: marinated octopus with rocket and artichoke crème, brochette of lamb with sea lavender, bulgur pilaf and thyme-lavender gravy, blood-orange sorbet. ƒ75.

De Vrolijke Abrikoos (The Jolly Apricot), Weteringschans 76, ✆ 624 4672 (*closed Tues*). Pastel shades, pine tables and bio-dynamic ingredients combined with subtlety and flair: giant roast mushroom with a creamy sauce, delicate oriental soups, or bass with a robust tomato sauce. There are tables outside in the garden. ƒ45.

De Witte Uyl, Frans Halsstraat 26, ✆ 670 0458. Big tables, comfortable chairs, a carefully chosen wine list, and a menu of imaginative medium-sized dishes. ƒ80.

Witteveen, Ceintuurbaan 256–258, ✆ 662 4368. Vast red, black and gilt interior, dressed-up waiters, and tables smothered with white linen. Formal setting for some of the best traditional Dutch cooking in town. ƒ70.

Zabars, Van Baerlestraat 49, 679 8888. It doesn't look much from the outside, but inside you'll find a cheery crowd enjoying wonderfully flavourful

Mediterranean food: Moroccan lamb casserole or crunchy Greek halva. *f*80.

◦ **Arena**, 's Gravesandestraat 51, ✆ 694 7444. Budget travellers chomp their way through stews and other tummy-filling fare in café-like surrounds. The occasional cloud of hashish smoke wafts by. *f*20.

◦ **Kong Kha**, Rijnstraat 87, ✆ 661 2578. Small, bustling restaurant and take-away, with authentic Thai home-cooking. Well worth a short ride on the number 4 tram. The fishcakes are delicious, and the chicken and coconut soup sweet and soothing. *f*25.

◦ **Riaz**, Bilderdijkstraat 193, ✆ 683 6453. Great Surinamese curries, eaten with rice or *roti*—a pancake in which you roll up your food and eat it with your fingers. *f*30.

◦ **Waroeng Asje**, Jan Pieter Heijestraat 180, ✆ 616 6589. Surinamese/ Indonesian take-away with a few tables near the Vondel park. The *soto soep* (spicy meat-and-veg soup with a bowl of rice alongside, *f*7) is a meal in itself. *f*25.

Vegetarian

◦ **Bolhoed**, Prinsengracht 60, ✆ 626 1803. Exotic Thai statues, quirky lamps, bright colours (soft lighting). The cuisine has a Mexican touch, and is imaginative and tasty. There are vegan dishes available, fish too, and the daily special three-course menu (*f*30) is excellent value. *f*35.

◦ **Golden Temple**, Utrechtsestraat 126, ✆ 626 8560. Simple décor, but tasty food with strong Indian flavours. Vegan options. *f*30.

◦ **De Waaghals**, Frans Halsstraat 29, ✆ 679 9609. Vegetarian cuisine with organic ingredients and international influences: Tunisian bean casserole, coconut and aubergine soup. Flavours sometimes rather bland. *f*45.

∞ **Zest**, Prinsenstraat 10, ✆ 428 2455. Trendy restaurant in fusion mode, offering good vegetarian choices: Thai risotto with sugarsnap peas and mushrooms. *f*55.

Restaurants that put special effort and imagination into the vegetarian options on the menu are: **Hemelse Modder** (Central); **Woeste Walmen** (Central); **De Luwte** (Jordaan); **De Vrolijke Abrikoos** (Further Afield); **Griet Manshande** (Further Afield).

Late Night

Some of these restaurants stay open until midnight: Further Afield: **Bodega Keyser** and **De Knijp**, Central: **Koriander**, **Sluizer** and **Saturnino**.

The downstairs Diner at the **Holland Casino** is open until 2am and serves good food. You don't have to buy a ticket to get in. **Bojo**, Lange Leidsedwarsstraat 51, is an Indonesian restaurant open until 2am (weekdays) and 5.30am (Fri and Sat). **Maoz**, Reguliersbreestraat, near Tuschinski Cinema, serves scrumptious *falafel* and salads all through the night. **Gary's Late-Nite Bagel Shop**, Reguliersdwarsstraat 53, sells genuine New York bagels, cheesecake and muffins until the wee hours.

Cafés and Coffeeshops

Cafés are at the centre of an Amsterdammer's social life. Wooden floors and furniture, and walls stained by years of cigarette smoke, have inspired the name 'brown café'. Here you can have a drink or just a coffee, nibble snacks or plough through hefty meals. But most of all you sit and talk, or while away the time leafing through the day's papers or glossy magazines. There's seldom any grating background music—though in friendly neighbourhood bars the clientele may burst into song. Whether it's in a tiny café supported by a handful of locals, or a stylish new bar with an arty crowd, you'll find that Amsterdammers create an atmosphere where they can relax and feel both *uit* and *thuis* ('out' and 'at home').

The term 'café' covers a wide range of establishments. At one end of the spectrum are the poky bars, where you go to knock back a few beers (with the odd *jenever* chaser); you might also be able to buy bread rolls, *tostis* (pale toasted sandwiches) or *bitterballen* (balls of meat purée, coated in breadcrumbs and deep-fried). At the other end you'll find enormous, airy **grand cafés** and places that offer such sumptuous fare that they're really indistinguishable from small restaurants. These often call themselves *eetcafés* (literally 'eating cafés') or even *petit restaurant cafés*. Some rather startling newcomers made an appearance during the 1980s: the **designer bars** are the complete antithesis of the brown café—hard metal furniture, bright light and colours and loud music—but are now very much part of the Amsterdam scene.

Most Amsterdammers drink beer. Ordering *een Pils* at the bar will get you a small glass of lager topped with a finger or two of froth. Or you might prefer a *jenever* (Dutch gin—oilier and weaker than its British counterpart, with a whiff of juniper berries). In this case ask for a *borrel*. You can have either *oud* (old—more mellow) or *jong* (young—sharper). *Jenever* may also be flavoured: *citroenjenever* (lemon) or *besenjenever* (blackberry) are popular. Ask for a *kamelenrug* (camel's back) and your glass will be filled to the rim. Traditionally, you knock back all of your *jenever* with a single gulp. Should you require both beer and gin simultaneously, request a *kopstoot* (literally: 'knock on the head'). On freezing winter's days a quick visit to a *proeflokaal* will warm your blood. These were once free tasting-houses attached to spirit-merchants and taphouses. These days you have to pay, but the procedure is much the same: walk in, drink up, walk out.

Coffeeshops serve tea, coffee and wonderful cakes and pastries. Sometimes they serve snacks and fuller meals, but never alcohol. Tea is seldom served with milk, unless you specifically ask for it. Coffee will come black or with strange processed *koffiemelk*, unless you order *koffieverkeerd* (literally 'coffee wrong'), in which case you'll get a delicious 50:50 mixture with fresh milk. Since the 1970s some coffeeshops (the so-called **smoking coffeeshops**) have openly sold marijuana. These are easily distinguishable at first glance/sniff. They are painted psychedelic colours, often have leaf designs on the windows and emit loud music and fazed customers.

Café-crawling is the best way to discover Amsterdam: between museum visits, on rainy afternoons, on long, hot summer evenings. There are nearly 1,500 cafés, and you're sure to rootle out a few favourites for yourself. Most cafés close at 1 or 2am at weekends. They begin opening their doors around 11am, though some don't get it together until 3 or 4pm. An asterisk (*) indicates cafés particularly recommended for their food. The letters in the margins are there to give you some indication of where the café is: **C**—the central area bounded by the main canals; **J**—the Jordaan and northwestern Amsterdam; **S**—south and southeast of the centre.

Cafés

(C) **In't Aepjen**, Zeedijk 1. A '*rariteiten-café*', crammed with antiques (*see* **Walk IV**).

(C) ***AmTricain**, American Hotel, Leidseplein. Splendid Art Deco grand café (*see* **Walk VI**).

(C) ***Aas van Bokalen**, Keizersgracht 335. Arty brown café (*see* **Walk VI**).

(J) ***Belhamel**, Brouwersgracht 60. Art Nouveau décor on a pretty canal (*see* **Walk II**).

(C) ***Eetcafé Van Beeren**, Koningsstraat 54, © 622 2329. Quiet neighbourhood café with an imaginative chef.

(J) **De Blaffende Vis**, Westerstraat 118. Cheery café (*see* **Walk III**).

(C) **Cul de Sac**, Oudezijds Voorburgwal 99. Down a side alley—one of the few good bars in the red-light district.

(C) **Dantzig**, Zwanenburgwal 15. Attractive corner of the ugly Stadhuis. A grand café that frequently fills with wedding parties (*see* **Walk III**).

(C) **De Druif**, Rapenburg 83 (near Maritime Museum). Dates from 1631 (*see* **Walk IV**).

(J) **Dulac**, Haarlemmerstraat 118. Fantasy grand café, inspired by the French fairy-tale illustrator Edmund Dulac (*see* **Walk IV**).

(S) ***De Duvel**, 1e van der Helststraat 59–61. Busy café with a large terrace near the Albert Cuyp market.

(C) ***1e Klas** (First Class), Platform 2B, Centraal Station. Lose yourself in the great age of rail travel (*see* **Walk I**).

(C) **Eik en Linde**, Plantage Middenlaan 22 (near Zoo). Brown café with mixed, arty crowd (*see* **Walk III**).

(C) **Eland**, Prinsengracht 296. Traditional brown café.

(C) ***Engelbewaarder**, Kloveniersburgwal 59. Writers gulp down pasta and scribble away on wooden tables. Heated discussions about art and life echo from the corners.

(C) **Gollem**, Raamsteeg 4. Home of a hundred (or more) beers.

(J) **De Gijs**, Lindengracht 249. Tiny eccentric two-tier bar.

(S) ***De Groene Olifant** (The Green Elephant), Sarphatistraat 510. Cosy bar flooded with light. The folk are friendly and the food delicious.

(C) **Het Hok**, Lange Leidsedwarsstraat 134. A refuge from the hordes, filled with quiet people playing chess.

(S) **Hollandse Manege Café**, Vondelstraat 140. Overlooks an exquisite 19th-century riding school arena (*see* **Walk VI**).

(C) **Hoppe**, Spui 18–20. Dates from 1670. Busy after-work (*see* **Walk I**).

(C) ***Huyschkamer**, Utrechtsestraat 137. Trendy café in a former male brothel (*see* **Walk II**).

(S) **De IJsbreker**, Weesperzijde 23. Attached to the contemporary music venue. Tranquil riverside terrace.

(C) ***De Jaren**, Nieuwe Doelenstraat 20. Light and airy grand café. Home of the arts and media set (*see* **Walk I**).

(C) **Karpershoek**, Martelaarsgracht 2. Claims to be Amsterdam's oldest café (*see* **Walk IV**).

(J) **De Kat in de Wijngaert**, Lindengracht 160. Quiet and friendly.

(J) **Koophandel**, Bloemgracht 49. Converted warehouse that fills up around midnight and throbs till dawn.

(C) ***Kort**, Amstelveld 2. Modern café with a quiet canalside terrace (*see* **Walk V**).

(C) **De Kroon Royal Café**, Rembrandtplein 17. Historic meeting place of variety artistes and agents, with a view over Rembrandtplein (*see* **Walk V**).

(C) **Luxembourg**, Spui 22–24. Grand café that attracts well-heeled office workers (*see* **Walk I**).

(C) ***Het Molenpad**, Prinsengracht 653. A brown café that sometimes crams a live jazz band into one corner. A smoky, dreamy place to while away a Sunday afternoon.

(J) **Nol**, Westerstraat 109. Outrageously kitsch bar. Locals, gangsters and visitors get swept into sing-songs.

(C) **L'Opera**, Rembrandtplein 19. Sedate Art Deco café on a bustling square (*see* **Walk V**).

(C) **Papeneiland**, Prinsengracht 2. Built in 1642, with a secret passage across the canal (*see* **Walk III**).

(C) **De Prins**, Prinsengracht 124. Pretty canalside pub popular with students.

(C) ***Van Puffelen**, Prinsengracht 377. Sawdust on the floor, and cherubs on the ceiling. A good restaurant at the back, a terrace on a barge on the canal in front, and a smart clientele.

(J) **Rooie Nelis**, Laurierstraat 101. A Jordaan institution. Bursting with locals and visitors having a good time.

(J) ***Rosereijn**, Haarlemmerdijk 52. Cosy brown café with a good selection of magazines and cheap, tasty food.

(C) ***Schiller**, Rembrandtplein 26. Cosy Art Deco bar tucked away from the rumpus of Rembrandtplein. Excellent cuisine. (*see* **Walk V**).

(J) **'t Smalle**, Egelantiersgracht 12. An 18th-century *proeflokaal* converted into brown café. Gets packed most evenings(*see* **Walk III**).

(J) **De Tuin**, 2e Tuindwarsstraat 13. Dim light, board games and a twinge of eccentricity. A classic brown café.

(C) **Twee Prinsen**, Prinsenstraat 27. Heated terrace and a friendly, alternative crowd who profess great rivalry with the 'yuppies' at the **Vergulde Gaper** on the opposite corner.

(C) **Twee Zwaantjes**, Prinsengracht 114. Electric organ music, accordions and unforgettable big ladies with big voices from the Jordaan.

(S) ***Vertigo**, Vondelpark 3. Wonderful terrace on Vondelpark and cosy cellar under Film Museum (*see* **Walk VI**).

(C) ***De Waag**, in the old weighing house) on Nieuwemarkt Vast candlelit café, decorated with medieval austerity.

(C) **Welling**, J. W. Brouwerstraat 32. Traditional brown café convenient for the Concertgebouw (*see* **Walk V**).

(C) **De Wetering**, Weteringstraat 37. A real log fire in winter and an ancient television for crucial football matches.

(S) **Wildschut**, Roelof Hartplein 1–3. Art Deco interior and noisy, smoky but none the less popular terrace.

Designer Bars

(C) **Esprit**, Spui 10. Aluminium and plateglass for the trendy (*see* **Walk I**).

(S) **Krull**, Corner of 1e van der Helststraat and 1e Jan Steenstraat). Friendly café near the Albert Cuyp market.

(C) ***Morlang**, Keizersgracht 451. Brittle, trendier-than-thou atmosphere, but good food.

(C) ***Het Land van Walem**, Keizersgracht 449. Friendlier than the Morlang next door, with a bigger terrace and a garden at the back.

(C) **Seymour Likely Lounge**, Nieuwezijds Voorburgwal 250. Real creation of a fictitious artist (*see* p.60), and one of the trendiest spots in town.

(C) **Schuim**, Spuistraat 189. Shopwindow café full of students during the day, and artsy types at night who admire their friends' paintings.

Proeflokalen

(C) **De Admiraal**, Herengracht 319. Enormous, with comfy chairs (*see* **Walk II**).

(C) **De Drie Fleschjes**, Gravenstraat 18. More traditional *proeflokaal*. Some nearby offices have their own marked barrels (*see* **Walk I**).

(C) **Het Proeflokaal**, Pijlsteeg 31. Delightfully cramped and crooked old *proeflokaal* with a range of flavoured *jenevers* and sticky liqueurs.

Coffeeshops

(C) **Backstage Boutique**, Utrechtsedwarsstraat 65–7. The zaniest coffeeshop in town (*see* **Walk II**).

(C) **Greenwoods**, Singel 103. Real homemade English afternoon tea.

(S) **Granny**, 1^e van der Helststraat 45. Near Albert Cuyp market. Some of the best *appelgebak* in town.

(C) **Pompadour**, Huidenstraat 12. Refined hand-made chocolates in a splendid setting (*see* **Walk VI**).

(C) **Puccini**, Staalstraat 17. Irresistible cakes and outrageous chocolates near the Waterlooplein fleamarket.

(J) **Reibach**, Brouwersgracht 139. German specialities, such as wickedly alcoholic fruit from the *Rumtopf* jar, and a view over a beautiful canal.

Smoking Coffeeshops

(C) **The Bulldog**, Leidseplein 13–17/ Oudezijds Voorburgwal 90. Oldest and most commercial.

(C) **Prix d'Ami**, Haringpakkersteeg 5. Deeply respectable-looking branch of a chain of coffeeshops.

(C) **Rusland**, Rusland 16. Privately owned, intimate and relaxedly scruffy.

(C) **Pink Poffertje**, moored at southern end of Oude Schans. Cosy boat that even sells marijuana beer.

Where to Stay

Hotels:

1. American Hotel
2. Amstel Hotel Intercontinental
3. Blakes
4. Hotel de l'Europe
5. Le Grand Amsterdam
6. Grand Hotel Krasnapolsky
7. Hotel Pulitzer
8. Amsterdam Hilton
9. Hilton International Schiphol
10. Seven One Seven
11. Hotel Ambassade
12. Golden Tulip Doelen
13. Dikker and Thijs Fenice
14. Jan Luyken
15. Schiller Karena
16. Acca International
17. Hotel Acro
18. Hotel Agora
19. Hotel Amsterdam
    Prinsengracht
20. Hotel Belga
21. Het Canal House
22. La Casoló
23. Hotel de Filosoof
24. Hotel Orlando
25. Owl Hotel
26. Hotel Seven Bridges
27. Quentin Hotel
28. Hotel Toren
29. Hotel Washinton
30. Hotel Wiechmann
31. Hotel de Admiraal
32. Hotel Adolesce
33. Hans Brinker
34. Hotel Brouwer
35. Hotel Engeland
36. Hotel de Harmonie
37. Hotel Hoksbergen
38. Hotel Impala
39. Hotel Prinsenhof
40. Hotel de Westertoren

Hostels:

h1. Vondelpark
h2. Stadsdoelen
h3. Arena
h4. Eben Haezer Christian Youth
     Hostel
h5. The Flying Pig Park

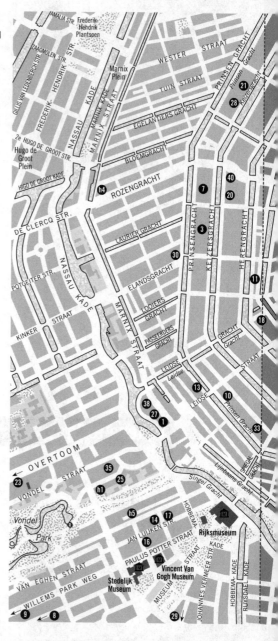

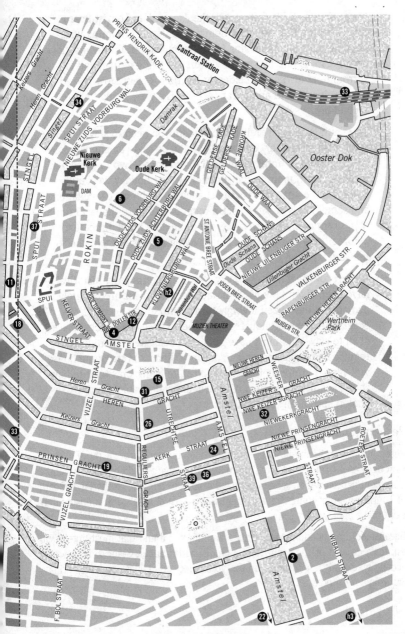

It's a summer Friday afternoon, the Amsterdam Tourist Board Information Office opposite Centraal Station is brimming with hopeful weekenders looking for accommodation. But by 4 o'clock Amsterdam is full. Frustrated visitors are being despatched to surrounding towns like Leiden or Haarlem—pretty towns, and commuting is swift and cheap, yet this is always going to be second best.

The truth is, to really relish Amsterdam you need to stay right in the centre, preferably on a canal, and to do that you should make sure you **book a hotel room well in advance**—two to three weeks at least, more in the summer or over holiday weekends. There is, of course, always the chance of catching a cancellation, and some hotels do keep back a room or two until the last minute. If you cannot book in advance, try calling the hotel direct just before noon—the witching hour between check-out and check-in—and try your luck.

All sorts of canal houses—poky, grand and resonantly historical—have been given new life as hotels. Many of these are privately owned and have been lovingly turned into little havens of *gezelligheid* or storehouses of antiques. These are the best places of all to stay—but most have built up a dedicated clientele and require booking some time in advance. Rooms in the same house will vary enormously in size and *en suite* bathrooms tend to have showers only. If you hear of a particularly desirable room, try to book it specifically by number.

Reservations

Reservations can be made, once you're in the country, through the VVV (*see* **Practical A–Z**, 'Tourist Information'. p.30). They charge a ƒ5 booking fee and a ƒ10 room deposit which is later deducted from your bill. The Netherlands Board of Tourism in your home country can give you a list of hotels, but unfortunately can't make bookings.

Because accommodation is at such a premium, you'll find that most hotels will ask for a deposit or the security of a credit card number. Some simply won't accept weekend reservations unless you book, or at least pay for, Friday, Saturday *and* Sunday.

Accommodation Categories

Standards of cleanliness and service are high, and unless you're scraping along at the very bottom of the price range, you're unlikely to find yourself sharing your room with local fauna, thumping faulty electrical equipment or speculating about the origins of the hairs on the sheets. Facilities can be quite spartan, however, and a lot of the smaller hotels offer rooms of the bed/bedside table/wardrobe only variety. Yet even these are usually tastefully done up and almost invariably impeccably clean.

Hotels are graded by the Benelux star system (one to five stars), though this isn't a particularly useful guide as it is based on an inventory of facilities and tells you nothing about location, service or ambience. Facilities vary in direct relation to price—you get what you pay for. Around the top end of the moderate range (*f*220—*f*280) you should be assured of at least a TV and telephone in your room. Beyond that lies the world of mini-bars, *en suite* jacuzzis and telephones in the loo.

As Amsterdam is such a compact city, hotels in this list are graded by price rather than area. Nearly all of them are within easy walking distance of the main tourist sites and museums, and have been chosen because of their pleasant atmosphere, location or historical significance.

The hotels in the 'expensive' range tend to be business hotels. Here you're paying for facilities like fax machines and meeting rooms. Such places are briskly efficient, but are often soulless and used to expense-account customers. You can be just as comfortable, and will probably be far happier, in one of the more idiosyncratic hotels from the top of the 'moderate' range. Price ranges given in this guide are as follows:

An asterisk (★) indicates hotels that are especially recommended.

∞∞∞	luxury	*f*450 and over
∞∞∞	expensive	*f*280–*f*450
∞∞	moderate	*f*175–*f*280
∞	cheap	under *f*180

These prices are for a double room with bath or shower *en suite* in season, and include services and taxes and (unless otherwise stated) Dutch breakfast. For prices of single rooms deduct 15–20 per cent. The addresses given below include the Amsterdam postcode.

Hotels

American Hotel, Leidsekade 97, 1017 PN, ☎ 556 3000, ✆ 625 3236. An Art Deco extravaganza of a hotel overlooking the thronging Leidseplein. The café downstairs was once the meeting place for Amsterdam's literati (*see* **Walk VI**). From ƒ475. Breakfast ƒ32.50.

*Amstel Hotel Intercontinental, Professor Tulpplein 1, 1018 GX, ☎ 622 6060, ✆ 622 5808. A gracious and sedate hotel on the banks of the Amstel. If you're stuck for transport you can use the hotel's motor yacht or limousine. ƒ850, breakfast ƒ42.50.

Blakes, Keizersgracht 384, 1016 GB, ☎ 530 2010, ✆ 530 2030. From ƒ550. Style diva Anouska Hempel brings her touch from London to a grand canal house. Bedrooms range from voluptous to Buddhist minimalist. Guests are rich and famous. Well, rich anyway.

*Hotel de l'Europe, Nieuwe Doelenstraat 2–8, 1012 CP, ☎ 531 1777, ✆ 531 1778. An elegant 19th-century hotel in the grand old style. Knocks spots off the Doelen down the road. From ƒ630. Breakfast ƒ35.

The Grand Amsterdam, Oudezijds Voorburgwal 197, 1001 EX, ☎ 555 3111, ✆ 555 3222. Built as an inn in 1578, then used as Admirality Headquarters, and finally serving as Amsterdam's city hall (from 1808 to 1988). Many fine 1920s interior fittings remain (including the Wedding Room in which Queen Beatrix plighted her troth), but some people are put off by the proximity of the red-light district. ƒ730 excl. breakfast.

Grand Hotel Krasnapolsky, Dam 9, 1012 JS, ☎ 554 9111, ✆ 626 1570. Excellent position, right in the centre of town. Very grand from the outside, and inside a mix of period charm and all mod cons. From ƒ620; breakfast ƒ37.50.

*Hotel Pulitzer, Prinsengracht 315–331, 1016 GZ, ☎ 523 5235, ✆ 627 6753. Twenty-four canal houses linked up to form a warren of oak-beamed rooms. The hotel has a peaceful garden and a magnificent 18th-century restaurant. From ƒ650; breakfast ƒ37.50.

Amsterdam Hilton, Apollolaan 138–140, 1077 BG, ☎ 710 6005, ✆ 710 6000. Modern building in the south of the city, not in the centre. Weekdays ƒ450 excl. breakfast, weekends from ƒ415.

Hilton International Schiphol, Herbergierstraat, 1118 ZK, ☎ 710 4000, ✆ 710 4080. Part of Schiphol complex around the airport. Shuttle bus from airport. From ƒ640 excl. breakfast; breakfast ƒ42.50.

Seven One Seven, Prinsengracht 717, 1017 JW, ☎ 427 0717, ✆ 423 0717. Superb, antique-filled suites on one of the smartest canals in town. The owners have aimed at creating a relaxed, cosy atmosphere—which is extremely chic and well-appointed. From ƒ550; special weekend rates from ƒ450. Price includes breakfast, afternoon coffee and drinks from the bar in the evening.

Hotel Ambassade, Herengracht (11) 335–353, 1016 AZ, ☎ 626 2333, ✆ 624 5321. Eight converted houses, dotted about with antiques and with a magnificent breakfast-room overlooking the canal. ƒ335; breakfast ƒ22.50.

Golden Tulip Doelen Hotel, (12) Nieuwe Doelenstraat 24, 1012 CP, ☎ 554 0600, ✆ 622 1084, telex 14399. One of Amsterdam's oldest hotels, though fading in grandeur. Rembrandt painted the *Night Watch* here in 1642. ƒ420.

★Dikker & Thijs Fenice Hotel, (13) Prinsengracht 444, 1017 KE, ☎ 626 7721, ✆ 625 8986. Plum in the middle of it all, in a hectically lively area of town. Modern furnishings in a 100-year-old shell. From ƒ415.

Jan Luyken Hotel, Jan (14) Luykenstraat 58, 1071 CS, ☎ 573 0730, ✆ 676 3841. Smart, efficient business hotel in quiet area near the Concertgebouw. From ƒ370.

★Schiller Karena Hotel, (15) Rembrandt-plein 26–36, 1017 CV, ☎ 554 0700, ✆ 626 6381. Decorated with the paintings of its 19th-century owner, the downstairs café was once the meeting place of actors and artists. The hotel itself is smart, comfortable and overlooks a lively square. From ƒ420; breakfast ƒ32.50.

Acca International, Van de (16) Veldestraat 3a, 1071 CW, ☎ 662 5262, ✆ 679 9361. Modern, functional hotel near the main museums. From ƒ195; breakfast ƒ10.

Hotel Acro, Jan Luykenstraat 44, (17) 1071 CR, ☎ 662 0526, ✆ 675 0811. Sparkling, simple, if a little soulless.

Set in the quiet museum district. ƒ175.

Hotel Agora, Singel 462, 1017 (18) AW, ☎ 627 2200, ✆ 627 2202. The owner is interested in fine furniture—and it shows. Rooms overlooking the canal or back garden are the best. Good value from ƒ215.

Hotel Amsterdam Prinsen- (19) **gracht**, Prinsengracht 1015, 1017 KN, ☎ 623 7779, ✆ 623 8926. Friendly staff, all mod cons and canal views, though the décor is a little bland. From ƒ190.

Hotel Belga, Hartenstraat 8, 1016 (20) CB, ☎ 624 9080, 623 6862. Unpretentious, family-run hotel in a quaint shopping alley. ƒ190 (ƒ160 without shower).

★Het Canal House, Keizersgracht (21) 148, 1015 CX, ☎ 622 5182, ✆ 624 1317. Stunning converted canal house, filled to the brim with the owner's carefully chosen antiques. The breakfast-room has a piano and a drippingly beautiful crystal chandelier. The hotel has the feel of a tastefully (if somewhat grandly) decorated private home, and it even has a lift (quite a rarity in these historic houses). From ƒ265 to ƒ345

★La Casaló, Amsteldijk 862, 1079 (22) LN, ☎ 642 3680, ✆ 644 7409. Romantic houseboat with a waterside terrace and just four rooms, all individually decorated. It's on the outskirts of town, so a car or bicycle is a good idea. From ƒ235 to ƒ275.

★Hotel De Filosoof, Anna (23) Vondelstraat 6, 1054 GZ, ☎ 683 3013, ✆ 685 3750. Each room is named after a well-known thinker, and decorated accordingly. The hotel can arrange consultations with one of Holland's practising philosophers, many of whom frequent the bar. From ƒ195.

∞ **Hotel Orlando**, Prinsengracht
㉔ 1099, 1017 JH, ☎ 638 6915, 🖷 625 2123. Canalside house with just five rooms, individually decorated in a modern style. Need to book well in advance. ƒ160 to ƒ260.

∞ **Owl Hotel**, Roemer Visscherstraat
㉕ 1–3, 1054 EV, ☎ 618 9486, 🖷 618 9491. Smart family hotel with large garden. In the museum neighbourhood. ƒ210.

∞ ***Hotel Seven Bridges**, Reguliersgracht 31, 1017 LK, ☎ 623 1329. No
㉖ fax. The most charming small hotel in Amsterdam. Beautifully decorated rooms—and breakfast served in bed. ƒ200 to ƒ340.

∞ ***Quentin Hotel**, Leidsekade 89,
㉗ 1017 PN, ☎ 626 2187, 🖷 622 0121. Popular with musicians playing at De Melkweg around the corner. Posters of past (now famous) residents adorn the walls. Spotless, tastefully decorated and good views over the canal. From ƒ220.50 excl. breakfast.

∞ **Hotel Toren**, Keizersgracht 164,
㉘ 1015 CZ, ☎ 622 6033, 🖷 626 9705. Seventeenth-century canal house with high moulded ceilings, and antiques scattered among the modern furniture. From ƒ225, breakfast ƒ17.50.

∞ **Hotel Washington**, Frans van
㉙ Mierisstraat 10, 1071 RS, ☎ 679 6754, 🖷 673 4435. Large 19th-century house on a peaceful avenue

near the Concertgebouw. Room furnishings are simple but tasteful, and there's a small back garden. A friendly, homey atmosphere much appreciated by visiting concert musicians. From ƒ185.

∞ ***Hotel Wiechmann**, Prinsengracht
㉚ 328–330, 1016 HX, ☎ 626 3321, 🖷 626 8962. Carefully converted canal houses with an air of old world charm, and a noble breakfast-room. From ƒ200.

◊ **Hotel De Admiraal**, Herengracht
㉛ 563, 1017 CD, ☎ 626 2150, 🖷 623 4625. Friendly owner, views over *two* canals, and a good breakfast. Around ƒ165 (ƒ110 without private bathroom); breakfast extra ƒ7.50.

◊ **Hotel Adolesce**, Nieuwe Keizers-
㉜ gracht 26, 1018 DS, ☎ 626 3959, 🖷 627 4249. Cheerful, simple hotel with a sunny breakfast-room. A good one if you have children, as it is one of the few establishments that genuinely welcomes them. From ƒ125–ƒ150, some rooms without bathroom.

◊ **Hans Brinker**, Kerkstraat 136,
㉝ 1017 GR, ☎ 622 0687, 🖷 638 2060. Prides itself on its no-frills good value and central situation. ƒ145.

◊ **Hotel Brouwer**, Singel 83, ☎ 624
㉞ 6358, 🖷 520 6264. A gem. Canal house with rooms tastefully done up with lovely old furniture. Most have a good view. ƒ154.

◊ **Hotel Engeland**, Roemer Vischer-
㉟ straat 30, 1054 EZ, ☎ 689 2323, 🖷 685 3148. English representative in a quaint row of 19th-century houses built to show seven different

national architectural styles. From ƒ175 (breakfast extra).

○ **Hotel de Harmonie**, Prinsengracht
36 816, 1017 JL, ℰ 625 0174, ℰ 622 8021. Bright, jolly, family-run hotel. ƒ130 (without bathroom) to ƒ140.

○ **Hotel Hoksbergen**, Singel 301,
37 ℰ 626 6043. ℰ 638 3479. No-nonsense knotty pine, some canal views, clean rooms, friendly management.

○ **Hotel Impala**, Leidsekade 77, 1017
38 PM, ℰ 623 4706, ℰ 638 9274.

Clean, laid-back hotel with young crowd. From ƒ130–ƒ140.

○ **Hotel Prinsenhof**, Prinsengracht
39 810, 1017 JL, ℰ 623 1772, ℰ 638 3368. Quiet, thoughtfully decorated hotel with friendly management. ƒ165 (ƒ125 without bathroom).

○ **Hotel de Westertoren**, Raadhuis-
40 straat 35b, 1016 DC, ℰ/ℰ 624 4639. Well-kept, if a little noisy. From ƒ140.

Bed & Breakfast

Despite their easy assimilation of things British, Amsterdammers do not seem much taken by B&B. When you do find private accommodation, it probably won't be all that much cheaper than (or very different from) a room in a small hotel.

Bed and Breakfast Holland, Theophile de Bockstraat 3, 1058 TV, ℰ 615 7527, ℰ 669 1573. Has a number of B&Bs on its books. Prices range from ƒ95 for a minimum 2-night stay and there is a ƒ20 booking fee per reservation. Advance bookings only.

Hostels

The two official International Youth Hostel Federation hostels are:

h1 **Vondelpark**, Zandpad 5, 1054 GA, ℰ 589 8999, ℰ 589 8955.

h2 **Stadsdoelen**, Kloveniersburgwal 97, 1011 KB, ℰ 624 6832, ℰ 639 1035. Members ƒ28 per person (including breakfast); non-members ƒ33; sheet hire ƒ6.25.

There are also:

h3 **Arena**, 's Gravesandestraat 51, 1092 AA, ℰ 694 7444, ℰ 663 2649. Erstwhile seedy hippy Sleep-In, which has now been considerably smartened up and attracts a very friendly crowd of backpackers. Double room ƒ135, dormitories from ƒ27.50, bedding ƒ5.

h4 ***Eben Haezer Christian Youth Hostel**, Bloemstraat 179, 1016 LA, ℰ 624 4717, ℰ 627 6137. Spotless, not oppressively religious and the best

value of the lot. ƒ27.50, including breakfast and bed linen. No membership required. There are lockers available.

h5 **The Flying Pig Park**, Vossiusstraat 46, 1071 AJ, ℰ 400 4187, ℰ 470 5159. Friendly crowd, clean dorms, free lockers and a cosy café beside the Vondelpark. Dorm beds from ƒ26.50 per person, double room ƒ120.

Campsites

Het Amsterdamse Bos, Kleine Noorddijk 1, 1432 CC, Aalsmeer, ☎ 641 6868 (*open April–Oct*). Bus 171 from Centraal Station, 169 from Schiphol. Good facilities but far out. ƒ8.75 per person, ƒ4.75 per car, ƒ6.75 caravans; ƒ4 per night electricity charge for camper vans and caravans.

Vliegenbos, Meeuwenlaan 138, 1022 AM, ☎ 636 8855 (*open April–Sept*). Bus 32 (10 minutes from Centraal Station). 'Youth Campsite'—all ages welcome but be prepared for late-night high spirits. From ƒ10 per person, cars ƒ5.50, electricity ƒ5.

Apartments

Amsterdam Apartments, Kromme Waal, 1011 BV, ☎ 626 5930, ✆ 626 9544. Privately owned flats around town—in fact usually flats let by Amsterdammers away on holiday—from ƒ700 per week.

GIS Apartments, Keizersgracht 33, 1015 CD, ☎ 625 0071, ✆ 638 0475. From the simple to the luxurious. From ƒ2,000 per month, minimum three months.

Global Home Network, Suite 205, 110-D Elden Street, Herndon, Virginia, USA, ☎ +1 703 318 7081, ✆ +1 703 318 7086, have a number of canalside apartments on their books, for short and medium-term lease. Prices on application.

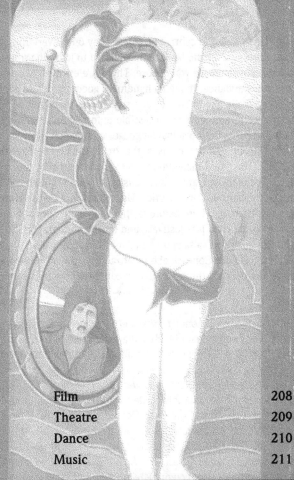

Amsterdam's nightlife centres on cafés. They offer everything from a quiet evening over the backgammon board to jolly sing-songs in just about any language you choose. There are even some cafés where you can dance, though a handful of good nightclubs serve those who really like to bounce and sweat. The more genteel spectator entertainments are accessible to foreigners. Films are usually shown in their original language, with Dutch subtitles; there's a strong tradition of visual theatre, and many performances in English; the new Muziektheater provides a venue for touring opera and dance companies, and Amsterdam has high international status in the various music worlds. Up and coming British rock bands test the water here before facing jaded audiences at home; there are some good jazz festivals, and recent immigration has upped the quality of salsa and Latin American music. The acoustically superb Concertgebouw attracts leading classical artists and conductors, and there's a healthy contemporary music scene.

Information

The tourist office publishes a monthly *What's On In Amsterdam* (ƒ4, available from the Amsterdam Tourist Board (ATB) and around town). The free monthly *Uitkrant* (from the ATB, AUB, libraries, museums and theatres) is more comprehensive and, although it's in Dutch, fairly easy to follow. An even better bet (also in Dutch) is the PS Weekend supplement to *Het Parool*. *Queer Fish* (ƒ2.50 from larger newsagents) is a twice-monthly guide to trendy Amsterdam, focussing mainly on clubs and with a strong gay slant. *Oor* (from newsagents) is the Dutch equivalent of *NME*, the British rock music newspaper. Both the Amsterdam Tourist Board and the AUB booking office (*see* **Practical A–Z**, 'Tourist Information' p.30) can reserve tickets. The AUB also has an up-to-the-minute What's On noticeboard (good for pop music) and masses of leaflets. *www.aub.nl* has up-to-the-minute information on shows and exhibitions, and a bookings service too. (Also *see* **Practical A–Z**, 'Festivals and Events', p.16)

Film

The Dutch are avid movie-goers. Most cafés and some restaurants have a list of the week's films pinned up on the wall. Home-grown products haven't, however, made much of an impact internationally—though director Paul Verhoeven is known for *Robocop* and *Total Recall*, and a Dutch film, *Antonia*, picked up the 1996 Oscar for Best Foreign Film. The British director Peter Greenaway operates largely with Dutch funding. You'll find most of the multi-screened **commercial cinemas** in the area around Leidseplein, where they offer pretty standard fare. The six-screen Tuschinski (*see* **Walk V**, p.159) must be a hot contender for the most beautiful cinema in the world and is worth a visit no matter what's showing. Cinema **prices** range from *f*10–*f*15 and there are often discounts on week nights. In the rare cases where an English film has been dubbed over you'll see *Nederlands Gesproken* on the publicity.

Amsterdam offers nothing to rival the internationally important **Rotterdam Film Festival** (held Jan/Feb; information from the ATB), but **art movies** get a good showing in some rather romantic old cinemas.

art houses

Desmet, Plantage Middenlaan 4, ✆ 627 3434. Ornate Art Deco cinema used by a Jewish cabaret company in the early years of the Second World War. These days known for its imaginative mini-festivals and weekend gay screenings.

Netherlands Film Museum, Vondelpark 3, ✆ 589 1400. Frequent changes of programme, usually with something from the museum's extensive archive—such as tinted silent movies (*see* **Walk VI** p.159).

Kriterion, Roeterstraat 170, ✆ 623 1708. Cult American movies and erotic French late-nights.

See also **De Melkweg**, p.214.

The Movies, Haarlemmerdijk 161, ✆ 638 6016. Some of the programming verges on the mainstream, but the 1920s interior is a delight and there's a vibrant café/restaurant (*see* **Food and Drink**, p.191).

Rialto, Ceintuurbaan 338, ✆ 675 3994. Good on retrospectives, science-fiction, animation and children's films.

De Uitkijk, Prinsengracht 452, ✆ 623 7460. Amsterdam's oldest cinema (dating from 1913), squashed into an even older canal house. It features a white grand piano that has long since tinkled its last notes, but is too big to be removed.

Theatre

Like England, the Netherlands experienced a 17th-century Golden Age of the theatre. Playwrights of that era, such as Vondel, Hooft and Bredero, are still performed in Holland. The 18th and 19th centuries saw the growth of extravagant stage spectacles. By the end of the 19th century, theatre had ossified from a popular into an élitist form. The 'Tomato Action' of 1968 put an end to that. A disgruntled new generation of actors began throwing tomatoes at their older colleagues during performances and sparked off a theatrical revolution. In the decade that followed, Amsterdam theatres like the **Mickery** and the **Shaffy** earned a worldwide reputation for high quality avant-garde work. Government cuts and changing tastes have curtailed the mud-wading and body-painting, but there is still a strong tradition of excellent, highly visual theatre (look for work by **Orkater Theatre Company** and spectacular outdoor romps by the **Dogtroep**).

There is no national theatre company; the chief mainstream company is the rather stolid **Toneelgroep Amsterdam**, resident at the Westergasfabriek. Two local English-speaking companies compete with foreign touring productions for the Amsterdam audience. The In Theatre presents small-scale productions, usually upstairs in a converted prop room at the Stadsschouwburg, and Boom Chicago offers improvised comedy in their own supper theatre next door. The Nes (off Damstraat) and the banks of the Amstel are traditionally theatreland, but these days no old warehouse, factory or stable is safe from troupes of eager actors.

The best thing to do is check the listings magazines for touring companies—and here's a short list of venues where you're likely to find good work in English.

't Fijnhout Theater, Jacob van Lennepkade 334, ✆ 685 3755. A popular theatre with English-language touring companies.

Koninklijk Theater Carré, Amstel 115-125, ✆ 622 5225. Built for a circus—a function it still performs over the Christmas period. The home of most big Amsterdam musicals, but more off-the-wall performances slip into gaps in the programme (*see* **Walk II**, pp.108–9).

Felix Meritis, Felix Meritis Building, Keizersgracht 324, ✆ 626 2321. A descendent of the Shaffy, which was at the forefront of the avant-garde during the 1970s and 1980s, and housed in a building with a rich cultural past. Still a place to catch exciting new work (*see* **Walk VI**, p.175).

De Stadsschouwburg, Leidseplein 26, ✆ 624 2311. Amsterdam's municipal theatre. A wide range of national productions and visiting international companies. There's a good **theatre bookshop** near the main entrance (*see* **Walk VI**, p.172).

See also **De Melkweg**, p.214.

Dance

Until recently, Dutch dance was sagging sadly, propped up by a rather unvivacious Nationale Ballet and the practically moribund Scapio Ballet. Only the Nederlands Dans Theater had the verve and energy to prevent complete artistic prolapse. But the tide has turned, inspired perhaps by the big stage at the new Muziektheater, an influx of foreign dancers and traditional rhythms from the former colonies. The Nationale Ballet has imported Canadian Wayne Eagling to be its artistic director, has expanded its repertoire, and is benefiting from the visits of touring companies who now have a suitable venue, the Muziektheater. The Scapio is dusting off the cobwebs and has appointed Ed Wubbe as their daring new choreographer; the Nederlands Dans Theater keeps up a salvo of fine ballet and modern dance. Look out also for work by **Djazzex** (jazz dance) and **Dansgroep Krisztina de Chatel** (vivid theatrical style).

Once again the listings magazines will tell you what's on, but the following venues are worth checking out:

Bellevue, Leidsekade 90, ✆ 624 7248. Modern dance touring companies.

Frascati, Nes 63, ✆ 626 6866. More established modern dance companies.

Muziektheater (Stopera), Waterlooplein 22, ✆ 625 5455. If you want to see something in this new opera house, ballet may be the best choice as the acoustics are a little iffy (*see* p.211).

Classical and Opera

After a lull during the 1980s, Dutch music seems to be undergoing a renaissance. Baroque and period instrument orchestras are reaching particularly high standards (try to catch the **Amsterdam Baroque Orchestra** or the **Orchestra of the 18th Century**). The Nederlandse Opera repeatedly comes up with sharp, adventurous productions, often of 20th-century works, and the contemporary music scene is very lively (look out for pieces by Louis Andriessen and performances by the refreshingly unorthodox Ricciotti Ensemble). The famed **Royal Concertgebouw Orchestra** first established its reputation before the Second World War under the baton of Willem Mengelberg. He built up a close working relationship with Mahler and Richard Strauss and devoted 50 years to establishing his orchestra as one of the greatest in the world, only to be sacked after the war for pro-German sympathies. In the 1960s the orchestra was propelled to even greater heights by Bernard Haitink. Now, conductor Riccardo Chailly is giving it new life.

Tickets will seem cheap if you're used to London or New York prices, but they sell out quickly. You can try for returns half an hour before a performance, but there are no last-minute discounts, and systems of selling return tickets (especially at the Muziektheater) can be disorganized. Churches are favourite venues for concerts and recitals: the Oude Kerk, the Nieuwe Kerk, the Engelse Kerk and the Waalse Kerk. Other venues include:

AGA Zaal and Yakult Zaal, Damrak 213, ✆ 627 0466. Home to the Netherlands Chamber Orchestra and the Netherlands Philharmonic respectively. Beautifully converted concert halls in the old Beurs van Berlage (see **Walk I**, p.85).

Concertgebouw, Concertgebouwplein 2–6, ✆ 671 8345. The Grote Zaal (Large Hall) has perfect acoustics and is used for orchestral concerts and visiting pop stars and jazz bands. Nervous students from the Sweelinck Conservatorium across the road make their professional debuts in the Kleine Zaal (Small Hall). Free lunchtime concerts on Wednesdays (see **Walk V**, pp.153–4).

De IJsbreker, Weesperzijde 23, ✆ 693 9093. A deservedly famous centre for con-

temporary music which offers a stimulating programme of local and international composers and improvisers.

Muziektheater (Stopera), Waterlooplein 22, ✆ 625 5455. Home to the national ballet and opera companies, but subject of one of the biggest architectural and property development controversies of the century, and of angry complaints by musicians and audience alike about the bad acoustics (see pp.69 and 160). It does, however, have an attractive, cosy auditorium—rare for a modern theatre. There are backstage tours (Wed and Sat 4pm; f8.50; book in advance on ✆ 551 8103 for English guide).

De Rode Hoed, Keizersgracht 102, ✆ 638 5606. Varied programmes in a converted church.

Rock and Pop

Chart-busters and stadium-packers like Madonna and Prince used to give Amsterdam a miss and head for the larger venues of Rotterdam. But in 1996 Amsterdam gained a state-of-the-art sports and entertainment stadium. The **Amsterdam ArenA** looks like a giant spaceship, hovering on the southeast outskirts of the city. It opened with concerts by Tina Turner and Michael Jackson, and has been packing in the audiences ever since. Keep an eye out also for Dutch stars who have made it internationally—such as Mathilde Santing, Eton Crop and the not-so-gently ageing Golden Earring—who have a loyalty to the old town and come back for a gig or two at venues in the centre.

Young British bands (who see an Amsterdam tour as the penultimate rung on the ladder to fame and glory) are often the best bet if you're looking for good rock. Many of these head for **Paradiso** or **De Melkweg**, though they often also strain the sound systems of smaller venues around town such as a new dance and concert hall called (confusingly) Arena. Many bands who have since made it big have a soft spot for Paradiso and De Melkweg. In 1995 The Rolling Stones popped in for an unscheduled 'unplugged' concert in Paradiso before a first-come-first-served audience of just 500.

Amsterdam's large Indonesian and Surinamese populations swell many a bar with pulsating ethnic rhythms—the Latin and South American music scene is especially lively. In the summer everyone heads for the **Vondelpark**, where good musicians give free concerts and the park swings with a party atmosphere.

The listings magazines are your best guide to what's on. Prices range from free entrance to around ƒ20 and starting times are usually between 9 and 11pm.

Akhnaton, Nieuwezijds Kolk 25, ✆ 624 3396. Recording studios, rehearsal facilities and a forum for much of the liveliest new music, hip-hop, Latin and ethnic bands.

Amsterdam ArenA, Arenaboulevard 1, ✆ 311 1333. Sports stadium that is the venue for visiting megastars.

Arena, 's Gravesandestraat 51, ✆ 694 7444. The old hippy Sleep-In has undergone a transformation into one of the trendiest music and dance venues in town.

Cruise Inn, Zeeburgerdijk 272, ✆ 692 7188. Flotsam from the 1950s shake, rattle and roll in an old wooden clubhouse.

Korsakoff, Lijnbaansgracht 161, ✆ 625 7854. A venue for headbanging post-punks, which nods towards heavy metal and gothic teeny-boppers.

Paradiso, Weteringschans 6–8, ✆ 626 4521. An institution. A gloomy looking church that has been converted into a bright and buzzing venue for good music—anything from big rock names to jazz, African, Latin and even contemporary classical.

See also **De Melkweg**, p.214, and 'Nightclubs', below.

Jazz, Latin and Folk

The mellow tones of jazz seem to suit the atmosphere of the brown cafés, and many have a live band on a Saturday night or Sunday afternoon. There are often special gigs around the same time as the Holland Festival (see **Practical A–Z**, pp.16–18). Surinamese and other South American immigrants crowd out a number of vibrant drinking and dancing venues around town. Bars and cafés with live music often don't charge entrance, but have more expensive drinks.

Jazzcafé Alto, Korte Leidsedwarsstraat 115, © 626 3249. Live jazz every night in a cosy brown café in a brash touristy street.

De Badcuyp, 1ᵉ Sweelinckstraat 10, © 675 9669. Neighbourhood café-cum-arts centre in a converted bathhouse. A lively venue for jazz and salsa.

Bimhuis, Oudeschans 73, © 623 1361. Major jazz venue. Visiting artists and the best locals; free sessions Mon and Wed.

Brasil Music Bar, Lange Leidsedwarsstraat 70, © 626 1500. Live Samba and a gyrating throng of Latin expatriates.

Casablanca, Zeedijk 26, © 625 5685. Café hosting mainstream and standard bands, with the occasional jam session.

Jazz Cruise, © 623 9886, starts at Rijksmuseum (April–Nov Sat 8pm and 10pm). An hour-and-a-half of jazz on a canal boat, with beer, wine and cheese thrown in.

Maloe Melo, Lijnbaansgracht 163, © 420 4592. Enduring, rather poky, blues café.

Meander, Voetboogstraat 3, © 625 8430. Lively café where student types swing to salsa, bop to funk and chill out to jazz.

Mulligan's, Amstel 100, © 622 1330. Rousing Irish sing-a-longs.

Soeterijn, Linnaeusstraat 2, © 568 8500. The top venue for music from Africa, Indonesia, Eastern Europe and the Middle East.

Odeon Jazz Kelder, Singel 460, © 624 9711. Trad jazz in an intimate atmosphere.

Rembrandt Bar, Rembrandtplein 3, © 623 0688. Dutch folk music.

Rum Runners, Prinsengracht 277, © 627 4079. Glitzy Caribbean bar/restaurant with live Latin bands (Sun pm and early evening).

For a real knees-up and noisy accordion visit **Café Nol** or **De Twee Zwaantjes** (see **Food and Drink**, 'Cafés').

Nightclubs and Dancing

Amsterdam nightclubbers don't suffer the fashion neuroses of their London or New York counterparts. You can dress up, down, wild or straight: there's seldom any need to shock or impress the doorman before you're let in. Entrance prices are low enough—and the city small enough—for you to wander from one club to the next. The mood is carefree and unpretentious—late-night clubbing seems just an extension of early-evening café life. There *is* a new club-culture scene that holds all-night warehouse parties in deserted areas of town, yet even here you'll find playful Dutch touches. Club nights on the beach at Zandvoort are the current focus of the summer dance scene. The *Queer Fish* booklet (on sale at larger bookstores) is a good source of information about one-nighters or parties. The

commercial discos (chart music, plastic palm trees, expensive drinks and posses of drunken men) cluster around Leidseplein. What follows is a list of places for those with rather different tastes. Most venues close at 4am (5am over weekends). You should tip the doorman as you leave (about ƒ5), and avoid using cabs cruising outside. Legal cabs will be found at a nearby rank—or the club may phone for you.

Dansen bij Jansen, Handboogstraat 11, ✆ 620 1779. A bit like a Students' Union bop. You usually need to prove membership of a college or university to get in. Frequent theme and fancy-dress nights.

Escape, Rembrandtsplein 11, ✆ 622 1111. A cavern of a place that's a hyper-trendy club, complete with shops and even a hairdresser.

Mazzo, Rozengracht 114, ✆ 626 7500. Comfortable club with a good atmosphere and an excellent range of music, often live with local bands.

Odeon, Singel 460, ✆ 624 9711. Multi-roomed venue in a converted canal house; often overpopulated by adolescent tourists.

See also **De Melkweg**, below.

Scandals Lounge, Reguliersdwarsstraat 13, ✆ 422 6220. Glitzy hip and garage.

Sinners in Heaven, Wagenstraat 3, ✆ 620 1375. Weird'n'wonderful décor; world-famous-in-Holland clientele.

Soul Kitchen, Amstelstraat 32, ✆ 620 2333. The sort of music that 30-somethings can dance to, in a friendly refreshingly untrendy atmosphere. No under 25s.

Trance Buddha, Oudezijds Voorburgwal 216, ✆ 422 8233. Young New Age crowd with appropriate soundtrack.

West Pacific, Haarlemmerweg 8, ✆ 488 7778. Fun, hip dance-café that is part of an arts complex in an old gasworks.

Arts Centres

De Brakke Ground, Nes 45, ✆ 626 6866. Attractive venue for Flemish art and performance. Excellent dance programmes.

De Meervaart Centrum, Meer en Vaart 1, ✆ 610 7498. A good variety of film, theatre, dance and music (classical and jazz).

De Melkweg (Milky Way), Lijnbaansgracht 234a, ✆ 624 1777. A vibrant centre for the arts converted in the 1960s from an old dairy. The theatre hosts companies from around the world (often in English) with extraordinarily imaginative plays. The small cinema shows a range of films from mainstream to cult. The concert hall stages excellent African and South American bands, and acts as a try-out venue for up-and-coming rock groups. At weekends an alternative disco takes over. The coffeeshop

was one of the first where the sale of marijuana was tolerated by the authorities. Consider taking out membership (ƒ15, valid three months) which gives you considerable discounts.

Amsterdam RAI, Europaplein 12, ✆ 549 1212. A business congress centre which houses large concerts and touring musicals. Venue for KunstRAI, an annual contemporary art fair (see **Practical A–Z**, p.18).

Westergasfabriek, Haarlemmerweg 8–10, ✆ 681 3068. Newest arts centre, in a converted gasworks. Home to the Toneelgroep Amsterdam (see above) and European base for the Cirque du Soleil. Visiting shows are usually experimental. Every night after 11pm customers bop until late.

Shopping

> *What is there that's not found here*
> *Of corn; French or Spanish wine*
> *Any Indies goods that are sought*
> *In Amsterdam may all be bought*
> *Here's no famine—the land is fat.*

> Constantijn Huygens, 17th-century Dutch poet

Amsterdam's prosperity in the Golden Age turned it into an exotic *emporium mundi*. The little shops below the decorative *uithangborden* (painted signs) were crammed with Nuremberg ceramics, Lyons silk, Spanish wines, mysterious Egyptian potions and an abundance of local pastries, cheeses, linen and boots. When Marie de Médicis made her grandiose entry into Amsterdam in 1638, the first thing she did when she had a moment's spare time (amidst the lavish ceremonies celebrating her arrival) was to swoop down on the Amsterdam shops where, apparently, she haggled with the adept confidence of someone reared in a market-place.

Amsterdam's markets, boutiques and eccentric speciality shops are still one of the city's greatest allures. The range of goods and oddity of the shops can keep you browsing for hours. The only barriers against your absolute financial ruin are the inconvenient opening hours. Calvinism wins over tourism—despite the recent relaxation of laws governing shop hours, you'll find very few places at all open on a Sunday. Amsterdammers enjoy their weekends, and the fun tends to overflow into Monday: many shops also stay closed on Monday mornings, if not for the whole day. However, most stay open late on Thursday nights. (Thursday, the night before the weekenders descend on the city, has a wild feeling of local festivity that dissipates under the influx of outsiders.)

Weekday **opening hours** are generally 9–6. On Saturdays shops close around 5. Some shops in the city centre now open from noon to 6 on Sundays. Many of the smaller shops can be quite idiosyncratic about when they open, but all have a little black and yellow timetable of opening hours posted on an outside window.

Dutch **sales tax** (BTW—17.5 per cent on most goods) is included in the marked price, though many stores offer **tax-free** shopping to non-EU tourists. They'll help with the paperwork.

After-hours Shopping

Most neighbourhoods have one or two shops that open around 5pm and stay open until between 11pm and 1am. Here you can buy, at a suitably inflated price, emergency groceries. Look out for signs reading *Avondverkoop* or *Nightshop*. Here's a selection of the more upmarket ones:

Baltus, Vijzelstraat 127.

Big Bananas, Leidsestraat 76. Big price tags. Rude assistants.

Heuft's First Class Nightshop, Rijnstraat, 62. Late-night oysters and champagne.

In addition to these, the **Albert Heijn Supermarket** on Koningsplein is open 10–10 Mon–Sat and noon–6 on Sunday. It is a conventional supermarket with normal prices. Some larger stores in the city centre (such as Hema and De Bijenkorf) are now also open on Sunday afternoons.

To locate a **late-night pharmacy** contact ℂ 694 8709.

Antiques

The **Rokin** (the street running from the Dam to Muntplein) was once the traditional stretch for antique dealers. Now there are only a few crusty die-hards here—the sort of shop where you have to ring a bell before they let you in.

These days the most stylish, outlandish and enticingly chaotic treasure-troves are to be found in the **Spiegelkwartier** (*see* **Walk VI** pp.173–4) and around the **Looiersgracht** (*see* 'Markets', p.220).

Books

Good **antiquarian bookshops** pop up all over the city, but especially around the university at the southern end of the red-light district. New books in English are usually quite expensive in Amsterdam.

American Book Center, Kalverstraat 185. After W.H.Smith's, the best stock in town of English fiction and non-fiction, magazines and children's books.

Architectura & Natura, Leliegracht 44. Just what it says, with an impressive collection of books on Amsterdam.

Atheneum, Spui 14–16. Stamping ground of the city's intelligentsia. Good selection of magazines and English non-fiction.

Book Exchange, Kloveniersburgwal 58. Essential in this town of outrageous prices.

a la Carte, Utrechtsestraat 110–112. Maps, streetplans and guide books.

English Bookshop, Lauriergracht 71. Carefully selected range, some second-hand.

Intertaal, Van Baerlestraat 76. Everything you need to learn Dutch or teach English.

Lankamp & Brinkman, Spiegelgracht 19. Children's books in English.

Lambiek, Kerkstraat 78. Cheery comic shop. Collectors' pieces and cartoon gallery.

Robert Premsela, Van Baerlestraat 78. Art books a cut above the museum shops.

De Slegte, Kalverstraat 48–52. Discount and antiquarian megastore.

Waterstones, Kalverstraat 152. Large well-stocked branch of the British chain.

Bicycles

't Mannetje, Frans Halsstraat 35. Tandems, three-wheelers and other curious designs, as well as repairs.

Macbike, Mr Visserplein 2. Second-hand bikes. Parts, repairs and sympathy.

Clothes

Dutch designers don't cause many tremors in world fashion, but you will find tasteful, well-cut clothes in fine fabrics at much lower prices than in other capitals. The second-hand clothes shops attract stall-grubbers from around the globe.

designer

P. C. Hooftstraat and Van Baerlestraat are the corridors of high fashion and the top designers—here you'll find international labels and Dutch designers.

Cora Kemperman, Leidsestraat 72. Slightly off-the-wall yet supremely stylish.

Edgar Vos, P. C. Hooftstraat 134. Nifty suits for high-powered businesswomen.

Fever, Prinsengracht 192. Hot little numbers for hot little people.

Sissy Boy, Van Baerlestraat 15. Middle-of-the-road elegance at fast-lane prices.

eyebrow-raisers

Rob & Rik, Runstraat 30. Leatherwear from functional to fetish.

Tothem, Nieuwezijds Voorburgwal 149. Swimsuits and sexy underwear for men.

La Culotte, P. C. Hooftstraat 111. Pricey, sensuous silk lingerie.

Clubwear House, Herengracht 265. Clubwear for the brave and the beautiful.

second-hand clothes

Clusters of second-hand shops rub elbow patches with each other in the zigzag of lanes from **Huidenstraat** to **Hartenstraat**. You could also try:

Petticoat, Lindengracht 99. Fifties retro, hats, shawls, cufflinks and zooty underwear.

Hans en Grietje, Overtoom 255. Ethnic and colonial bits and bobs.

shoes and accessories

If you're into something demure, head for **P.C. Hooftstraat** again. Or try:

Big Shoe, Leliegracht 12. Unisex.

Candy Corson, St Luciensteeg 19. Stylish leather bags and belts.

Shoebaloo, Koningsplein 7–9. Glitz, ruffs and teetering heels for the oddly shod (unisex).

children

Bam Bam, Magna Plaza, Nieuwezijds Voorburgwal 182. For trendy toddlers.

Oilily, P. C. Hooftstraat 133. For tiny tots whose mums and dads have big pockets.

Department Stores

De Bijenkorf, Dam 1. 'The Beehive'—aptly named. Bustling shop with a wide range of good quality merchandise, and no pretensions to being Harrods.

Hema, Kalvertoren, Kalverstraat (and all around town). The Dutch Woolworth's or five-and-dime—but all in good taste. An excellent one-stop shop to stock up on essentials.

Metz & Co., Keizersgracht 455. Liberty prints, stylish kitchenware and design-museum furniture. Superb view from the glass-walled café on the top floor.

Delftware, Clogs and Gifts

Rinascimento Gallerie d'Arte, Prinsengracht 170. Old and new Delftware (the real thing, not souvenir shop tat). Watch the designs being painted on by hand.

De Klompenboer, Nieuwezijds Voorburgwal 20. Clogs and other wooden goodies carved on the premises. Also pewter and lace.

Diamonds

Where you buy depends on your personal taste, but do shop around and stick to established dealers. You can watch diamonds being cut in a number of shops.

Rokin Diamonds, Rokin 12.

Van Moppes, Albert Cuypstraat 2–6.

Coster Diamonds, Paulus Potterstraat 2–6 (*see* **Walk VI**).

Food

Look out for two kinds of **bakery**. A *warme bakker* sells breads and biscuits and a *banketbakker* sells pastries and all the wonderful creamy things that the doctor forbids. Many also sell hand-made chocolates. In the better **cheese shops** you'll be given a sliver to taste before buying. Choose from mild *jong* (young), or the more tangy *belegen* (matured) or *extra belegen*.

Hendrikse, Overtoom 472. Tarts and cream cakes fit for Queen Beatrix.

C. O. Hotkamp, Vijzelgracht 15. Mouthwatering goodies close to the town centre.

Runneboom, 1ᵉ van der Helststraat 49. Delicious ryebread, Greek village loaves, healthy wholemeals and crispy white rolls.

Pasteuning Deliwijn, Willemsparkweg 11. Traditional Italian deli with a good selection of wines.

A Taste of Ireland, Herengracht 228. Irish and British provisions for the homesick.

Arxhoek, Damstraat 19. Farm cheeses.

Natuurwinkel, Weteringschans 133, and all around town. Everything from organic vegetables to vitamins and tofu-burgers.

De Bierkoning, Paleisstraat 125. Cosy shop behind the palace. Glasses of all shapes and around 750 brands of bottled beer.

Hart's Wijnhandel, Vijzelgracht 3. Wide range of wines and spirits.

Albert Hein is the most popular supermarket chain. You'll find branches on Waterlooplein, Koningsplein and Vijzelstraat. The largest—the one behind the Royal Palace—is also open on Sundays.

Markets

Albert Cuyp Markt, Albert Cuypstraat, *Mon–Sat 9–4.30*. Foodstuffs, clothes and hardware (*see* **Walk V**).

Bloemenmarkt (Flower Market), Singel, between Muntplein and Koningsplein, *Mon–Sat 9–6*. Amsterdam's floating flower market (*see* **Walk III**).

Boerenmarkt, Noordermarkt, Sat 10–3. Organic produce, ethnic crafts.

De Looier Indoor Antiques Market, Elandsgracht; *Mon–Thurs 11–5, Sat 9–5*. mid-price antique market. There's also a *rommelmarkt* (junk market) just around the corner (*see* **Walk VI**).

Nieuwmarkt, *May–Sept, Sun 10–5*. Good quality antiques in the shadow of a medieval city gate and weighing house.

Noordermarkt, *Mon 7.30–1.30*. Pile upon pile of junk. Get there early for a treasure hunt.

Oudemanhuis Book Market, Oudemanhuispoort, *Mon–Sat 10–4*. A dim alley smelling of musty binding and yellowing paper.

Stamp Market, near Nova Hotel, Nieuwezijds Voorburgwal 276; *Wed, Sat 11–4*. Grizzled collectors swap stamps, currency, medals and esoteric jokes.

Waterlooplein; *Mon–Sat 10–4*. The city's famous fleamarket (*see* **Walk III**).

Lapjesmarkt, Westerstraat, *Mon 7.30–1*. Bargain clothes and spectacular fabrics.

Lindengracht; *Sat 9–4*. Small general market, but the best.

Specialist Shops

Amsterdam abounds in idiosyncratic speciality shops: old family businesses, and outlets for the fantasies of quixotic visionaries. Here are but a few:

De Beestenwinkel (The Animal Shop), Staalstraat 11. Stuffed bunnies, tiger puppets and teddy bears to put your pyjamas in.

Brillenwinkel, Gasthuismolensteeg 7. Classic spectacle frames, from Mahatma Gandhi to Dame Edna.

Condomerie Het Gulden Vlies, Warmoesstraat 141. Condom as consumer item.

Joe's Vliegerwinkel, Nieuwe Hoogstraat 19. Kites weird and wonderful.

Hangmatten Maranón, Singel 488–490. Bright and breezy hammocks from around the world.

P. G. C. Hajenius, Rokin 92–6. Tobacconist with famed house-brand cigars.

The Head Shop, Kloveniersburgwal 39. Accessories for dope devotees.

Kitsch Kitchen, 1e Bloemdwarsstraat 21. Gaudy plastic goodies, brightly patterned enamel bowls and curious implements.

Knopenwinkel, Wolvenstraat 14. Buttons of all shapes and periods.

Kramer, Reestraat 20. Candles and candlesticks—ethnic to high altar.

Klamboe Imports, Prinsengracht 232. Mosquito nets—the best way to ward off the pests.

Olivaria, Hazenstraat 2a. Entirely devoted to olive oil; there's even a tasting bar.

Poppendokter, Reestraat 20. Dolls and parts of dolls.

Vlieger, Amstel 34. Pencils, pigments and piles of inspiring paper.

Waterwinkel, Roelof Hartstraat 10. Over 100 types of mineral water from around the world, and mud from the Dead Sea.

De Witte Tanden Winkel, Runstraat 5. Champagne-flavoured toothpaste and toothbrushes, toothbrushes, toothbrushes.

Gay

In the heady social upheaval of the 1960s and 70s, when pixie-hatted members of the Gnome Party held protest meetings on the Dam and troupes of hippies camped out in the Vondelpark, Amsterdam's lesbians and gays joined in the frolic. Homosexuality had been decriminalized in 1811, but the gay community wanted a city free of the petty prejudices and subtle discrimination they ran up against in day-to-day life. In many ways they succeeded. Today Amsterdam is known as the Gay Capital of Europe. Gay bars and cafés, though often in clusters, aren't in ghettos. Nobody bats an eyelid if two men kiss or hold hands in public. The city was quick off the mark in coping constructively with AIDS, the council housing department gives gay couples the same status as married heterosexuals, and in 1987 the world's first memorial to persecuted lesbians and gays, the Homomonument, was unveiled (the three triangles of pink granite between the Westerkerk and the Keizersgracht are the focal point of many a party, protest or commemoration service).

There are gay bars, clubs, hotels, bookshops and restaurants all over town. You'll find most of the heavier leather bars lurking up the north end of **Warmoesstraat**, ribbons of coffeeshops, restaurants and bars along **Kerkstraat** and **Reguliersdwarsstraat**, a jolly throb of clubs and pubs along the **Amstel** off Rembrandtplein, and scores of local neighbourhood cafés. Despite accusations that the Amsterdam gay scene is stagnating, gay tourists flock to the city. Over weekends, the hunk at the end of the bar is more likely to be a computer programmer from South London than a local lad. Many Amsterdammers respond to this invasion by staying at home, venturing out on Thursdays and Sundays when the occupying forces are thinner on the ground.

The atmosphere, though, is friendly and welcoming. Most gay venues distribute free **maps of gay Amsterdam**, leaflets and free magazines (such as *Rainbow*) giving you an idea of what's on about town; but as people are so open and chatty, word-of-mouth is often the best way to find out what the evening might have in store.

Here is an idiosyncratic selection of places to go; some are well known but others are quirky, local establishments, out of the tourist maelstrom.

Cafés, Coffeeshops and Restaurants

Backstage Boutique (a.k.a. 'The Twins'), Utrechtsedwarsstraat 75; *open Mon–Sat 10am–6pm.* Not exclusively gay, but with an atmosphere of stratospheric camp that shouldn't be missed (*see* 'Lunch and Cafés', **Walk VI**).

Café Secret, Kerkstraat 346; *open Sun–Thurs 9pm–3am, Fri–Sat 9–4.* Cosy café that sometimes has live entertainment.

COC, Rozenstraat 14; *coffeeshop open Wed–Sat 1pm–5pm.* Spartan but amiable haven in Amsterdam's lesbian and gay 'culture centre'.

Downtown, Reguliersdwarsstraat 31; *open daily 10–8.* A friendly day-time coffeeshop, popular with tourists and locals, in one of Amsterdam's gay streets. It serves food and has a sprawl of pavement tables on sunny days.

Getto, Warmoesstraat 51; restaurant/café *open Wed–Sat noon to 1am, Sun noon–midnight; closed Mon and Tues.* A young, friendly crowd and good food make this one of the most popular recent additions to the gay scene.

Le Monde, Rembrandtplein 6; *open daily 8am–midnight.* Tiny, cheery snack café with a terrace on Rembrandtplein. The sister restaurant along the square does good Dutch food.

La Strada, Nieuwezijds Voorburgwal 93; *open daily noon–1am.* Brown café with good food and friendly staff, popular with local lesbians.

Reibach, Brouwersgracht 139; *open daily 10–8, but closes 6pm Oct–Mar.* Trendy café with a Germanic edge, great cakes and a pleasant, small terrace on one of Amsterdam's most tranquil canals.

Bars

Argos, Warmoesstraat 95; *open Mon–Thurs 9pm–3am, to 4pm at weekends.* Amsterdam's oldest leather bar sweats with bikers' jackets, cowboy chaps and denim. As you wander into the dimmer recesses, what the gay guides coyly term 'action' becomes quite lively.

April, Reguliersdwarsstraat 37; *open daily 2pm–1am.* More than double its previous size (and more attractively designed) after a 1996 renovation. Popular with young Amsterdammers during the week. Over the weekend tourists swell numbers until the bar bursts into a street party.

Amstel Taveerne, Amstel 54; *open daily 3pm–1am, to 2pm at weekends.* Beer mugs and bric-a-brac hang everywhere.

Dutch reproductions on the walls. Dutch originals around the bar. A provincial pub in the middle of the city with sing-alongs and good cheer (all Dutch).

Havana, Reguliersdwarsstraat 17; *open daily 4pm–1am, to 2am at weekends.* Comfortable café/bar with an exhausting constellation of beautiful people. There's a small dance floor upstairs, so you can pop up for an early bop.

Casa Maria, Warmoesstraat 60; *open Sun–Thurs noon–1am, Fri–Sat noon–2am.* In the heart of the red-light district. A jukebox full of uproarious kitsch, a gregarious Spanish owner, and a picture window that offers the best people-watching possibilities in town.

Le Shako, 's Gravenlandseveer 2; *open daily 9pm–2am, to 3am at weekends*. A miniscule bar that attracts students, writers, academics and a good load of local scruffs. Cheap beer on Tuesdays and free snacks on Thursdays.

Montmartre, Halvemaansteeg 17; *open daily 4pm–1am, to 2am on Fri and Sat*. Dancing barmen, original 1920s décor, loud music and a tight squeeze.

Clubs

De Trut, Bilderdijkstraat 165; open Sun 11pm–4am. A trendy, but relaxed and pose-free club with a wide range of music, a (mainly) young crowd and a mix of lesbians and gay men. The Trut is in the cellar of what was once one of Amsterdam's biggest squats. The entrance is unmarked, but if you turn up between 11 and midnight, you'll see where to go. Often the club gets so full you have to wait for someone to leave before you're allowed in.

COC, Rozenstraat 14. Amsterdam's Gay Centre runs a disco on Friday nights (10pm–2am) which attracts a local crowd and ingénues from the provinces.

C'ring (or Cockring), Warmoesstraat 96; open daily 11pm–4am, to 5am on Fri and Sat. Steamy, sweaty, swarming venue for emergency sex.

Exit, Reguliersdwarsstraat 42. April's busy disco-sister.

Accommodation

Hotels are forbidden by law to discriminate against gay couples, but here's a selection of specifically gay places to stay. The prices are for a double room with shower in season, with breakfast included. (Addresses are given with the Amsterdam postcode.)

Amsterdam House Hotel, 's Gravelandseveer 3, 1011 KM; ✆ 624 6607, ✉ 624 1346. Friendly canalside hotel just minutes from gay hotspots. From ƒ140.

International Travel Club/ITC, Prinsengracht 1051, 1017 JE; ✆ 623 0230. Quiet hotel overlooking one of Amsterdam's finest canals, popular with an older crowd. From ƒ140.

Jordaan Canal House, Egelantiersgracht 23, 1015 RC; ✆ 620 1545, ✉ 638 5056. Beautifully situated, exclusively gay 17th-century canal house. From ƒ170.

Hotel New York, Herengracht 13, 1015 BA; ✆ 624 3066. Swish hotel with all mod cons, hiding behind three 17th-century canal houses at a tranquil end of Amsterdam's grandest canal. From ƒ250.

GIS Apartments, Keizersgracht 33, 1015 CD Amsterdam; ✆ 625 0071, offers furnished apartments from ƒ150–250 per night.

Many of Amsterdam's best 'straight' hotels are sympathetic places to stay, and many are gay-owned. *See* especially the **Quentin Hotel** (which has a large lesbian clientele), **Seven Bridges Hotel** and **Hotel Engeland** under **Where to Stay**.

Lesbian Amsterdam

Lesbians are not as well catered for as gay men in Amsterdam, but there's a lively, friendly scene in places such as:

Sarah's Grannies, Kerkstraat 176; *Mon–Sat 9am–6pm*. Offers good Dutch meals in a relaxed atmosphere. Not exclusively gay, but popular with local women.

Café Saarein, Elandsstraat 119; *open Mon 8pm–1am. Tues–Thurs and Sun 3pm–1am, Fri and Sat 3pm–2am*. A cosy local café, currently the citadel of Amsterdam's lesbian life.

Café Vive-la-Vie, Amstelstraat 5; *open daily noon–1am, to 2am at weekends*. Sociable crowd in a vaguely Art Deco bar with music that increases in volume as the night wears on.

COC (*see* under 'clubs' above) holds a house-oriented women-only disco on Saturdays from 8pm–2am.

You II, Amstel 178, *open Thurs to Saturday 11pm to 5 am; Sunday 4pm to 1am*. More of a disco than Vive-la-Vie, and less heavily house than COC. Much-needed hip, yet pretty, relaxed lesbian meeting place.

Other Attractions

If the sun's shining, the place to be is **Zandvoort**, on Amsterdam's **gay beach**. Zandvoort is not the forgotten patch in the dunes that such places usually are, although it's a bit of a trek to reach it. There are two gay bars (**Eldorado** and **Sans Tout**) on the beach. Both are open from 8am until midnight. You can get there by train from Centraal Station (about 30mins, frequent trains right through the day). Once you get to the beach, walk south along the promenade and then on past the '*Naakt Strand*' (nudist beach) for about 5km.

There's a **gay cinema** every Saturday and Sunday at Desmet, Plantage Middenlaan 4a, ✆ 627 3434. It shows a selection of popular and independent films and attracts a local crowd.

You can spend hours browsing around **gay bookshops** like Intermale, Spuistraat 251—mostly for men—or Boekhandel Vrolijk, Paleisstraat 135, which has a wide selection of literature, biographies and non-fiction of interest to lesbians and gay men. The American Discount Bookshop, Kalverstraat 185, has a good gay section.

Mandate, Prinsengracht 715 (*open Mon–Fri 11am–10pm; Sat noon–6pm, Sun 2pm–6pm; daily membership ƒ18, six visits ƒ63*) is a well-equipped **gay gym** with a busy coffee bar; and the notorious Amsterdam **saunas** are Thermos Day, Raamstraat 35 (*open Mon–Fri noon–11pm, Sat and Sun noon–10pm; adm ƒ30*) and Thermos Night, Kerkstraat 60 (*open daily 11pm–8am; adm ƒ30*).

Information

COC is Amsterdam's lesbian and gay social centre (Rozenstraat 14; ✆ office 626 3087/information ✆ 623 4079; *open Mon–Thurs 9am–5pm; for disco and coffeeshop hours, see* 'Clubs' *and* 'Lesbian Amsterdam' *above*).

Gay and Lesbian Switchboard (✆ 623 6565; *open 10am–10pm*) gives information and advice in English.

Day Trips from Amsterdam

Hélène Müller loved art. Her husband, Anton Krüller, loved nature. She was heiress to a blast-furnace industry; he married the boss's daughter. Together they developed the family firm into a prosperous multinational and used their fortune to realize a dream. Between 1909 and 1914 Anton bought up tracts of wild land near Arnhem. Hélène built up a superb and inspired collection of late 19th and early 20th-century art. They restocked the land with game, planted copses, built a lodge to live in and a museum for the paintings. Today the Kröller-Müller Museum, set in the vast and varied landscape of De Hoge Veluwe national park, is one of the most delightful places to visit in the Netherlands. The estate now covers 5,500 hectares (13,000 acres) of land, the art collection is still growing and there really is something for everyone. You can picnic in forests or lie about on dunes, gallop through the fens on horseback or cycle sedately along leafy lanes. You can bird-watch, look for wild boar or nestle in animal hides waiting for red deer. The airy, intimate museum is a pleasure to walk around, and the collection is one of the best in the country. The sculpture park could detain you for hours and the Lodge is unstuffy and well-preserved. There are all the cafés, restaurants and children's playgrounds you could wish for, without the horrid ambience of a theme park or tourist trap. On the outskirts of the park is Paleis Het Loo, a royal residence for three centuries, now open to public view.

Getting There

The easiest way to get there is by **car**. You can drive about in the park, and abandon the car where you wish. Take the A1 to Apeldoorn or the A2 and A12 to Arnhem. There are gates to the park at the villages of Otterlo, Schaarsbergen and Hoenderloo. The journey takes about 1½ hours. The nearest **railway** stations are at Arnhem and Apeldoorn. Both are served fairly frequently from Centraal Station (though less so over weekends) and the journey takes around 1½ hours. The Netherlands Railways often offer special excursion tickets (check at Centraal Station information desk). From late June to early August there's an hourly **excursion bus** from Arnhem railway station. Once in the park you can get about on the (free) white **bicycles**. Out of season you'll need to take the **VAD bus** 107 from Arnhem, or the 110 from Apeldoorn.

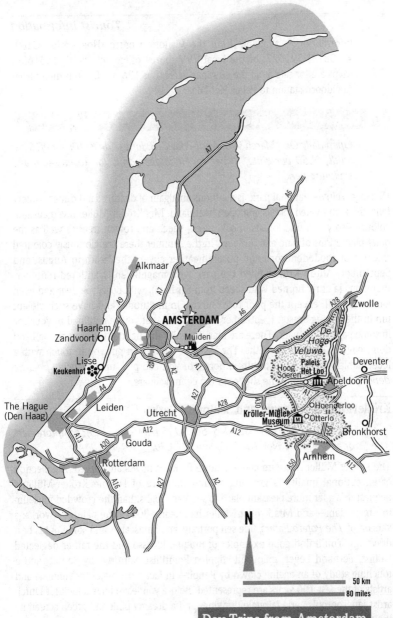

Alkmaar

AMSTERDAM

Muiden

Haarlem
Zandvoort

Lisse
Keukenhof

The Hague
(Den Haag)

Leiden

Utrecht

Gouda

Rotterdam

Zwolle

De
Hoge
Veluwe

Hoog
Soeren

Paleis
Het Loo

Deventer

Apeldoorn

Hoenderloo

Kröller-Müller
Museum

Otterlo

Bronkhorst

Arnhem

N

50 km
80 miles

Day Trips from Amsterdam

Information is available from the Visitors' Centre (Hoenderloo Gate), ✆ (0318) 591627, or the local VVV tourist office, ✆ (0900) 1681636. Maps are for sale at all the entrance gates. Bus 126 or 104 runs direct from Apeldoorn station to Paleis Het Loo.

De Hoge Veluwe National Park

Open daily Oct–March 9–6, April–May 8–8, June–Aug 8–10; adm f10 per adult, f4.50 per child, f8 per car (includes admission to museum and sculpture park).

De Hoge Veluwe national park is a curious amalgam of drifting sand dunes, watery fens, thick cultivated forests and open heathland. Mrs Kröller-Müller loved autumn colours—so you'll find forests of oak, birch, beech and rowan trees as well as the older plantations of pine and junipers. In the summer there are gloriously coloured thickets of rhododendrons and purple heather covers the heath in August and September, Anton Krüller filled the park with magnificently antlered red deer, moufflons (a curly horned wild sheep from Sardinia), wild boar, roe deer and even kangaroos. All, except the poor roos, survive in multitudes and have such violent fun in the rutting season (September to October) that you're confined to your car in some parts of the park. There are marked walks throughout the area, though you don't have to keep to the paths. The Visitors' Centre can put you in touch with a local stables if you'd like to hire a horse, or you can pick up a bicycle (*free, no deposit necessary*) from the shelter in the central square.

Kröller-Müller Museum and Sculpture Park

Museum open Tues–Sat 10–5, Sun 11–5 (Nov–Mar 1–5); sculpture park open 1 April–1 Nov 10–4.30, Sun 11–4.30.

The Kröller-Müller Museum and Sculpture Park are now state-owned. A collection of exceptional quality is growing around the core of Hélène Kröller-Müller's bequest. It's a far more pleasant place to see Van Goghs than the crowded museum in Amsterdam—and Mrs Kröller-Müller had nearly 300 of the painter's works: a version of *The Potato Eaters*, fine self-portraits and landscapes and some of his best drawings. You'll find good examples of Braque, Picasso and the rather neglected Cubist, Fernand Léger, colourful stippled Pointillist paintings by Seurat, and a touching study of an ageing clown by Renoir—in fact most major movements and artists of the last 100 years are represented. Before you leave have a look for Dutch artist Jan Toorop's eerie fairytale drawings and a dreamy pink and green screen by the French Symbolist painter, Odilon Redon.

Out in the **Sculpture Park** you'll find pieces not only by old familiars like Rodin, Henry Moore and Barbara Hepworth, but also exciting work by contemporary artists. The Park reflects Hélène Kröller-Müller's vision of the way art, nature and architecture can interrelate. The long, low, stone and glass museum blends perfectly into the surrounding landscape. In the pond outside, Marta Pan's enormous, curvaceous, abstract white *Swan* is gently blown about by the wind. In a little hollow, over a hill, rusty iron sheets seem to grow up from the soil. Boulders hang suspended in rope hammocks between the trees; giant, seed-shaped balls of clay, slate igloos and odd tent-like structures are scattered about open grass patches. A frail needle of aluminium pipes and steel wire towers 27m (92ft) into the sky, higher than most of the trees. Anyone under the age of 12 makes a beeline for Jean Dubuffet's *Jardin d'Email* (1972/3). From the outside it's a tall white wall, but once you climb the narrow stairs you're in a big, bumpy white landscape cut up by irregular black lines. Bemused adults sit around the edges, while children tear about, trip over the mounds and bang their heads.

Jachthuis St Hubertus

Open April–Oct, guided tours every ½ hour 10.30–11.30 and 2–4.30.

Before leaving De Hoge Veluwe, pay a quick visit to the Jachthuis St Hubertus, St. Hubert Hunting Lodge. The Kröller-Müllers' family home and its artificial lake were built in 1914 by H. P. Berlage, the father of modern Dutch architecture (see p.63). It's a compact brick building with an ugly, incongruous tower. Inside, however, the house has a cosy 'lived-in' atmosphere—and some superb Art Deco furniture. Coloured bricks and brightly glazed tiles abound, and the motifs on hunting, of the story of St Hubertus (the patron saint of hunters), and of the sun, run throughout the interior design.

Paleis Het Loo

Open Tues–Sun 10–5, adm f12.50.

Adjoining the national park is the Koninklijke Domeinen (Royal Estate) and the magnificent Baroque Paleis Het Loo (Het Loo Palace). Built in 1685 as a hunting lodge for Stadhouder William III (of 'William and Mary' fame), the palace was used as a royal residence until 1962. Nowadays it is open to the public. You wander through a succession of lavishly decorated state rooms and boudoirs. Each is done up using furniture that reflects the taste of one of the royal occupants, in sequence from the 17th century to the 1930s. But most splendid of all are the gardens, laid out again in the 1980s following the 17th-century plans by Daniel Marot, who also originally designed the palace interior. View the exquisite formal layout from the roof of the palace, then descend to stroll among rose bushes, brush against fragrant herbs and wander through the gazebo.

Lunch and Cafés

The **Museum Café** sells light snacks and cakes and has a sunny terrace, the **Koperen Kop** (*open daily*) is the main restaurant and serves fuller meals, the smaller **Rijzenburg** closes during the week over winter. The best thing to do is to take a picnic—you can have it anywhere you like.

Outside the park, visit the leafy village of **Hoog Soeren** (near Paleis Het Loo) for a game lunch at Café-Restaurant Hoog Soeren, ✆ 055 519 1231, or follow the A1 towards Deventer, and branch off to Bronkhorst (you have to cross a river by punt to get there). It's the smallest village in the country, with just over 60 inhabitants, and it has an inn with an excellent restaurant, **De Goude Leeuw**, ✆ 0575 451 231. You can also eat in the palace itself, in a grand but inexpensive restaurant.

Bulbs, Woods and Beaches

Keukenhof

Open late March–late May, daily 8–8; adm f18. Centraal Station will usually have details of special discount offers on a combined rail/bus ticket to the Keukenhof. Alternatively, you could combine a visit to the gardens with a trip to Leiden or Haarlem—there's a bus connection from both to the Keukenhof in the season (details from VVV). The cafés around the Keukenhof are crowded and unexciting. Pack a picnic.

In spring, the fields of North Holland blaze with the colours of millions of tulips and other bulbs, and attract nearly that number of tourists. Coachloads pour out of Amsterdam, to return traumatized by the sight of great cutting-machines churning through the bulbfields scrunching up the flowers. (Most plants are grown for the bulb rather than the bloom, and a swift blade to the stalk makes the bulb subdivide.) The VVV tourist office and various agencies around the station can help with organized tours (see p.230), but it's far better to go on your own by train or car. The town to head for is Lisse, and the garden to see is the Keukenhof.

The Keukenhof (literally 'Kitchen Garden') was, in the 15th century, the herb and vegetable patch of the Countess Jacoba van Beieren. Whatever she grew there enabled her to get through four husbands (including a Duke of Gloucester and a Dauphin of France) before her own death at the age of 35. In 1949 a group of Dutch bulb-growers took over the land as a shop-window for the bulb industry. It turned out to have a much wider appeal. Today there are some 30ha (74 acres) of nearly 7 million plants and a further 5000sq m (54,000sq ft) of flowers under glass. The best time to go is from mid to late April, when tulips, daffodils, narcissi and hyacinths are all flowering at once.

Amsterdamse Bos (Amsterdam Woods)

You can get to the Amsterdam Woods (*open 24 hours; adm free*) by bus—nos.170, 171, 172—but a quainter way to go is by antique tram. On Sundays, and some other afternoons from March–September, a variety of old trams run from Haarlemmermeer Station in west Amsterdam. There's one every 20 minutes (but contact the Amsterdam Tourist Board for full details).

You don't have to go so far afield for a bit of greenery. The wilds of the Amsterdamse Bos are only a tram ride away from the centre of town. The Amsterdamse Bos was created in the 1930s, providing jobs for the hundreds of unemployed needed to produce it, and a new recreation space for the expanding city. The Bos Museum, Koenenkade 56, in the northeast corner of the Bos (*open daily 10–5; adm free*) tells the story of how it all happened. You can go for secluded walks, cycle (there are bikes for hire at the main gate), go boating on one of the vast stretches of water, or visit the buffalo reserve. There are lots of places to picnic, or you can have a pancake amongst live peacocks on the terrace of the Boerderij Meerzicht (*open summer months 10–7*), an old farmhouse near the museum. The Bos is the ideal place to go if the children are getting small-space fatigue.

The Beach

Canal water can be pretty poisonous, so if the weather is hot and you feel like an outdoor swim, you can join the flocks of Amsterdammers heading for the beaches at Zandvoort. Although Zandvoort is just beyond Haarlem (another 15 minutes on the train) it has achieved the honorary status of being 'Amsterdam's beach'. It's a crowded and commercial resort, though if you wander further up the coast you'll find a nudists' beach, a gay beach and lots of quieter spots among the dunes.

Muiderslot (Muiden Castle)

Guided tours only, every half-hour, duration one hour; open May–Oct Tues–Fri 10–5, last tour at 4, Sat and Sun 1–4, last tour at 3, Nov–April Sat and Sun only; adm f8. Muiden is just 20mins' drive from Amsterdam along the A1. Alternatively, take bus 136 from Amstel Station (50mins), or a local train from Centraal Station to Weesp, then bus 153 (45mins). There's a café at the castle, or you could stop off for pancakes or a light lunch at Graf Floris V, Herengracht 72, in the village.

Muiderslot stands firmly fixed in the national psyche for two reasons. It was here in 1296 (a date as familiar to Dutch schoolchildren as 1066 is to British) that Count Floris of Holland was imprisoned and murdered. Over three centuries later, the castle was the focus of the Muiderkring (Muiden Circle), the country's most famous ever literary circle, centring on the poet P. C. Hooft. It was here that Tesselschade, the doyenne of 17th-century letters, sparkled (*see* pp.76–7). For 'castle' in Holland you can usually read 'stately home'. But Muiderslot is very much in the moated, turreted, impenetrable stone wall mould. Most of the building dates back to the 13th and 14th centuries, though inside it has been restored in a style which rather effectively recreates an atmosphere that would have been more familiar to members of the Muiderkring. You can see the chamber where Floris met his fate, and the desk at which P.C. Hooft wrote his poems, standing up. The rooms are filled with such curiosities as a 'money table' (you detected counterfeit coins by clinking them on the limestone top), and a family box-bed (children in drawers underneath, parents shut into a wardrobe above, with a cord to pull that opened a vent when it all got a bit too pongy). Keep an eye open for a painting in which human figures have cabbages for heads—done a good 400 years before Magritte came up with the idea.

After visiting the castle you can wander through its attractive formal garden, then stroll along fortified walls beside the river Vecht into the village of Muiden—a cluster of dinky gabled houses along the waterfront.

The language spoken in the Netherlands is Nederlands. In the Middle Ages it was known as Dietse or Duutsc (hence the English 'Dutch'), an equivalent of the German Deutsch meaning 'the language of the people' (as opposed to Latin—the language of scholars and the Church). You can hear variations spoken in Belgium (Flemish or Vlaams) and South Africa (Afrikaans).

The standard form of the language goes by the rather grand title of Algemeen Beschaafd Nederlands (General Cultured Netherlandic or ABN), though there are a multitude of regional dialects. Most of the Dutch you'll hear in Amsterdam will be ABN. But relax in a neighbourhood bar, or wander through one of the markets, and you'll hear the noisy rasping vowels of what detective story writer Nicolas Freeling called the rooks' caw of the Amsterdam dialect.

Historically, Dutch is the same language as German, a descendant of the language spoken by West Germanic tribes and the Salic Franks. Even today there are many similarities of sentence structure and vocabulary between the two languages. But Dutch doesn't have the gloss and edge of German. It's a softer, cosier, muddy language that seems to have grown out of the bogs and polders. Dutch is not an easy language to grapple with. However, to a short-term visitor to Amsterdam this need present no problem, as nearly everyone you meet will speak such good English that you could almost consider it to be the city's second language. The list of words and phrases below will help the polite and adventurous who wish to master everyday courtesies, interpret the menu, or disentangle themselves from sticky situations.

Pronunciation

Pronunciation is a question of tackling some rather difficult vowel sounds. Happily, spelling is phonetic, so once you've learned the sounds you'll be able to make a pretty accurate stab at pronouncing anything you read. The stress in Dutch, as in English, generally falls on the first syllable of a word.

Consonants

Most consonants are pronounced the same as they would be in English. However, *p*s, *t*s and *k*s aren't aspirated (i.e. they're pronounced without the accompanying puff of air). Say *ch* and *g* as in the Scottish 'loch' (*g* is more strongly voiced in northern parts of the country). Good luck in getting your tongue around the combined *s* and *ch* sounds in words like *schip* (ship), *school* (school) or *schrijter* (writer). You have a choice for *r*—you can roll it at the back of your mouth or trill it behind your teeth, but you must *always* pronounce it. Say *w* halfway between the English 'w' and 'v', except before *r*, when you pronounce it 'v'. The Dutch *v* is closer to English 'f'. Say *j* as English 'y'; *sj* as English 'sh' and *tj* as English 'ch'.

Language

Vowels

Pronounce the basic *a, e, i, o, u* sounds the same as you would in English, but *much shorter* (*a* as in 'hard', but shorter). Say *ie* as in 'neat', *oo* as in 'boat' and *oe* as in 'pool', but make all the sounds shorter. *aa* is like the 'a' in 'cat', but longer and *ee* is similar to the vowel sound in 'hail'. Say *eu* to rhyme with 'err', but round your lips tightly, and say *uu* as English *oo* in 'hoot'. The combination *ij* is a distinct letter in the Dutch alphabet, and is pronounced 'ay', whether it begins a word like *ijs* (ice/ice-cream), or comes in the middle, as in *wijn* (wine). The stretch of water north of Centraal Station is Het IJ, 'het ay'. The diphthong *ui* is a killer. In getting their tongues around the streetname Spui, Americans usually come up with 'Spew-ee' and the Brits manage 'Spow'. The Dutch sound is closer to the way a French person would say *œil*. If that leaves you none the wiser, try running together 'er-ee', but with no hint of an 'r' sound.

Here are some practice sentences:

Dag! Ik wil graag een fles wijn
darHg! ik vil HgrahHg ayn fles veyn
(Hello, I'd like a bottle of wine, please)

Waar is de wc?
Vahr iss de vay say?
(Where is the loo?)

Echt? Wat leuk!
EHgt? Vut lerk!
(Really? How nice!)

Useful Words and Phrases

do you speak English?	*spreekt u Engels?*	there is/there are	*er is/er zijn*
I don't understand	*Ik begrijp het niet*	there isn't/aren't	*er is/zijn geen*
could you speak more slowly?	*kunt u wat langzamer spreken?*	I have	*ik heb*
		I don't have any	*ik heb geen*
hello/goodbye	*dag*	I'd like	*ik wil graag*
hi	*hoi* (grating to some ears)	we'd like	*wij willen graag*
		I like it	*ik vind het leuk*
'bye	*doei* (grating)	I don't like it	*ik vind het niet leuk*
goodbye	*tot ziens*		
see you later	*tot straks*	where	*waar*
good morning/ afternoon/night	*goede morgen/ middag/nacht*	what	*wat*
		when	*waneer*
good evening	*goedenavond*	which	*welk*
yes/no/maybe	*ja/nee/misschien*	who	*wie*
please	*alstublieft*	why	*waarom*
thank you/thanks	*dank u wel/bedankt*	where is the lavatory?	*waar is het toilet?*
don't mention it	*niets te danken*	may I	*mag ik*

can you	*kunt u*	I'm lost	*ik ben verdwaald*
how much is this/that?	*hoeveel kost dit/dat?*	call a doctor quickly	*roep vlug een dokter*
expensive	*duur*	call the police/ an ambulance	*roep de politie/ een ambulance*
cheap	*goedkoop*	entrance/exit	*ingang/uitgang*
can you help me?	*kunt u mij helpen?*	push/pull	*duwen/trekken*
I'm hungry/thirsty	*ik heb honger/dorst*	open/closed	*open/gesloten (dicht)*
I'm in a hurry	*ik heb haast*		

Meeting People

how do you do?	(say your name and surname clearly)	may I get you a drink?	*mag ik u iets te drinken aanbieden?*
how are you?	*hoe maakt u het?*	do you have a light?	*hebt u/je een vuurtje?*
very well, thank you	*uitstekend, dank u*		
fine, thanks	*heel goed, dank je*	really?	*echt?*
and you?	*en u/jij?*	shall we go?	*gaan we?*
my name is...	*mijn naam is . . .*		
what are you having?	*wat neem je?*		

Hotel

single room	*eenpersoonskamer*
double room	*tweepersoonskamer*
with private bath/shower/toilet	*met privé bad/douche/toilet*
may I see the room?	*mag ik de kamer zien?*
did anyone telephone for me?	*heeft er iemand voor mij gebeld?*
may I see the manager, please?	*mag ik de directeur spreken, alstublieft?*

Transport

airport	*luchthaven/vliegveld*	how can I get to...?	*hoe kom ik bij...?*
customs	*douane*	where is...?	*waar is...?*
railway station	*trein station*	the ticket office	*het loket*
platform	*perron*	I'd like a ticket to...	*ik wil graag een kaartje naar...*
platform five	*spoor vijf*		
car	*auto*	single/return	*enkeltje/retourtje*
bicycle	*fiets/rijwiel*	change (trains)	*overstappen*
ticket	*kaartje*	when does the next/ first/last train leave?	*wanner vertrek de volgende/eerste/ laatste trein?*
occupied/reserved	*bezet/gereserveerd*		
where can I get a taxi?	*waar kan ik een taxi krijgen?*	how long does it take?	*hoe lang duurt het?*
what's the fare to...?	*wat kost het naar...?*	near/far	*dichtbij/ver weg*
take me to this address	*breng me naar dit adres*	left/right/ straight ahead	*links/rechts/ vooruit*
I want to go to...	*ik wil naar...*		

Driving

car hire	*auto verhuur*	parking place	*parkeerplaats*
petrol/diesel	*benzine/diesel*	parking garage	*parkeer garage*
leaded/unleaded	*lood/loodvrij*	no parking	*verboden te park*
filling station	*benzinestation*		*eren/niet parkeren*
garage (for repairs)	*garage*	speed limit	*snelheidslimiet*

Numbers

nought	*nul*	seventy	*zeventig*
one/two/three	*een/twee/drie*	eighty	*tachtig*
four/five/six	*vier/vijf/zes*	ninety	*negentig*
seven/eight/nine	*zeven/acht/negen*	hundred	*honderd*
ten/eleven/twelve	*tien/elf/twaalf*	two hundred and	*tweehonderd-*
thirteen, fourteen etc.	*dertien/veertien* etc.	twenty	*twintig*
twenty	*twintig*	thousand	*duizend*
twenty-one	*eenentwintig*	million	*een miljoen*
twenty-two	*tweeëntwintig* (etc.)	first/1st	*eerste/1e*
thirty	*dertig*	second/2nd	*tweede/2e*
forty	*veertig*	third/3rd	*derde/3e*
fifty	*vijftig*	fourth/4th	*vierde/4e*
sixty	*zestig*	eighth/8th	*achtste/8e*

Time

what time is it?	*hoe laat is het?*	tomorrow	*morgen*
one o'clock	*een uur*	morning/afternoon	*morgen/middag*
a quarter past one	*kwart over één*	evening/night	*avond/nacht*
half past one	*half twee* [sic]	Monday	*maandag*
a quarter to two	*kwart voor twee*	Tuesday	*dinsdag*
ten to/past three	*tien voor/over drie*	Wednesday	*woensdag*
twenty past five	*tien voor half zes*	Thursday	*donderdag*
twenty-five to eight	*vijf over half acht*	Friday	*vrijdag*
I'll come at 2 o'clock	*ik kom om twee uur*	Saturday/Sunday	*zaterdag/zondag*
today	*vandaag*	day/week/month	*dag/week/maand*
yesterday	*gisteren*	year	*jaar*

Menu Guide

may I see the menu/wine list?	*mag ik de spijskaart/wijnkaart zien?*
bon appétit	*eet smakelijk*
it tastes good/bad	*het smaakt lekker/niet lekker*
may I have the bill, please?	*mag ik de rekening, alstublieft?*
waiter/waitress	*ober/serveerster*
service	*bediening*
starter	*voorgerecht*

soup	soep
main course	hoofdgerecht
dish of the day	dagschotel
dessert	nagerecht

Drinks

a beer, please	een pils, alstublieft	fizzy mineral water	spa rood (brand)
a bottle of wine	een fles wijn	still mineral water	spa blauw
red/white	rode/witte	coffee (with milk)	koffie (verkeerd)
sweet/dry	zoete/droge	tea	thee
fresh orange juice	jus d'orange	(with milk/lemon)	(met melk/citroen)
tomato juice	tomatensap		

Fish

cod	kabeljauw	herring	haring
bass	zeebaars	trout	forel
eel	paling	salmon	zalm
halibut	heilbot	sole	tong

Meat, Poultry and Game

veal	kalfsvlees	duck	eend
lamb	lamsvlees	turkey	kalkoen
beef	rundvlees	rabbit	konijn
pork	varkensvlees	venison	wild
chicken	kip		

Vegetables

garlic	knoflook	spinach	spinazie
mushrooms	champignons	potatoes	aardappelen
carrots	worteltjes	potato chips	patat frites
asparagus	asperge	salad	sla

Dessert

whipped cream	slagroom	ice-cream and	
fruit	vrucht	chocolate sauce	dame blanche
ice-cream	ijs		

Preparation

poached	gepocheerd	grilled	geroosterd
fried	gebakken	stuffed	gevuld
roast	gebraden	rare	rood
boiled	gekookt	medium	half doorbakken
braised	gestoofd	well-done	gaar

Dutch Specialities

amandelbroodje	sweet roll with almond-paste filling
appelgebak	world-famous apple pie
appelmoes	apple sauce (with everything)
belegd broodje	bread roll with variety of fillings
bitterbal	ball of meat purée covered in breadcrumbs and deep fried
blinde vink	slice of veal rolled around stuffing
boerenomelet	omelette with vegetables and bacon
drie-in-de-pan	fluffy pancake with currants
erwtensoep	thick pea soup with sausages in it
frikandel	meatballs
hete bliksem	potatoes, bacon and apples cooked in butter, salt and sugar
Hollandse nieuwe	freshly caught filleted herring
hutspot	hotchpotch (beef and vegetable stew)
kroket	croquette (with any filling imaginable)
pannekoek	pancake
poffertjes	mini doughnut-like pancakes
rolpens	fried slices of beef and tripe with apple
speculaas	spiced almond biscuit
uitsmijter	bread, ham and fried eggs (and variations)
vla	custard, served with everything that doesn't have *appelmoes* (q.v.)
Vlaamse karbonade	braised beef and onions—usually with beer
wentelteefje	bread fried in egg batter, then sprinkled with cinnamon and sugar

Indonesian Dishes and Terms

ayam	chicken
babi pangang	roast suckling pig with sweet and sour sauce
bami goreng	casserole of noodles, vegetables, pork and shrimps
daging	beef
gado gado	vegetables with peanut sauce
goreng	fried
ikan	fish
kroepoek	fluffy deep-fried prawn crackers
loempia	enormous spring roll
nasi	rice
nasi goreng	fried rice (with meat and vegetables)
nasi rames	mini *rijsttafel* on a single plate
pedis	spicy (tongue-searing)
pisang	banana
rendang	beef stewed in a dry, fiery sauce
rijsttafel	plain rice, and up to 30 side dishes of spicy meats, vegetables, sauces and fruit
sambal	hot chilli paste
saté	skewered meat with peanut sauce
seroendeng	spicy, fried coconut
tauge	bean sprouts

History/General

Bakker, B. (ed.), *Amsterdam: the history of a city and its people* (Waanders, 1988). A short, anecdotal, well illustrated glossy pamphlet. Good café reading.

Cotterell, Geoffrey, *Amsterdam* (Saxon House, 1972). Readable romp through the history of the city right up to the 1960s.

Geyl, Pieter, *The Revolt of the Netherlands 1555–1609* and *The Netherlands in the 17th Century 1600–1648* (Cassell, 1988). Definitive histories of the uprising against Spain, the unification of the Netherlands and the Golden Age.

Hibbert, Christopher, *Cities and Civilizations* (Weidenfeld & Nicolson, 1987). Interesting chapter on everyday life in the 17th century.

Farber, Jules, *But give me Amsterdam* (Kosmos, 1995/6). Full of interesting tidbits.

Kistemaker, Renée and Van Gelder, Roeloef, *Amsterdam: The Golden Age* (Abbeville Press, 1975). Wittily written illustrated account of 17th-century Amsterdam.

Kruizinga, Jaap, *Het XYZ van Amsterdam* (2 vols., Amsterdam Publishers, 1995/6). Detailed encyclopaedia of the city; a lifetime's work. At present only in Dutch, but keep an eye open for the translation.

Schama, Simon, *The Embarrassment of Riches: An interpretation of Dutch culture in the Golden Age* (Abbeville Press, 1975). An erudite book that wears its immense research very lightly. A wonderful read.

Art and Architecture

Clark, Kenneth, *Civilisation* (BBC Publications, 1969). Accessible and perceptive chapter on the Golden Age.

Derwig, Jan and Mattie, Erik, *Functionalism in the Netherlands* (Architectura & Natura, 1995). An informed, sympathetic view of concrete-and-glass architecture.

Fromentin, Eugène, *The Masters of Past Time: Dutch and Flemish painting from Van Eyck to Rembrandt* (Phaidon, 1981). Impressions of an articulate art critic wandering about the towns and galleries of 19th-century Netherlands. A gem.

Fuchs, R. H., *Dutch Painting* (Thames & Hudson, 1978). By the current director of the Stedelijk Museum. A good general introduction, if at times a little disjointed.

Jaffe, H. L. C., *De Stijl 1917–1931* (Alec Tiranti, 1956). Comprehensive history of the Netherlands' most influential modern art movement.

Janse, Herman, *Building Amsterdam* (De Brink, 1994). Helpfully illustrated beginner's guide to Amsterdam architecture.

Kloos, Maarten (ed.), *Amsterdam: An architectural lesson* (THOTH, 1988). Lectures by renowned architects on modern Amsterdam architecture.

McQuillan, Melissa, *Van Gogh* (Thames & Hudson, 1989). Life, letters and works.

Meischke, R. et al., *Huizen in Nederland: Amsterdam* (Waanders, 1995). Photos and floor plans of most of the historical buildings in town. Text in Dutch.

Further Reading

Rosenberg, Jakob et al., *Dutch Art and Architecture 1600–1800* (Penguin, 1978). Comprehensive, clearly written account of the Golden Age and beyond.

Stone, Irving, *Lust for Life* (Methuen, 1980). Interesting semi-fictional (though at times cringingly awful) biography of Van Gogh.

White, Christopher, *Rembrandt* (Thames & Hudson, 1988). Easy and wide-ranging account of Rembrandt's chaotic life and his work.

Guides

Kemme, Guus, *Amsterdam Architecture: A guide* (THOTH, 1989, revised 1996). Photographs and brief accounts of important buildings in the city—from the oldest standing, up to the 1990s.

Stoutenbeek, Jan, and Vigeveno, Paul, *A Guide to Jewish Amsterdam* (De Haan, 1985). Every nook and cranny of the city with a significance to Jewish people listed and discussed. Now sadly out of print, but still available second-hand.

Amsterdam in Cameracolour (Ian Allen, 1980). Good photos and witty snippets of text.

Fiction

Dutch fiction is unjustifiably neglected by the English-speaking world. Authors mentioned below are very much worth exploring. Penguin Books has a good Dutch list.

Carmiggelt, Simon, *I'm Just Kidding* (publ. in English 1972). Wry observations on life in Amsterdam—an anthology of pieces he wrote weekly for the newspaper *Het Parool* under the penname 'Kronkel'.

Frank, Anne, *The Diary of Anne Frank* (Pan). No matter how many times you read it, you'll be moved by its honesty and awed by its perception.

Freeling, Nicolas, *Because of the Cats, Love in Amsterdam* etc. (Penguin, 1963). The creator of Van der Valk of the BBC TV series writes good classic detective stories—many set in Amsterdam.

Hillesum, Etty, *Etty* (Triad Grafton, 1985). War diary of a young Jewish woman who died in Auschwitz. More knowing than Anne Frank's diary, and not as compelling.

Mulisch, Harry, *Last Call* (Penguin, 1985). From one of Holland's foremost authors. The story of an old actor unearthed to play Prospero in *The Tempest*—it examines the national guilt about the lack of intervention to save the Jews in the Second World War. (Mulisch also wrote *The Assault*, which was made into an Oscar-winning film.)

Multatuli, *Max Havelaar: or the coffee auctions of the Dutch Trading Company* (Penguin, 1987). Neglected Dutch classic, a satirical indictment of Dutch colonialism which shocked 19th-century Holland.

Nooteboom, Cees, *A Song of Truth and Semblance* (Penguin, 1990). Two different fictions, separated by centuries, interweave. A witty novel that seems to reveal the essence of Dutch writing. (Try also *Rituals* and *In the Dutch Mountains*.)

Wolkers, Jan, *Turkish Delight* (Marion Boyars). Deliberately offensive misogynistic work by one of Holland's most provocative writers and artists.

Main page references are in **bold**; page references to maps are in *italic*.

Index